BRAZILIAN NATIONAL CINEMA

D0714010

Brazilian cinema is one of the most influential national cinemas in Latin America and this wide-ranging study traces the evolution of Brazilian film from the silent era to the present day, including detailed studies of more recent international box-office hits, such as *Central Station* (1998) and *City of God* (2002).

Brazilian National Cinema gives due importance to traditionally overlooked aspects of Brazilian cinema, such as popular genres, ranging from musical comedies (the *chanchada*) to soft-core porn films (the *pornochanchada*) and horror films, and also provides a fresh approach to the internationally acclaimed avant-garde *cinema novo* of the 1960s.

Lisa Shaw and Stephanie Dennison apply recent theories on stardom, particularly relating to issues of ethnicity, race and gender, to both well-known Brazilian performers, such as Carmen Miranda and Sonia Braga, and lesser-known domestic icons, such as the Afro-Brazilian comic actor Grande Otelo (Big Othello) and the *uber*blonde children's TV and film star, and media mogul, Xuxa.

This timely addition to the National Cinemas series provides a comprehensive overview of the relationship between Brazilian cinema and issues of national and cultural identity.

Lisa Shaw is Reader in Portuguese and Brazilian Studies at the University of Liverpool. She is author of *The Social History of the Brazilian Samba* (1999), co-author of *Popular Cinema in Brazil* (2004) and co-editor of *Latin American Cinema: Essays on Modernity, Gender and National Identity* (2005).

Stephanie Dennison is Reader in Brazilian Studies at the University of Leeds. She is co-author of *Popular Cinema in Brazil* (2004) and co-editor of *Latin American Cinema: Essays on Modernity, Gender and National Identity* (2005) and *Remapping World Cinema: Identity, Politics and Culture in Film* (2006).

National Cinemas
Series Editor: Susan Hayward

Australian National Cinema
Tom O'Regan

British National Cinema
Sarah Street

Canadian National Cinema
Chris Gittings

German National Cinema
Sabine Hake

French National Cinema
Second Edition
Susan Hayward

Italian National Cinema 1896–1996
Pierre Sorlin

Nordic National Cinemas
Tytti Soila, Astrid Söderbergh Widding and Gunnar Iversen

Spanish National Cinema
Núria Triana-Toribio

Irish National Cinema
Ruth Barton

Chinese National Cinema
Yingjin Zhang

Mexican National Cinema
Andrea Noble

Brazilian National Cinema
Lisa Shaw and Stephanie Dennison

Forthcoming titles:

South African National Cinema
Jacqueline Maingard

BRAZILIAN NATIONAL CINEMA

Lisa Shaw and Stephanie Dennison

LONDON AND NEW YORK

First published 2007
by Routledge
2 Park Square, Milton Park, Abingdon, Oxon, OX14 4RN

Simultaneously published in the USA and Canada
by Routledge
270 Madison Ave, New York, NY 10016

Routledge is an imprint of the Taylor & Francis Group, an informa business

© 2007 Lisa Shaw and Stephanie Dennison

Typeset in Galliard by
Keystroke, 28 High Street, Wolverhampton
Printed and bound in Great Britain by
Antony Rowe Ltd, Chippenham, Wiltshire

All rights reserved. No part of this book may be reprinted or reproduced or utilised in any form or by any electronic, mechanical, or other means, now known or hereafter invented, including photocopying and recording, or in any information storage or retrieval system, without permission in writing from the publishers.

British Library Cataloguing in Publication Data
A catalogue record for this book is available from the British Library

Library of Congress Cataloging in Publication Data
A catalog record for this book has been requested

ISBN10: 0–415–33815–8 (hbk)
ISBN10: 0–415–33816–6 (pbk)

ISBN13: 978–0–415–33815–8 (hbk)
ISBN13: 978–0–415–33816–5 (pbk)

FOR LILLIE AND EDDIE
FOR DAD AND CHRISTINE

CONTENTS

FIGURES

The above were reproduced with kind permission. While every effort has been made to trace copyright holders and obtain permission, this has not been possible in all cases. Any omissions brought to our attention will be remedied in future editions.

PREFACE

Quotations from primary and secondary sources are given in English translation. Film titles are given in the original Portuguese, with an English translation provided by the authors in parenthesis the first time the title appears in a given chapter. Thereafter the title is given in Portuguese alone within that chapter. Where a film has been exhibited abroad under an English title, the latter is given in italics. In addition, the Filmography provides a list of all the films referred to in the book, together with an English translation.

ACKNOWLEDGEMENTS

The research that gave rise to this book was greatly facilitated by the support of the Universities of Leeds and Liverpool. Essential archival work in Brazil was only possible thanks to generous research grants from the British Academy and the Arts and Humanities Research Board. We would like to express our gratitude to the following institutions, colleagues and friends, all of whom helped to bring this book to fruition: Maite Conde, João Luiz Vieira, Júlio César Miranda, John Gledson, David Treece, Ismail Xavier, Lúcia Nagib, Vinícius Chiappeta Braga, Diana Holmes, Marie-Louise Banning, Caroline Dawson, Rogério Ferraraz, Claire Williams, Andrea Noble, Tatiana Heise, the World Cinemas group of the University of Leeds and, in particular, Song Hwee Lim, Clóvis Molinari (Arquivo Nacional), Carlos Augusto Calil, the Biblioteca Nacional, the Fundação Getúlio Vargas, the Cinemateca of the Museu de Arte Moderna and the Museu da Imagem e do Som, Rio de Janeiro, the Cinemateca Brasileira, São Paulo, and the Tempo Glauber, Rio de Janeiro. We are grateful for the assistance given in the acquisition of illustrations for the book from Maria Byington, Rosângela Sodré (Centro Técnico Audiovisual), Anwen Rees (BBC Wales), Rafael Luna (the Cinemateca of the Museu de Arte Moderna), and Sara Rocha (Tempo Glauber). Our visits to Brazil were often only feasible thanks to the wonderful hospitality of Elmar Pereira de Mello, Hilda White Rössle de Mello, Maria Helena and Júlio César Senna, Barbara and Mike Thornton, Carmen and Durval Barros, Ellen Ostoff and Miguel Magalhães, and Maria Helena da Silveira Caldeirat.

Staff at Routledge have been unfailingly helpful and patient – thanks especially to series director Susan Hayward for her support and encouragement, and to Charlotte Wood.

Last, but never least, we would like to say thank you to our families for their love and support.

INTRODUCTION

The 'national' in the Brazilian context

In a recent examination of approaches to understanding national cinema, Valentina Vitali and Paul Willeman write: '[a]s a rule, books on specific national cinemas acknowledge that it is impossible, or at least difficult, to write film history in terms of national cultural formations, only to proceed to do precisely that'.[1] Finding ourselves slipping into this rather irresistible approach, and thus searching for reasons why *not* to speak of Brazilian national cinema, we were at once struck by how much less problematic the 'national cinema' question appeared to be in the Brazilian context when compared to that in other volumes in this Routledge series. Unlike the case of Australia, Brazil's national language (Portuguese) sets its cinema clearly apart from the dominant international cinema (Hollywood), and unlike, for example, British and Spanish cinema, and despite Brazil's size (the fifth largest country on the planet), Brazilian cinema operates almost exclusively in that language. The Portuguese language also sets Brazilian cinema apart from film production elsewhere in Latin America, despite (mostly Euro-American) academics' insistence on lumping all Latin American cinemas in together as one.[2] That said, it is possible to view the Brazilian *cinema novo* as part of a supra-national body of filmic work in the Spanish- and Portuguese-speaking countries of the Americas in the 1960s and 1970s: the so-called 'continental project' of New Latin American cinema.[3] So too is it increasingly useful to situate a still relatively small number of contemporary Brazilian (or part-Brazilian) films within the context of filmmaking across the continent and beyond, given the impact of Ibermedia and other international co-production initiatives.[4] But these are just other ways of thinking about Brazilian films – they do not, as we see it, make it either 'impossible' or even 'difficult' to write Brazilian film history in terms of a 'national cultural formation'. As we hope to reveal, Brazilian films can still most usefully be viewed first and foremost as products of their local cinematic culture and socio-political context, and for this reason a discussion of Brazilian cinema as national cinema appears to make perfect sense.

Furthermore, there are no sub-state cinemas[5] to complicate notions of the national in Brazil. Brazil's sovereignty has remained unchallenged since the birth of cinema (an issue complicating a text like *German National Cinema*). Like that of Mexico, the Brazilian diaspora may be growing, but unlike the Mexican situation there is no real Brazilian filmmaking tradition being forged outside Brazil. Of course, as many other recent studies of national cinemas have also revealed,[6] in Brazil the concept of transnationality is gradually transforming both the filmmaking scene and the ways in which films are related to the society that produces them. That said, the transnational is not something traditionally associated with Brazilian cinema. For example, despite his own plans for developing a 'tri-continental cinema', the films made by acclaimed *cinema novo* director Glauber Rocha in Europe are seen (by both Europeans and Brazilians) as unproblematically part of the Brazilian canon, because they form part of his auteurist body of work.[7] On the other hand, a film such as Walter Salles's *Diarios de motocicleta* (*The Motorcycle Diaries*, 2004) is seen in Brazil as a foreign film directed by a Brazilian, and its highly suggestive transnationality is, for the time being, a source of interest almost exclusively among foreign observers.[8] Thus, with the possible exception of the experience of Brazil's indigenous populations, the optic of the 'transnational' has not yet become the most rewarding and logical way to examine Brazilian cinema.[9]

With regard to the rather mundane issue of statistics, filmmaking in Brazil also fulfils the remit of a national cinema comfortably. With the exception of falls in production rates during times of international and economic crisis, as witnessed in most of the world's cinemas, film production in Brazil has been steady since its inception in the last decade of the nineteenth century. It is a cinema that is capable of exciting the interest of domestic audiences (over 12 million people went to see *Dona Flor e seus dois maridos* (*Dona Flor and Her Two Husbands*) when it was released in 1976) and audiences abroad (*Cidade de Deus* (*City of God*, 2002) is the third highest-grossing foreign language film of all time to be screened in the UK). Brazilian films have been winning international prizes regularly since the 1950s,[10] and Brazilian cinema can boast its own critically acclaimed and highly influential avant-garde/art-house film movement – the aforementioned *cinema novo* – thus bolstering the case for the existence of a 'national cinema' in Brazil.

Brazil seemingly presents no real difficulties with regard to the limits of the national in terms of borders or governance. Brazil gained its political independence from Portugal in 1822, and by the mid-nineteenth century the process of cultural nation-building was under way. With the overthrow of the monarchy in 1889, the First Republic (1889–1930) had settled the many border disputes that had remained unresolved throughout much of the century by the time cinema became established in the country. That said, it has been argued that, as a result of Brazil's neo-colonial Third World status, one of the manifestations of which is the foreign domination of the film market, filmmakers have been necessarily concerned with the ramifications of nationalism.[11] As Stam, Vieira and Xavier put it,

> Given the foreign domination of the market, and given the immense obstacles to making films, the cinema, for better or worse, has been habitually evaluated in terms of its service to 'development' and 'national liberation'. The filmmakers express their creative personalities,

> but they also see themselves as part of a larger collective project: the consolidation of a national cinema.[12]

Elsewhere, Randal Johnson writes:

> In purely practical terms, the cinema is demanding because of its unique situation among the arts in Brazil. It industrial base, dependent on imports, renders it more capital-intensive than other sectors of cultural production, and the fact that it must compete against highly organized and highly capitalized foreign film industries makes its very survival problematic without state assistance. Therefore its stance of economic and cultural nationalism is more pronounced than other areas of cultural production.[13]

The result of this neo-imperial threat,[14] whether real or imagined, is a greater concern with *the national*. Thus, while the Brazilian government has traditionally sought, through the sponsorship of the film industry, the promotion of language and culture (a practice common to many 'national' film industries), Brazilian film-makers do not turn to considerations of the national solely in order to gain financial support. Their primordial desire to place the nation on the big screen sets them apart from many other national film cultures and facilitates greatly any discussion of national cinema.

One of the results of this is that the rhetoric promoting the national film industry has changed little down the years. In a speech on the state of the film industry delivered to the Brazilian Senate in 2000, but which would not have looked out of place in the early 1960s, when suspicion of the United States dominated left-wing politics in Brazil, filmmaker Carlos Diegues stated the following:

> It is no exaggeration to say that the role of American film in today's global culture is the same as that of the conquistadors of the Renaissance . . . If Brazil cannot produce its own image and occupy a few screens with that image, Brazilians will become living archaeological mysteries, unknown both to others and to themselves.[15]

This sense of cinema's onerous responsibility for defending Brazilian national cultural interests is echoed in the words of José Álvaro Moisés, Brazil's Audio-Visual Secretary from 1999 to 2002:

> The country understands, more every day, how important it is for us to look at ourselves in a cinematic 'mirror'. We realise that we need that fundamental function of self-identification which is made possible by the projection of our common experiences on a screen, to understand each other better and to define with more clarity what we want for ourselves in the new millennium.[16]

This widely held belief of the importance of a 'cinematic mirror' to combat the neo-imperial intentions of Hollywood is coupled with the conviction that foreign filmmakers (and for foreign read Hollywood) cannot be trusted to do the job of making films about Brazil,[17] and it therefore behoves Brazilian filmmakers to depict the nation on screen. The result of this conviction, which dates from the cultural invasion of Latin America by the USA via the Good Neighbour Policy of the 1930s and 1940s, and the disastrous attempt on the part of Hollywood to woo South American audiences with cod depictions of an invented and ultimately offensive homogeneous 'Latin American-ness', has, as we shall see in subsequent chapters, had an impact on the choice of national themes dealt with in Brazilian films.[18]

We regard the *national cinemas* model as offering an opportunity to be as wide-reaching in our study as possible, in terms of filmmaking styles and practices, and it can thus help us avoid falling into the trap of just looking at 'a critical (and implicitly left-wing) cinema, a radical cinema, or a cinema characterized by questioning and enquiry',[19] an approach that so often characterises both studies of national cinemas by foreign academics and studies of Brazilian cinema in general.[20] Instead, we are following very much the definition laid out by Tom O'Regan in what is perhaps the most cited introduction in the Routledge 'National Cinemas' series. O'Regan sees national cinemas as a series of sets of relations between national film texts, national and international film industries, and the films' and industries' socio-political and cultural contexts.[21] Seen as such, the national cinemas model gives us the scope to discuss in hitherto unseen detail the impact, for example, of screen stars on the Brazilian film industry and beyond, and to ensure that something more than lip service is paid to popular cinema.

O'Regan suggests that:

> rather than talk about nationalism and national cinema as exclusive terms we should seek to investigate the way in which society as a national whole is problematized and the kind of nation that has been projected *through* such problematization. In this regard we can begin to see cinema as an effect of and as affecting that problematization.[22]

The films and film contexts we look at in this volume thus contribute to the debate on what 'national' means in the Brazilian context in a variety of ways: by simply staging, or by contesting, established notions of national identity, or by dint of the fact that the filmic product has been sponsored in one form or another by the Brazilian state. It is interesting to note that most of the filmmakers we discuss were either tied to a studio system with nationalist pretensions[23] or have received financial support from the State via financial initiatives with nationalist pretensions.[24]

It is also worth bearing in mind that Brazilians themselves use the adjective 'national' (*nacional* or *nacionais* in the plural) when describing Brazilian films, which, albeit superficially, lends some credibility to a national cinema analysis approach when discussing cinematic production in Brazil. However, the use of the term ultimately belies what is arguably a heightened awareness on the part of

Brazilians of the origins of things consumed within the country (at least when compared to somewhere like the UK) and the tradition of privileging the foreign over locally produced goods (whisky and cars being key examples). In terms of displays in bookshops, music stores and video and DVD rental stores, the 'nacional' is always separated from the 'internacional'. The adjective traditionally has negative connotations, and suggests a process of (unfavourable) comparison with the foreign, the imported and the international. It is interesting to note by contrast that one of the modern musical genres that Brazilians are most proud of, MPB or *Música Popular Brasileira*, avoids using the adjective 'nacional', as does the national football squad.[25] Brazilian rock music, dismissed as inferior to American and British rock and pop, is tellingly referred to as *Rock nacional.*

Rather than use the rest of this introductory chapter to project a highly theorised and thus overdetermined definition of national cinema on to Brazilian cinematic practices,[26] we will concentrate instead on features of these practices that need some explanation, providing a context for appreciating the different sections that this book encompasses. We see these features as falling broadly into the following areas: the development of cinephilia in Brazil, the issue of inclusion (the *bête noire* of the national culture argument) and, following on from this, the perennial problem of both identifying and maintaining an audience for Brazilian cinema.

Cinephilia in Brazil

Paulo Emílio Salles Gomes once declared wistfully that there is no such thing as cinema, only films, but there is, and has been at least since the 1950s, a Brazilian 'film culture' which arguably needs to exist to make the case for a bona fide national cinema (and as it happens Salles Gomes, despite his words, played a key role in the development of film culture – and as an extension national cinema – in Brazil). For example, there are a number of spaces (congresses, specialist journals, daily newspapers) afforded to filmmakers to express their ideas on cinema and the state of the film industry, but interest is not limited to their opinions on film. Filmmakers' views on political, social and cultural issues are regularly sought by the press: they are thus regarded in Brazil as intellectuals and important opinion formers. While some may express political opinions that are clearly personal,[27] and while there has always been a healthy amount of divergence of views between different elements of the film industry, Brazilian cineastes have, as Jean-Claude Bernardet argues, a 'corporativist' vision of themselves.[28]

Although some observers complain that contemporary filmmakers are loath to be drawn into debates on the state of Brazilian cinema, and that an ultimately counter-productive unanimity of purpose exists at present, the tradition in Brazil is very much of the active participation of filmmakers in film criticism, in developing policy for supporting the industry, and of contributing to cultural debates in general. For example, filmmakers in the 1950s and 1960s, such as Alex Viany and Glauber Rocha,[29] left an influential body of film criticism, and were instrumental in the creation of a national film culture in Brazil. In terms of theorists par excellence of national film culture, there are two names that stand out among others for their lasting contribution to film culture: Paulo Emílio Salles Gomes (1916–77) and Jean-Claude Bernardet (b. 1936).

Paulo Emílio Salles Gomes

Paulo Emílio Salles Gomes is one of the most important names in Brazilian film history, for his contribution to the creation of cinephilia and cinematheque culture in Brazil, and to the setting up of influential film courses, and for understanding Brazilian film, and culture in general.[30] Having been imprisoned in the 1930s for his communist views, and after successfully digging a tunnel to freedom, Salles Gomes headed for France, where he studied literature, sociology, journalism and, later, aesthetics at some of the most prestigious higher education institutions in Paris. On his return to São Paulo at the beginning of the Second World War, Salles Gomes set up the Clube de Cinema de São Paulo, along the lines of the influential Cercle du Cinéma that he had frequented in Paris, where intellectuals and university lecturers would meet informally and debate films, often in French. The Clube de Cinema was eventually deemed subversive and closed down by Getúlio Vargas's neo-fascist New State, the *Estado Novo* (1937–45). Salles Gomes's contact with Henri Langlois, founder of the Cinémathèque Française, proved instrumental in setting up in 1948 and running the first cinémathèque in Brazil, at the Modern Art Museum in São Paulo (later to become the Cinemateca Brasileira). Salles Gomes was also a key player in the organisation of an international film festival in São Paulo in 1954, to commemorate the four hundredth anniversary of the city. Together with Jean-Claude Bernardet, he founded in the early 1960s the Film Studies programme at the University of Brasília, and in 1968 he set up what is now the foremost Film Studies school in the country, the Escola de Comunicação e Artes (ECA) at the University of São Paulo. Ismail Xavier, considered to be one of the most important film scholars and professors in Brazil today, was one of his first pupils.

Salles Gomes was known to influential French film critics, directors and thinkers for his contributions to *Cahiers du Cinéma*, and for his acclaimed work on Jean Vigo, published in France in 1957 and later translated into English and Portuguese.[31] Salles Gomes's interest in Brazilian cinema was sparked by the *cinema novo* movement: he was one of its greatest defenders. As well as an important text on early filmmaker Humberto Mauro,[32] Salles Gomes has left an important legacy for scholars of Brazilian cinema in the form of seminal essays on Brazilian film culture. The most well known and most frequently cited of these is 'Cinema: trajetória no subdesenvolvimento' (Cinema: A Trajectory within Underdevelopment),[33] in which he argues that Brazilians:

> are neither Europeans nor North Americans. Lacking an original culture, nothing is foreign to us because everything is. The painful construction of ourselves develops within the rarified dialectic of not

> being and being someone else. Brazilian film participates in this mechanism and alters it through our creative incapacity for copying.[34]

Salles Gomes's essay begins with a summary of Brazilian history, in which the country is placed clearly in a Western cultural tradition. As a result of miscegenation, there was in Brazil no possibility of forcing out the colonisers as the Algerians went on to do with the French in 1962. Salles Gomes argues that Brazil's colonisers are to be found elsewhere,[35] in a clear reference to economic dependency, and clearly inspired by dependency theory, so much in vogue at the time of writing and still influential in contemporary discussions of national cinema.[36] Thus Salles Gomes's tract sees Brazilian cinema first and foremost in relation to Hollywood.[37] It also reiterates the notion of Brazilian cinema as having an onerous and 'worthy' role in terms of the preservation and promotion of Brazilian culture. For Salles Gomes, the role of Brazilian cinema was to express 'the complex reality of our culture',[38] and the best of Brazilian cinema 'nourishes an identification with the oppressed and maintains a critical distance from the oppressor'.[39]

Jean-Claude Bernardet

A less idealistic approach to reading Brazilian films can be found in the work of Jean-Claude Bernardet. Bernardet, a Belgian-born French national, moved to São Paulo in 1949 aged 12 and was naturalised Brazilian in 1964.[40] Bernardet's fascination with cinema (and Brazilian cinema in particular) began with his involvement in the Cinemateca Brasileira in the 1950s (both as a spectator and, later, as an employee). He has been a regular contributor to film criticism pages of a large number of newspapers and magazines since the 1960s. Like Salles Gomes, he studied in France (in his case on a semiology course led by Christian Metz). He has produced a number of key texts on Brazilian cinema, including an early study of the *cinema novo* movement (*Brasil em tempo de cinema*, 1967), a seminal film history title (*Cinema brasileiro: propostas para uma história*, 1979) and the recent *Historiografia clássica do cinema brasileiro* (1995), in which he analyses the contribution made to Brazilian film history by its critics. As well as taking on minor acting roles in films, Bernardet has, since the 1960s, been writing film scripts: his most successful work in this field to date is co-adapting *Um céu de estrelas* (*A Starry Sky*, Tata Amaral, 1996).

Bernardet's *Historiografia clássica* makes a number of potentially controversial observations that bear relevance for understanding Brazilian cinema as national cinema. The first two chapters set out to debunk two of Brazilian cinema's most cherished foundational myths: its 'birth', to which we shall return later in this chapter, and its so-called Belle Époque (the Bela Época).[41] The myth of the Bela Época, which even Salles Gomes bought into wholesale, states that the early years of the twentieth century represented an idealised time in filmmaking in Brazil. Bernardet argues that, as in the case of many other aspects of Brazilian film history that are taken as read, there is no proof that (a) more Brazilian than foreign films were being screened at the time and that (b) these films found an audience.[42] It is interesting that Brazil's filmmaking Belle Époque, mythical or otherwise, pre-dates the domination by Hollywood of world cinema. As Vitali and Willeman remind us, the national cinema model was created by Hollywood, since in the early years of cinema no one much cared about the nationality of a film.[43]

Cineclubes

As well as being influenced by the work of Brazil's 'intellectual' filmmakers, critics and academics, the development of a culture of film loving has been influenced by film clubs. The *cineclube* phenomenon has existed in Brazil since at least 1917, but the first legally constituted club appears in 1928 (the Chaplin Club).[44] The Cineclube de Marília, a small town in the state of São Paulo, was the longest-running (from 1952 until well into the 1990s).

The year 1956 was an important one for the founding of different film clubs, especially in Rio de Janeiro, but the movement really took off in the 1960s when the Catholic Church began to sponsor a number of more local clubs. At the height of the military dictatorship in 1968, at a national meeting of *cineclubes* in Brasília, representatives declared themselves to be against the regime. As a result, within a year, most of the 300 *cineclubes* in the country had disappeared owing to pressure from the State. When they re-formed, it was with much more specifically political objectives (watching a film, especially one that had experienced problems with the censors, became a political act and a challenge to the status quo). Partly as a result of this and partly as a result of the critical success of *cinema novo*, the *cineclubes* began to focus their attention on Brazilian cinema. Such was their concentration on national cinema that many clubs felt they had lost their purpose (to combat the dictatorship) by the time of redemocratisation in 1985, with apolitical films dominating the national industry.

Nowadays, the likes of *Estação* and *Espaço* art-house cinema groups in Rio de Janeiro and São Paulo have taken the place of the *cineclubes*. While many consider that such cinema halls have been totally de-characterised by neo-globalisation[45] and that the democratic thrust of the old *cineclube* movement has been lost among the audiences these venues attract, they are arguably no more elitist than the early *cineclubes*, where discussions of French cinema in the French language were de rigueur.

Cinematecas

With the growth of cinephilia and the *cineclube* movement, it was only a matter of time before the first *cinemateca*, in the style of the French cinémathèques, was founded.[46] The *filmoteca* attached to Modern Art Museum of São Paulo was the first of its kind, and was also the first to organise a retrospective of Brazilian cinema in 1952. Until the arrival of the *filmoteca* film preservation was carried out by concerned individuals. As no one had much of an idea of how to store films, they frequently caught fire. Hernani Heffner estimates that around 50 per cent of the films made in Brazil to date have been lost.[47]

In 1984 the *filmoteca* was separated from the Modern Art Museum and became the Cinemateca Brasileira, the most important in Brazil (and Latin America) in terms of holdings of filmic material, personal archives and so on, and in terms of public screenings of both national and international films. Although more financially supported than many other cultural institutions, both the original *filmoteca* and the Cinemateca Brasileira have nonetheless relied on the dedication of a small number of cinephiles: Paulo Emílio Salles Gomes, Jean-Claude Bernardet, filmmaker and critic Gustavo Dahl, and Lúcia Nagib all worked there at the beginning of their careers in film criticism.

The *cinemateca* of the Modern Art Museum of Rio de Janeiro (MAM-RJ) opened as late as 1957, and has been dogged by financial and other problems ever since. Despite the responsibility placed on Brazilian cinema to preserve the nation's cultural heritage, no real effort has been made at national level to preserve Brazil's film heritage. Given the fact that there is no national policy of film preservation, cinémathèques often function as very expensive charities, reliant on sponsorship by State-run or mixed-ownership companies and State and municipal governments, which are more likely to lend their support to high-profile film events (the remastering of old classics, for example) than improvements in storage infrastructure. Already strapped for cash and in a poor state of repair, the Rio cinémathèque came close to shutting for good in 2002, and was granted a last-minute reprieve in 2003 when it was incorporated into the cultural heritage scheme of the city of Rio de Janeiro.[48]

The question of inclusion

If there is one issue which problematises the *national*, where the stitching of the neat fit of the national cinemas 'pattern' on the Brazilian filmmaking body comes undone, it is the question of inclusion. Brazil has one of the worst records of wealth distribution in the world, which, together with its resulting pattern of unequal development and a centuries-long history of African slavery,[49] has helped to create a large section of the population that is ultimately disenfranchised. Perhaps the most obvious and startling example of this is Brazil's indigenous populations: traditionally ignored and only recently afforded the same rights of citizenship as other Brazilians.[50]

Thus, the argument for a national cinema is complicated by the fact that the vast majority of the population is removed from the opportunity and process of writing, directing, producing, starring in and even watching films. Given the at times seemingly insurmountable difficulties in making films in Brazil, most filmmakers are well-off, privately educated and white individuals (mostly men) with their own private incomes. Even with the supposed increase in access to alternative filmmaking technologies, there is no hard evidence to suggest that films on video, super-8, digital and so on are being made by communities traditionally beyond the reach and protection of the State.

A further example of this process of exclusion is the fact that Afro-Brazilians continue to be severely under-represented on cinema screens, being frequently substituted by light-skinned mixed-race stars.[51] Likewise, indigenous populations, North-Easterners and 'poor ethnic others' are frequently represented by white actors: their own appearance on screen is usually limited to 'ethnographic' documentary-filmmaking.

Since the days of Getúlio Vargas's authoritarian *Estado Novo*, the large immigrant populations in Brazil have been discouraged from cultural production aimed at their own communities, the result of which is a lack of tradition of making films aimed at 'specialised' audiences. As Stam, Vieira and Xavier observe, 'the view of the nation as a unitary subject muffles the "polyphony" of social and ethnic voices characteristic of a heteroglot culture'.[52]

The (elusive) audience

Jean-Claude Bernardet argues that European film historians date the 'birth' of cinema from the Lumière brothers' film screening in the Grand Café in Paris in 1895. Filming and screenings had taken place before then, but this event is acknowledged as the 'birth' of cinema because it was the first *successful* and *paid* public session. By contrast, Brazilian cinema's 'birth' is dated from the first filming. In this way, filming and screening were separated from each other from the outset. Bernardet sees this as more than a coincidence: 'By making such a choice, historians privileged production in detriment to exhibition and contact with the public.'[53] Thus in Brazil, Bernardet argues, when we talk about cinema we are talking about making films.[54] It has to be said that, as a rule, in academic work on Brazilian cinema scant attention is paid to audiences and questions of spectatorship.[55]

Ultimately, when we talk about Brazilian cinema we are talking about an exclusive art form, produced by, and increasingly for, an elite (and select) group of consumers. In terms of access to films of any nationality shown at theatres, the figures are bleak:

> Only about 70 million cinema tickets are sold in Brazil each year, to about 10 million consumers. This means that only 6 percent of the Brazilian population goes to the cinema. There are some 1400 cinema theatres in Brazil, which make it the country with the second highest ratio of inhabitants to theatres.[56]

Perhaps as a result of the kind of separation between the filmmaking process and the screening of films that Bernardet describes, the relationship between the filmmaking community and the film audience has, at best, been ambivalent. For a start, given the lack of information available on early audiences, they and their relationship with national cinema were invented by historians.[57] Working-class audiences of the *chanchada* films, the mainstay of Brazilian cinema throughout much of the 1940s and 1950s, were demonised by many observers for their popular tastes. Those who went in their millions to watch the soft-core *pornochanchada* comedies of the 1970s were dismissed as perverted hypocrites.[58] And, as filmmaker Carlos Diegues sees it, cinema-going in Brazil in the twenty-first century has become a typical middle-class leisure pursuit, because cinemas can now be found almost exclusively in shopping centres:

> [Cinema] is targeted precisely at the section of the population who, fuelled by dreams and fantasies of a hypothetical 'first world', refuse to recognise or take part in the realities of the country. They equally have difficulty in accepting their Brazilian cultural identity, a pre-requisite for understanding any audio-visual material produced in Brazil.[59]

By contrast, the once-vilified working-class audience is praised for its traditional support of the film industry in Brazil:

> The people who have stopped going to the cinema are precisely those who traditionally have always ensured the box-office success of Brazilian films, during all the previous cycles of the country's film production. Popular audiences who want to see themselves represented on screen have always been, historically and statistically, the key consumers of Brazilian films.[60]

As we shall see in Chapter 6, the irony here is that popular audiences of Brazilian cinema were frequently accused of watching nothing but poor imitations of Hollywood films, and of thus denying their Brazilian cultural identity in much the same way that middle-class cinema audiences are said to be denying theirs. Diegues may have attacked audiences before the recent resounding box-office success of Brazilian films such as *Cidade de Deus* (2002), *Carandiru* (2003) and *Dois filhos de Francisco* (*Two Sons of Francisco,* 2005), all of which outperformed Hollywood films on their release, but one only has to consider the highly successful music and television industries in Brazil, which more often than not enjoy a larger following than their foreign competitors, a following made up more often than not by the same middle class that allegedly dreams of a 'hypothetical first world', to question to what extent filmmakers and their representatives really know the audience.

The one great success story in all this is, of course, *Cidade de Deus,* a critical and commercial success, both at home and abroad, and, as revealed in Chapter 9, it is a film that strove to tackle head on the issue of exclusion of subaltern groups from the filmmaking process. But *Cidade de Deus* is very much the exception that proves the rule that the exclusion of a large proportion of the nation is taken as read in Brazilian national cinema. Thus, while it is, in fact, relatively easy to define Brazilian national cinema, that ease is in itself not necessarily something that Brazil's filmmaking community can be proud of.

Structure of this book

This volume is divided into four parts, the first of which, 'Cinema and the State', examines the relationship between central government and its institutions and the evolution of a cinema industry in Brazil. The official legislation relating to cinema, however ineffective in practice, provides an essential framework for understanding the Brazilian State's attitude towards the film medium since 1889. As Triana-Toribio notes, 'Even if the demands for a national cinema made in official and popular documents and magazines are not wholly met by the cinema itself, these demands are themselves a crucial part of the story of . . . national cinema.'[61]

Part II, 'Defining "national" cinema, 1896 to 1960', concerns itself with four pioneers of filmmaking in Brazil, two men, Adhemar Gonzaga and Humberto Mauro, and two women, Carmen Santos and Gilda de Abreu. Gonzaga and Mauro had very different visions of what direction Brazilian cinema should take, but both were in agreement on one issue: the colour of Brazil's 'skin'. Their films were peopled with photogenic white-skinned stars, and Afro-Brazilians and members of indigenous communities were conspicuous by their absence. Carmen Santos's ambitious project *Inconfidência mineira* (Conspiracy in Minas Gerais, 1948), which she produced and directed, dealt with Brazil's first attempt to assert its independence from Portugal in the eighteenth century. Her epic film thus constitutes an equally emblematic foundational myth of 'Brazilianness' the letter of Pero Vaz Caminha that documented the arrival of Portuguese navigators in the New World in 1500, depicted in similarly epic proportions in Mauro's *O descobrimento do Brasil* (The Discovery of Brazil, 1937). Both these historical melodramas memorialised the 'birth' of the nation in a manner that could not have been more acceptable to the propagandists of President Getúlio Vargas's New State (1937–45). Both Santos and Gilda de Abreu contributed to the consolidation of the star system in Brazilian film, and Abreu is equally remembered as the pioneering female director of one of the most commercially successful Brazilian films of all time, *O ébrio* (The Drunkard, 1946). Part II concludes with an examination of what is sometimes called the only truly Brazilian cinematic genre, the *chanchada* or musical comedy, which dominated film production in Brazil in the 1940s and 1950s. As Bastos has shown, the *chanchadas* encouraged audiences all over Brazil to situate themselves within a national identity symbolised by carnival and Copacabana, metonyms for the city of Rio de Janeiro, the then federal capital of Brazil and from the 1940s the site of both an eager modernity and an unrivalled glamour.[62] It is interesting to note that the ethos of *malandragem*, so central to the *chanchada*'s comic protagonists and plots, was traditionally seen as a characteristic trait solely of the inhabitants of Rio de Janeiro, the *cariocas*. With the diffusion of the *malandro* character, epitomised by countless roles played by Oscarito, via Atlântida's films, *malandragem* became associated with the Brazilian people as a whole, a badge of national belonging.[63] As Bastos concludes, 'For decades, when people talked about "being Brazilian", it was the stereotype of the Rio *malandro*, so well characterised in the Atlântida *chanchadas*, that populated their imaginary.'[64]

In Part III, 'Defining "national" cinema since 1960', we consider first the contribution made by *cinema novo* to the notion of national cinema in Brazil. Produced in the 1960s and early 1970s, the *cinema novo* represents the best-known, most analysed and most critically acclaimed group of Brazilian films. Although the *cinema novo* played an essential role in putting Brazilian cinema on the world cinematic map and has helped to increase its international dissemination and popularity ever since, it did not inspire the Brazilian cinema-going public at the time. What did was a series of soft- and later hard-core porn films (to the chagrin of cinephiles), some of which were funded by Embrafilme, the State production and distribution agency. The *pornochanchada* reflected on changing sexual mores at a crucial period of Brazilian history (military dictatorship), and their popularity at the box office can be read as a reaction on the part of cinema audiences to the 'respectable' official versions of the nation expounded by the military regime. We then turn our attention to the representation of the nation in the cinema of the *retomada*, which revisits the commonplaces of *cinema novo*, namely the *sertão* (arid interior of Brazil's North-East) and the *favela* (urban slum), but to bring those two specific loci of Brazilianness up to date in a cinematic language accessible to as broad a cross-section of the domestic audience, not to mention foreign spectators, as possible. That is not to say that this is the only portrayal of the realities of modern life; indeed, the *retomada* years have witnessed a steady output of middle-class, urban romantic comedies which contrast sharply with dystopian depictions of Brazilian cities and their inhabitants.[65] Some of these have enjoyed commercial success within Brazil, alongside *City of God* and *Carandiru*,[66] but did not reach foreign audiences. For the international viewing public, Brazilian cinema today is synonymous with hard-hitting stories of urban violence and deprivation. As Triana-Toribio has noted, certain film styles can be taken to embody a particular national identity.[67] To what extent this has created a kind of generic expectation among non-Brazilian audiences, and thus dictated the selection of films for international distribution, is open to debate, not least in Brazil.

Part IV, 'Brazilian identities on screen: stars', examines the star personae of some of the nation's most emblematic cinematic icons since the 1940s in order to answer a series of questions about national representation. If we accept that, as Richard Dyer argues, the star texts of a given society's movie stars betray the underlying tensions of that society's ideology, what does a whiter-than-white female star wearing an Afro-Brazilian costume reveal about Brazilian society in the 1940s and 1950s? What can we conclude from the fact that a film genre, the *chanchada*, which drew heavily on black culture (samba) in its soundtrack shockingly under-represented Afro-Brazilian performers and held up a Hollywood ideal of white beauty for its predominantly black or mixed-race, low-brow audiences? And what about a star system that tolerates a handful of black leading performers, such as the exceptionally gifted Grande Otelo, but excludes them from top billing and from magazines like *Cinelândia*, and denigrates them with racially inspired nicknames such as Big Othello, Chocolate, Little Black Prince and Black-out? As in Hollywood, whiteness is normativised in the *chanchada*, in keeping with the reigning 'pigmentocracy' of 1950s Brazil.[68] As Stam writes, 'the veiled presence of Afro-Brazilian music and dance in numerous films paradoxically marks Afro-Brazilian *absence* from the screen'.[69] This absence continues into the 1970s and beyond, with, as we argue, dark-skinned 'white' actresses representing the mixed-race and black peoples that make up the majority of Brazil's population. This section makes clear the extent to which screen stars, despite their absence from studies of Brazilian film history to date, have both been the main driving force behind the film industry in Brazil and formed the link with other media and varieties of popular entertainment, such as music hall, the recording industry and all-pervasive television.

Part I

CINEMA AND THE STATE

1

THE FIRST REPUBLIC (1889–1930)

Film and the law

The arrival of the moving image in Brazil in 1896 came less than a decade after the abolition of slavery in that country, the subsequent fall of the monarchy, and the establishment of the First Republic (1889–1930).[1] The first films to be shown in Brazil together with the new technology itself, as in other Latin American countries, were part of what has been termed a 'cinema of attractions',[2] which showcased movement and modernity and was based on an 'aesthetics of astonishment'.[3] The earliest home-grown films emulated this 'cinema of thrills and surprises',[4] such as Vittorio de Maio's *Chegada de um trem a Petrópolis* (Arrival of a Train in Petrópolis, 1897), which evidenced the great impact of Lumière's *Arrivée d'un train à La Ciotat* (*Arrival of a Train at La Ciotat Station*, 1895). However, Brazil's relative economic backwardness hindered the development of cinema until 1900, the year that marked the beginning of the so-called Belle Époque of Brazilian filmmaking.[5] Between 1900 and 1912, the new medium gained a firm foothold in national life. Brazilian films dominated the domestic market, thanks to a vertically integrated system of production, distribution and exhibition, and attained an annual production of over one hundred films covering a wide range of genres. 'Documentaries and newsreels, made with amazing rapidity and dealing with current events of local interest, fostered a public habit of frequent movie going.'[6] Under the First Republic's federal structure, the regulation of forms of public entertainment was the responsibility of individual states rather than the nation as a whole, and the cinema was clearly seen as an essentially local form of diversion, in need of little official sanction. It was not until the outbreak of the First World War (1914–18) that Brazilians turned their attentions to the use of film as a way of fostering nationalist sentiments, but this did not prevent isolated cases of censorship, such as when the Ministry of the Navy confiscated the film *A vida do cabo João Candido* (The Life of Corporal João Candido, 1912), directed by Carlos Lambertini,[7] which dealt with the true story of a black corporal who led an army revolt against corporal punishment in November 1910, known as the *Revolta da Chibata* (Revolt of the Whip).

There were a small number of similar State interventions into the sphere of the cinema prior to 1914. Itinerant trades of all kinds were outlawed during the urban reforms in Rio de Janeiro in the first decade of the twentieth century, and the *ambulantes* or travelling projectionists who had staged film screenings in makeshift locales and outdoors in towns and cities[8] were forced out of business, being replaced by the first movie theatres, which benefited from dramatic improvements in the urban infrastructure, not least the arrival of electricity. These premises were, however, prone to outbreaks of fire, leading the press to depict cinema-going as a dangerous activity. Consequently, in 1909 the state of Rio de Janeiro decreed that entertainment venues, including bars, indoor theatres and cinemas, had to comply with certain safety procedures.

The First Republic's light touch with regard to the regulation of the cinema and its overwhelming disregard for the medium's potential use as a propaganda tool did not always result in respect for the political regime on the part of filmmakers or their audiences. One of the most commercially successful so-called *falantes e cantantes* (literally 'talking and singing' films, made between 1907 and 1910, for which actors provided dialogue and songs from behind the cinema screen) was *Paz e amor* (Peace and Love, 1910), a tongue-in-cheek critique of national politics and Rio's social elite. This film combined music and light-hearted satire, and is best remembered for its caricature of then president Nilo Peçanha dressed as a fictitious king named Olin I, a thinly veiled anagram that leaves no doubt as to the intended allusion.[9]

Film and nation building

Aside from isolated pieces of legislation, there was no significant attempt to direct film production until the mid-1910s, when the notion that the new medium could be put to the service of nation building began to gain credence. This development was a direct consequence of the arrival in Brazil of newsreels and propaganda films from abroad, and was fostered by journalists writing for national newspapers and magazines such as *Para Todos* and *Careta*. Independent filmmakers took the initiative, rather than the State, establishing film studios such as Pátria Filmes, Brasil Filmes, Ipiranga Filmes and Guanabara Filmes, which produced newsreels and propaganda films for private companies and for the State. The patriotic names of these early attempts at industrialisation clearly indicate the wider vision of cinema as a national project,[10] and represent what Núria Triana-Toribio has termed a 'proto-national cinema'.[11] During the war years several of Brazil's most well-known novels that centred on national myths were adapted for the screen[12] and, as Maite Conde writes, this 'cinematic adaptation of what Doris Sommer has termed "foundational fictions" in effect constituted an early attempt to construe film as a "national art form" in Brazil'.[13] Conde goes on to argue that the patriotism that underpinned the reconfiguration of film was partially due to the conflict in Europe. Brazil joined the Allies in 1917, triggering an outbreak of fervent nationalism that was encouraged by filmmakers who documented national events such as the

Brazilian army's departure for the front,[14] and encouraged young men to enlist in the armed forces.[15]

The Brazilian army's involvement in documenting the realities of life in Brazil's Amazonian territories, under the command of Colonel Cândido Rondon, gave rise to a screen representation of a hitherto invisible component of the Brazilian nation. With the creation of the *Comissão Rondon* (Rondon Commission) in 1912, charged with building telegraph lines across more than 800 miles of the Amazonian Basin, Major Luís Tomás Reis was dispatched to Europe to acquire the latest filmmaking technology with which to film on location the explorations of Brazil's latest pioneers. The Commission also implemented official policies regarding relations between the State and Brazil's indigenous peoples. To this end Reis kept statistical records of the physical characteristics of the tribe members that he encountered, and his close-up shots of these people evidence his intent to scientifically document racial characteristics, in addition to cultural aspects of their lives.[16] His ground-breaking documentaries, such as *Rituais e festas Bororo* (Rituals and Festivals of the Bororo People, 1916), amply suggest that he saw his role as one of educating the people of Brazil about the origins of the nation's first inhabitants. As Reis wrote,

> archaeology still hasn't come up with anything conclusive about the origins of primitive American man. We still don't know for sure whether American man migrated here from another continent in very remote times or if he is native to here.[17]

Reis's moving images constitute an essential component of the Rondon Commission's public relations work directed at creating a unified community of Brazilians.

In the 1920s the political regime continued to have minimal involvement with the cinematic medium. The presidential candidate Arthur Bernardes contracted two filmmakers, the Botelho brothers, to film his political campaign, and they were subsequently employed by the government to shoot official events.[18] Furthermore, the young director Humberto Mauro managed to interest the state governor of Minas Gerais, Antônio Carlos, in the activities of his filmmaking debut in Cataguases. In 1928, when visiting the area, the governor visited the Phebo film studio, founded by Mauro, during the filming of *Sangue mineiro* (Blood of Minas Gerais, 1930), and expressed his enthusiasm for its initiatives, hinting at government support in the form of a loan that was never to materialise. Schvarzman argues that it was as a result of this implicit promise of state support that the final version of *Sangue mineiro* began with ultra-patriotic intertitles that extolled the virtues of Belo Horizonte and the culture of Minas Gerais.[19]

In 1910 the film archive (*filmoteca*) of the National Museum (Museu Nacional) was created, and over the following decade a number of educational films were commissioned for exhibition in primary and secondary schools on an ad hoc basis. In 1928 the first legislation was introduced to regulate the use of these teaching materials in schools within the federal district of Rio de Janeiro. In 1929 the first Exhibition of Educational Cinema took place, at a time when censorship was still only imposed by the police at the level of individual states.[20]

Cinema and morality

During the First Republic, calls for controls to be placed on the cinema formed part of wider debates on morality, particularly with regard to women, and principally focused on the physical space of the cinema, deemed as a site of unsavoury amorous activities. Attention was directed towards regulating the composition of audiences, rather than the content of the films that were exhibited. Although there was no rating code, exhibitors chose to advertise certain films as 'only for men' or 'unsuitable for ladies', thus limiting women's access to the public sphere of the cinema theatre.[21] As Conde argues, 'the high percentage of women in early audiences must have presented a threat to the traditional and patriarchal organisation of public space'.[22] The *Liga de Moralidade* (Morality League) used the fledgling medium to denounce what it saw as the vices of the modern age, commissioning a number of religious films, such as *Nossa Senhora da Aparecida e seus milagres* (Our Lady of Aparecida and Her Miracles, Mário Leite, 1919), which became a stock feature of Sunday services. The Catholic Church made its own films, such as *O dedo da justiça* (The Finger of Justice, 1919), a melodrama that emphasised the need for strong moral values and family life in the face of modern vices.[23]

Ironically, true-life crime cases, however unsavoury, were a popular and seemingly acceptable subject for silent movies. As early as 1908, *Os estranguladores* (The Stranglers), the first widely popular Brazilian film,[24] re-created a crime that had involved two Italians employed in a city-centre jeweller's murdering the owner's nephew and that had horrified the people of Rio de Janeiro. This cinematic vogue continued into the 1910s, giving rise to self-evident titles such as *O crime da mala* (The Suitcase Murder, 1912) and *O crime de Paula Matos* (The Paula Matos Murder, 1913).

Foreign influences

During the First Republic US movie companies such as Fox, MGM and Paramount opened offices in Brazil, and by the end of the First World War North American films dominated the country's movie screens, representing 85.9 per cent of the total market.[25] Hollywood movies were promoted in the Brazilian press, as were their stars, particularly in illustrated publications, such as *Careta* and, later in the 1920s, *Cinearte*.[26] Ironically, it was foreign immigrants who played a dominant role in the emerging national film industry[27] and, as Ana M. López has argued, the cinema as a commercial product provided a vital means by which first-generation Brazilians could achieve social mobility and assert new national affiliations.[28] The Spanish-born Francisco Serrador, for example, founded the *Companhia Cinematográfica Brasileira* (Brazilian Film Company) in 1912, which obtained the rights to distribute and redistribute the films of more than thirty movie companies throughout Brazil.[29] Serrador ploughed his profits into constructing or renovating numerous cinema theatres in Rio's city centre, culminating in the inauguration of the self-styled Cinelândia, an area of downtown dedicated to movie-going. Housed in five-storey buildings, his theatres seated an average of 800 spectators.[30]

As Johnson and Stam argue, Brazilian films of the 1920s and 1930s display a wide array of foreign influences, ranging from homages to Hollywood genres like the western, to outright parody of such traditions:

> Parody articulated the mingled affection and resentment with which Brazilians regarded the success of foreign films. Through parody Brazilian filmmakers could make fun of foreign films, laugh at their own inability to emulate their glossy production values, and indirectly capitalize on their success.[31]

European avant-garde film also made an impact on Brazilian cinema, giving rise, for example, to *São Paulo: sinfonia da metrópole* (São Paulo: Symphony of the Metropolis, 1929) 'in transparent homage to European city-symphony films like Walter Ruttmann's *Berlin, Die Symphonie Einer Grossstadt* (*Berlin, Symphony of a Great City*, 1927) and Alberto Cavalcanti's *Rien que les heures* (1926)'.[32] Although inspired by the foreign films that he avidly consumed at his local cinema in rural Minas Gerais, Humberto Mauro, who began making films in the latter half of the 1920s and was responsible for the so-called Cataguases Cycle of regional cinema, was very conscious of the need to create a cinema with clearly identifiable national characteristics:

> Cinema here in Brazil will have to emerge from our Brazilian milieu, with all its qualities and defects . . . If American cinema already accustomed us to the luxuriousness and the variety of its productions, it has not yet robbed us of our natural enthusiasm for the faithful representation of everything we are or that we wish to be.[33]

The year 1930 saw the demise of the First Republic in the form of the coup that brought Getúlio Vargas to power. Over the ensuing fifteen years the first Vargas regime tightened the State's grip on the media and the arts, not least film, as examined in the following chapter. Paradoxically, the Vargas era also witnessed the consolidation of the *chanchada*, and its central tenet of irreverent humour at the expense of the authorities.[34]

2

THE VARGAS YEARS (1930–45 AND 1951–54)

The advent of sound cinema in Brazil coincided with the installation of the Second Republic (1930–45). Getúlio Vargas came to power via a military coup in 1930, just a year after the production of the first Brazilian sound film, *Acabaram-se os otários* (No More Suckers, 1929).[1] *Coisas nossas* (Our Things, 1931) was released just a year after Vargas's ascension to the presidency and, as the following advertisement for the film reveals, home-grown movies that benefited from the latest Hollywood inventions were a source of considerable pride: 'Our customs, our music, our songs, our artists! A Brazilian film, a talkie, a musical, made here in Brazil.'[2]

Prior to 1930, film had already proved to be an important means of communication, second only to the press, and had been recognised as a key educational tool. Furthermore, the nascent Vargas regime believed that cinema could transmit a nationalist ideology and help to foster a sense of belonging to the wider national community. President Vargas's provisional government (1930–33) passed the first legislation in support of national cinema, making it compulsory to screen one Brazilian short film in every cinema programme, and giving a tremendous boost to short film production. In a speech given in 1934, Vargas, as honorary president of the ACPB (*Associação Cinematográfica de Produtores Brasileiros* – Association of Brazilian Film Producers), declared:

> Among the most useful educational agents available to the modern state is the cinema. An element of culture directly inspiring reason and imagination, it sharpens the qualities of observation, increases scientific resources, and knowledge . . . Thus cinema will become a book of luminous images through which our coastal and rural populations will learn to love Brazil, and it will raise confidence in the fortunes of our fatherland. For the many who do not read it will be the perfect pedagogical tool, the easiest and most impressive. For the educated, for those responsible for the success of our administration, it will be an admirable [teaching method].[3]

There is little doubt that the first Vargas regime was more interested in the educational and patriotic potential of filmmaking than the development of a film industry. The utilisation of didactic film as part of education and civic nationalism in both democratic and totalitarian regimes was observed with interest in Brazil. Personal contacts were made and correspondence exchanged with representatives of Italy's *Instituto Luce* and National Socialist Germany's *Reichstelle für den Unterrichtsfilm*.[4] In a letter addressed to 'Dr. Getúlio', dated 22 September 1934 and written in London, Luiz Simões Lopes, one of Vargas's closest aides and a special envoy, described his recent visit to Germany, where he had studied the activities of the Ministry of Propaganda of the Third Reich.[5] He tells of having obtained a copy of the most recent German legislation on labour and propaganda, and states:

> What most impressed me in Berlin was the systematic, methodical propaganda of the government . . . In the whole of Germany there is not a single person who does not experience on a daily basis contact with Nazism or Hitler, whether in the form of photography, the radio, the cinema, through the entire German press, through the Nazi leader himself, through party organisations or even, at the very least, through seeing everywhere the uniforms of the SA [assault troops] or the SS [Hitler's personal protection troops].[6]

Simões Lopes goes on to write: 'The organisation of the Ministry of Propaganda is so fascinating that I take the liberty of suggesting the creation of a smaller-scale version here in Brazil.' In his accompanying report, he sets out his proposal for the creation of a Ministry of Propaganda in Brazil. The first medium that he approaches is the cinema, stating:

> The cinema possesses an incalculable power to elucidate and persuade. It can teach us about everything, science and the arts, social events, geographic aspects. Furthermore, it exerts, with its dramatic force, its capacity for making people laugh and moving them, with its numerous and varied evocative elements, a powerful influence over the moral education of the masses.[7]

In the first half of the 1930s State-imposed censorship focused on issues of morality and depictions of national identity, rather than using cinema for any overt political purpose.[8] Anecdotal evidence points to a clear agenda of ethnic cleansing on the part of the censors of the first Vargas regime when it came to cinematic images. During the filming of *Favela dos meus amores* (Shantytown of My Loves, 1934), Humberto Mauro (later to become the de facto official filmmaker of Vargas's authoritarian *Estado Novo* or New State) was questioned by the police over his pioneering use of Afro-Brazilian non-professional actors in location shooting in a Rio shantytown.[9] As Mauro explained:

> It was the funeral scene in the shantytown, an extremely important scene, that the censors wanted to cut, on the grounds that we were

> showing lots of black people, and it was too downbeat.[10] It was a tremendous battle, but I managed to ensure that the film remained intact.[11]

The INCE

The INCE (*Instituto Nacional de Cinema Educativo* – National Institute of Educational Cinema) was established on 13 January 1937, under the headship of Edgard Roquette-Pinto. The institute was created in response to the fears of Gustavo Capanema, head of the Ministry of Education and Health between 1934 and 1945, that the unfettered growth of commercial film threatened to erode moral and educational standards. The INCE's slogan was 'educational cinema in Brazil must be the school for those who never went to school',[12] and it produced or acquired hundreds of educational films for free distribution to schools and cultural institutions across Brazil. The regime also made it compulsory for movie theatres to show such short films before every screening of a commercial feature film. Decree 21, 240/32 gave a flexible definition of 'educational film', which embraced:

> not only films that have as their purpose the diffusion of scientific knowledge, but also those concerned in their musical or figurative composition with the development of artistic motifs, directed at revealing to the public the great aspects of nature or of culture.[13]

The INCE clearly took some of its inspiration from the film institutes created under authoritarian regimes in Europe, and Roquette-Pinto visited France, Italy and Germany in December 1936 to study the use made in each country of educational film. He sent a letter and a detailed accompanying report back home to Capanema, in which he outlined his findings. In it he mentions briefly the German newsreels (*Wochenschau und Aktualitäten*), and concludes: 'From these notes one can see that the INCE . . . did not slavishly copy any of the great models adopted in Europe. I endeavoured to find other practical solutions more suited to the conditions in Brazil, without dismissing these precursors.'[14] The INCE films, some of which were of feature length, were exhibited in schools, cultural centres, sporting associations and workers' organisations, and provided regular work for actors and technical staff, as well as helping Brazilian cinema fulfil the demands of the quota system introduced by the Vargas regime, discussed in more detail below. As early as 1938 the acclaimed director Humberto Mauro, who produced and directed more than 200 documentaries for Roquette-Pinto's organisation, took some of his productions to the Venice Film Festival. In 1939 INCE films that showcased scientific accomplishments in the combating of diseases were shown in the Brazilian Pavilion at the World's Fair in New York, implicitly asserting Brazil's status as a modern, developed nation, as well as a land of tropical exuberance as exemplified in the musical performances by Carmen Miranda and her band in the Pavilion.[15]

The establishment of the *Estado Novo* in November 1937 signalled a turning point in the regime's attitude towards educational film; the incentives that had previously been suggested for involving private enterprise in the production of such films were forgotten, being replaced by an overwhelming emphasis on the INCE, particularly in association with the talented director Humberto Mauro.[16] The INCE's productions fell into two distinct camps: on the one hand, instructional films to be used in the classroom and, on the other, educational films that documented patriotic ceremonies or historical events, adaptations of literary and musical works, engineering feats, medical advances and so on.[17] Unlike its Italian and German counterparts, the INCE remained true to its pedagogical ambitions and never strayed into the realm of propaganda film.

Censorship and the DIP

The year 1939 proved to be a key one for the *Estado Novo*'s relationship with Brazil's fledgling film industry. Keen to enhance the nation's image abroad, the Vargas regime introduced a law in September of that year to prohibit the export of films that gave an unfavourable view of Brazil or posed a threat to national security.[18] This legislation also raised the screen quota for Brazilian films to a minimum of one full-length feature film and one short film per year in every cinema theatre, casino and sporting association in the country.

The *Departamento de Imprensa e Propaganda* (DIP – Department of Press and Propaganda), established on 27 December 1939 under the direction of Lourival Fontes, sought to control the image of Brazil and its president created by the press, the arts and popular culture, for both domestic and foreign consumption. The DIP actively promoted the production of films that valorised the natural beauty of Brazil, key historical events and the achievements of the regime. Its cinema and theatre division controlled prior censorship of all films, the organisation of competitions to co-opt filmmakers, and the production of the official newsreels, the *Cine Jornal Brasileiro*, enforcing the latter's screening before all feature films, in every cinema theatre in Brazil. '[T]he DIP participated in every stage of film production, promoting, rewarding and punishing, censoring, registering, licensing and, finally, supervising the exhibition of the end product.'[19]

The *Cine Jornal Brasileiro* newsreels were produced between October 1938 and September 1946, first by the *Departamento Nacional de Propaganda* (DNP – National Department of Propaganda) and subsequently by the DIP. Production totalled 250 films between October 1938 and August 1941, and in 1944, of the 1,600 cinema theatres in Brazil, the official newsreels were exhibited in 608 of them, in 278 cities in thirteen different states.[20] In the early 1940s the DIP, which had previously worked with private companies, created a national film distribution agency to ensure the widespread exhibition of its productions, the *Cooperativa Cinematográfica Brasileira* (Brazilian Film Cooperative).[21] In spite of such measures, recent studies have questioned the efficacy of the DIP in imposing the regime's ideologies on the nation and silencing dissent.[22] According to José Inácio

Mello Souza, the DIP's newsreels were by no means guaranteed blanket exhibition across Brazil and were particularly hit by competition from foreign counterparts.[23] In order to make films the DIP initially had to rely on the facilities offered by studios such as Adhemar Gonzaga's Cinédia, and the government body only acquired its own filmmaking equipment and laboratory in 1945, precisely at the moment when the regime it was designed to ideologically underpin was in its death throes.

With the introduction of decree law 4,064 on 29 January 1942, the Vargas regime created the National Film Council (*Conselho Nacional de Cinematografia*), within the DIP. This law effectively gave the DIP the authority to increase the screen quota for Brazilian films, but the regime gave only token assistance to Brazilian filmmakers, even lowering the tariff on imported films and placing much greater emphasis on co-option, State propaganda and censorship. The makers of feature films were largely left to fend for themselves and thus most studios concentrated on the money-spinning, low-budget *chanchadas* or musical comedies that appealed to mass audiences.[24]

The *Cine Jornal Brasileiro*

The *Cine Jornal Brasileiro* newsreels centred on a patriotic, militaristic discourse that revolved around the iconic figure of President Getúlio Vargas. The president remained central to the official celebrations captured on film, even when he was not present in person. The newsreels cultivated the impression that Vargas could be in several places at once, and thus had a thorough knowledge and understanding of the entirety of his land and people that equipped him to best take care of their needs. Official visits by Vargas, who is said to have logged 90,000 miles visiting every corner of Brazil during his first government,[25] and those made by his representatives to varied regions of Brazil are often evocatively titled.

The mainstay of the State-sponsored newsreels was footage of national celebrations, usually involving a display by the armed forces or commemorations of military feats. The *Semana da Pátria* (Fatherland Week) military celebrations held on 7 September provided an annual focus for national pride. The mise-en-scène was impressive, with a cast of thousands, highlighting the omnipotence of Vargas and all that he represented. Like any military parade, it was above all a show of force, in keeping with the view that 'Vargas and his era were built around the metaphor of war.'[26] Another dominant theme of the *Estado Novo* newsreels was modernity, and the films frequently showcased industrial progress and public works schemes, such as the construction of dams in Brazil's arid North-East, and of hospitals, highways and road tunnels. Aviation was a particularly favourite topic in the first half of the 1940s, with footage of the inaugurations of aerodromes, and the arrival in Rio of new aircraft for military use. Industrial development was clearly framed in patriotic discourse.

Film under democracy

Ousted from power by the military in 1945, Vargas was replaced by the democratic regime of General Eurico Gaspar Dutra, Brazil's president from 1946 to 1951. The provisional government that preceded the election of Dutra replaced the DIP with the DNI (*Departamento Nacional de Informações* – National Information Department), which, in December 1945, increased the annual screen quota for Brazilian films from one to three. Decree 20,493 passed in January 1946 confirmed this new quota and reasserted the government's right to censor the cinema and other forms of entertainment.[27] Dutra went on to consolidate the position of the cinema within Brazilian society, not least by introducing tax incentives for Brazilian film companies in August 1949. He also opened up Brazil's borders to mass imports of US consumer goods, and the increasing popularity of Hollywood movies, in addition to the rise of the home-grown *chanchada*,[28] was reflected in the rapid increase in the number of cinema theatres in Brazil – by 1950 the total number had risen to 3,033, as opposed to just 1,317 five years earlier.[29] The Dutra regime continued to produce newsreels, now called the *Cine Jornal Informativo* (literally, Informative Newsreels). After the demise of the *Estado Novo* in 1945, however, the INCE became something of an anachronism, as the Brazilian State turned its attention away from education and towards economic development in the post-war context.[30]

After Vargas returned to the presidency in 1951, his democratically elected regime continued to draw on the support of the *Cine Jornal Informativo*, within which there was a resurgence of civic themes. However, these newsreels were a much weaker ideological force than those produced during the earlier Vargas years, as the following example indicates: the 1951 newsreel entitled *Dia da Pátria* (Fatherland Day) shows a choir performing in the gardens of the Ministry of Education and Culture under the direction of Heitor Villa-Lobos, in marked contrast to the eponymous newsreels of the first Vargas regime that showcased grandiose military parades. The INCE continued in operation until 1964, although it produced few films in the 1950s, depending increasingly on co-productions with other bodies. After Vargas's return to power by democratic vote, scant resources were directed to the Institute, but the president's attention did turn to State involvement in feature film production. For this Vargas sought the advice of the acclaimed Brazilian filmmaker Alberto Cavalcanti, who had worked in England since the 1920s.[31]

In August 1952 the president submitted the initial proposal for the creation of the INC (*Instituto Nacional de Cinema* – National Cinema Institute), which would promote national film production by running filmmaking courses, offering grants and awarding annual prizes for the three best shorts and feature-length films. (In practice, the INC was only established in 1957.) Vargas also introduced decree law number 30,179 on 19 November 1951, the so-called 'eight for one' law, which made it compulsory for all cinema theatres in Brazil to show at least one Brazilian film for every eight foreign ones. This legislation, together with the populist Vargas government's decision to keep cinema ticket prices artificially low in spite of high inflation,[32] greatly assisted the commercial success of the home-grown musical comedies known as *chanchadas*, discussed in detail in Chapter 6.

3

FILMMAKING AND THE DICTATORSHIP (1964–84)

Introduction

In Brazil the years 1964–84 were the most intense in terms of State-sponsored financial support for the arts, and in particular cinema, which, as it happens, coincided with a period of military rule in Brazil. The origins of the two State-supported initiatives that we will concentrate on in this chapter, the National Cinema Institute (INC) and the Brazilian Film Company (Embrafilme), despite their associations with the dictatorship, can be found in the cultural euphoria of the developmentalist period of Brazilian history associated with President Juscelino Kubitschek de Oliveira (1956–61).

By the end of Juscelino Kubitschek's presidential term, the Brazilian economy had begun to slow down and the newly elected President, Jânio Quadros, was faced with the difficult task of continuing with the nation's modernisation programme, while at the same time keeping the needed flow of cash from foreign banks coming into the country. When the International Monetary Fund demanded the introduction of economic austerity measures, Quadros surprised the Left by giving in to these demands, such as the freezing of salaries. At the same time, however, he pursued an independent foreign policy, as witnessed in his support for the Cuban revolution. As a result, the Right gradually abandoned him and the Left did not have enough seats in Congress to give him and his policies the support that he needed. Quadros then took the surprising step of resigning, only eight months into his term of office, in the hope of being granted greater power by Congress. Unfortunately for him, his plan backfired and the government accepted his resignation. Quadros's vice-president, João Goulart, on an untimely trip abroad to socialist China, was prevented by military and conservative elements (with the support of the outgoing president himself) from assuming the presidency automatically and, instead, a parliamentary system was instated in the country, giving the president reduced powers. A universal plebiscite, encouraged by Goulart, returned Brazil to the presidential system in 1963, and Goulart was voted back into a position of real strength with the support of trade unions, progressive sectors of society, the working class and left-wing parties. Such support, along with his centre-left programme of limited land reform, redistribution of income, laws to protect the less well-off and nationalisation schemes, was enough to provoke a conspiracy among the military and right-wing politicians to overthrow the government. When troops surrounded Brasília in 1964 and Goulart fled to Uruguay, leaving the presidency vacant (there was, of course, no vice-president to take his place), the nation's military leaders carried out a coup and seized temporary control of government. General Humberto Castelo Branco was quickly elected by Congress.

It was, then, in the context of a very clear distinction between Left and Right that the 1960s got under way, and such distinctions would inflect discussions of national culture, and the State's relations with cultural production, throughout the decade and beyond. The first attempt at regulating the film industry in the 1960s was the founding in 1961 of the *Grupo Executivo da Indústria Cinematográfica* (GEICINE), the 'first of many commissions or groups designed to study problems of the film industry to have executive powers'.[1] Although considered a failure, GEICINE was instrumental, in the context of policy creation for Brazilian national cinema, in establishing a lasting definition for Brazilian film, and in introducing a co-production programme which, while limited in terms of its success at the time, would inspire subsequent funding policies for national cinema. As John King observes, 'GEICINE's measures did not have time to have much effect, but pointed to the beginning of a state intervention which was to increase greatly after the coup.'[2]

In Brazil there was no legal definition of what constitutes a national film until 1961, whereafter it was defined as being produced by a Brazilian firm, spoken in Portuguese, with at least two-thirds Brazilian (or foreigners resident in Brazil for more than two years) in the technical crew and cast. Studio shots had to be filmed in Brazil, and film had to be developed and mixed in the country. This definition changed little for the next twenty-five years or so.[3] Meanwhile, the goal behind GEICINE's co-production programme was to encourage foreign distributors to invest in Brazilian cinema. Perhaps unsurprisingly, the policy did not go down well with nationalist sectors of the industry. But, as Randal Johnson points out, GEICINE itself was dominated by a 'universalist', as opposed to nationalist, group, with a clear internationalist mentality: hence their concept of industrialisation through foreign investment.[4] At first, the co-production programme was unsuccessful, given that there was no real financial incentive for foreign distributors to get involved. However, between 1966 and 1969, when the scheme was eliminated by Embrafilme, thirty-eight films benefited from foreign involvement in their production, including a number of important Leftist *cinema novo* films, such as Joaquim Pedro de Andrade's *Macunaíma* (1969), Nelson Pereira dos Santos's *Como era gostoso o meu francês* (*How Tasty Was My Little Frenchman*, 1971), and Carlos Diegues's *Os herdeiros* (*The Heirs*, 1970): 'The co-production program, in fact, became an important source of financing for Cinema Novo directors in a period when production capital was increasingly difficult to come by.'[5]

Instituto Nacional de Cinema

The National Cinema Institute (INC), created in 1966, had much greater powers as a regulatory agency. Given that it was set up after the installation of the military dictatorship, it was closely associated with the authoritarianism of the government of the time, whereby 'state intervention in the cultural arena fitted in with the ideology of national security'.[6] Initially (unlike GEICINE, which could rely, at least, on the support of the so-called 'universalists'), the INC was not popular with anyone. It was described by the *Jornal do Comércio* as a 'birth control pill of cinematic activity that will transform one of our most promising manufactured goods into a condemned fetus'.[7]

The INC was greeted with suspicion because filmmakers feared loss of freedom of expression and creativity, given its associations with the dictatorship and the undemocratic way it was brought into existence (by executive decree). For others, it represented unjustifiable government interference in the free enterprise system.[8] Both of these complaints, of course, continue to be heard to this day from different sectors of the industry with regard to State film policy in Brazil. Johnson notes that, once the executive decree by which the INC was created became law, industry professionals settled down and sought to gain some benefit from its policies.

The main direct benefit that filmmakers derived from the creation of the INC was access to production subsidies, based initially on box-office returns and, from 1970, offered to films at both the higher and the lower end of the scale of commercial popularity. A further modification to the subsidy programme was carried out in 1973, in order to encourage production of children's films, historical films and films based on literary works of 'undeniable value'.[9] Although ultimately unsuccessful in terms of shifting the focus of cinematic production, this was the first time that the State had attempted to stimulate the production of specific kinds of films.[10] The government thus revealed its preference, for example, for patriotic films that recuperated in an epic format Brazil's past, such as Carlos Coimbra's popular historical costume drama *Independência ou morte* (Independence or Death, 1972), which portrayed Emperor Pedro I's battle for and declaration of independence as above all a brave and nationalist gesture.[11] This can be contrasted with Joaquim Pedro de Andrade's censored *Os inconfidentes* (*The Conspirators*, 1972), a historically revisionist film that debunked the government's goal to produce more historical films.

As well as more efficient fiscal policies (to do with ticket pricing, box-office returns and so on), which producers had been demanding for some time, filmmakers and producers also benefited from INC-sponsored film festival prizes and, more significantly, 'quality awards', which provided additional income for, on average, 15 per cent of the total Brazilian film production.[12] In this, Johnson sees no real evidence of politically motivated partiality, citing the frequency with which *cinema novo* films received the awards.[13] But he does admit that between 1970 and 1973 hardly any explicitly political films were awarded prizes.[14] To this we should add the observation that hardly any explicitly political films were *made* in the period cited, attesting, perhaps, to the existence of a certain co-optation by the State of filmmakers and producers, through such production subsidies and prizes.

Embrafilme

Castelo Branco and other moderates within the military intended only to stay in power until the so-called radical elements of Brazilian society had been brought under control. But in 1967 Castelo Branco was replaced in power by General Arthur da Costa e Silva, the first in a line of extreme right-wing presidents that ushered in a period of oppression in 1968, referred to as 'the coup within the coup', which lasted until the mid-1970s and the so-called *abertura* or political opening up. This period saw a strengthening of the resolve of the military to counter sedition, with greatly increased censorship of the arts, and the imprisonment, torture and 'disappearance' of political prisoners (although nowhere near as many as in Argentina and Chile):

> it was within a context of political repression that state policy toward the film industry changed direction in the early 1970s, moving away from the relatively neutral, technical solutions of the 1960s toward a form of state capitalism in which the government became an active agent and productive force in the industry.[15]

The Empresa Brasileira de Filmes SA (Embrafilme) was created in 1969, with its powers being both increased and diversified in 1974. As with the INC, no one was consulted on its creation. Initially Embrafilme worked alongside the INC, its function being to encourage consumption of national films at home and abroad, but already by 1970 the responsibility for financing films had passed from the INC to Embrafilme, and in 1973 it began distributing films. Embrafilme was nominally a mixed-ownership company, but in reality the bulk of its shares were owned by the government. As in the case of the INC, despite the State's seeming intense involvement in the directing of cinematic production, cineastes more often than not did not complain, as through Embrafilme they received generous financial support, exhibition quotas, market reserves, effective distribution of their films, and so on.

In terms of the number of Brazilian films made and their box-office success, the 1970s was one of the most important decades in the history of Brazilian cinema. The role of Embrafilme in this success (after 1973) should not be underestimated, given that, as a film distribution agency, it followed a strictly commercial rationale.[16] Embrafilme became the first central distributor for Brazilian films to be established on a national, rather than regional, basis.[17] At one point it was the second largest distributor in the country.[18]

During the directorship of film producer Roberto Farias (1974–79) the organisation's budget rose from $600,000 to $8 million. Embrafilme was responsible for the distribution of over 30 per cent of Brazilian films in the 1970s, and for between 25 and 50 per cent of annual film production. As a result, the market share of Brazilian cinema increased from 15 per cent in 1974 to more than 30 per cent in 1980, while the number of spectators of Brazilian films doubled.[19] Three films, *Xica da Silva* (*Xica*, 1976), *Dona Flor e seus dois maridos* (*Dona Flor and Her Two Husbands*, 1976) and *A dama do lotação* (*Lady on the Bus*, 1978), each partly financed and/or distributed by Embrafilme in the mid-1970s, set box offices alight, and have been quoted ever since as proof of the success of Embrafilme and the importance of State intervention in the national cinema industry. During the dictatorship, cineastes were happy to support a cultural agency of the government, in exchange for that agency's backing against a greater enemy: an invading foreign cinema.

In terms of financial support for production, in 1970 Embrafilme began by granting loans to well-established production companies, turning its attention to co-production in 1973, and to full production (that is, taking on financial risk) in 1975. Between 1970 and 1979, eighty-two films by fifty-six different production companies had been supported by Embrafilme. By supporting production companies rather than 'making qualitative or ideological judgments about the films in question',[20] Embrafilme (and the government that funded it) could deflect accusations of co-optation and interference in cultural production.

There can be no disputing the fact that the 1970s represent a high point in the production of Brazilian films. On average seventy national films were released per year during the first half of the decade, almost twice as many as during the second half of the 1960s.[21] This figure rose again in the second half of the 1970s, peaking at 104 in 1979. The number of spectators paying to see national films also rose considerably over the decade, with over 50 million tickets sold per year on average from 1975 onwards. The number of days that Brazilian cinema halls were obliged to show Brazilian films increased from 63 days in 1969 to 112 days in 1975.[22] While the box-office charts at the time were dominated by the Trapalhões movies,[23] as well as the 'big three' Embrafilme productions mentioned above, the importance of the soft-core porn films known as *pornochanchadas* has to be recognised in terms of the sheer increase in production and general viewing figures, much to the dismay of many working within the industry at the time.[24]

The close relationship that *cinema novo* had with the INC continued with Embrafilme, whereby nearly all films by *cinemanovistas* were either co-produced or distributed by Embrafilme.[25] The first film to be distributed by Embrafilme was Leon Hirszman's *São Bernardo* (1971), while the first film contracted for co-production was Nelson Pereira dos Santos's *O amuleto de Ogum* (*The Amulet of Ogum*, 1974). The final feature films of Glauber Rocha and Leon Hirszman, *A idade da terra* (*The Age of the Earth*, 1980) and *Eles não usam black-tie* (*They Don't Wear Black Tie*, 1981), were 100 per cent financed by Embrafilme. *Cinemanovistas* have always argued that accepting money from the State in no way implies support of other policies of the government.[26] Likewise, the financial support offered to *cinema novo* by Embrafilme in no way implied support of the politics of the leftist filmmaking movement. For a start, the government vetoed at the last minute the choice of erstwhile *cinema novo* producer Luiz Carlos Barreto as head of Embrafilme in 1974.[27] But the most convincing proof of the lack of support a governmental level of *cinema novo* is the movement's troubled relationship w the censor, creating a situation in which films were financed by the government with one hand and censored with the other. For example, Leon Hirszman's politically inflected *São Bernardo* may have been co-produced by Embrafilme, but it was held up by the censors for seven months, causing the bankruptcy of Hirszman's own production company Saga Filmes. As a result, it took Hirszman nearly ten years to raise enough funds to make another feature film.

While Randal Johnson suggests that Embrafilme did not exert direct ideological control over filmmakers and film projects,[28] it is likely that some form of self-censorship on the part of filmmakers and producers would have been exerted, influenced both by the generous financial support on offer from Embrafilme and by the financial cost of getting into difficulties with the censor. By way of illustration, when filming *Lúcio Flávio, passageiro da agonia* (*Lucio Flavio*, 1977) and *Pixote: a lei do mais fraco* (*Pixote*, 1981), both hard-hitting dramas that can easily be read as highly critical of Brazil's socio-political status quo, and both of which involve scenes of police violence, director/producer Hector Babenco sought the advice of the police, in order to minimise future censorship problems.

After an extended period of political opening up (*abertura* or *distenção*), which began around 1974,[29] (indirect) elections brought a civilian to power in 1984, heralding the end of the dictatorship. By then, the Embrafilme bubble had burst. For a start, with recession and competition from TV and video, the number of cinema halls had fallen from 3,276 in 1975 to 1,553 in 1984.[30] As well as losing considerable credibility amid accusations of corruption and favouritism,[31] the organisation was plunged into debt by the severe economic recession and attendant rising production costs. According to Randal Johnson, between 1980 and 1984, of the 109 films released by Embrafilme, only twenty got 700,000 spectators or more, the absolute minimum number required for a film to make a profit.[32] Spectators for national films dropped 40 per cent between 1980 and 1984.[33]

As well as facing criticism from within the production side of the industry, Embrafilme had throughout its existence had to deal with severe criticism from the exhibition sector. Writing in 1987, Johnson observed that:

> Brazilian cinematic legislation stipulates that exhibitors must show national films at least 140 days per year, that they must pay a minimum of 50 percent of net income for those films, that they must make payments within fifteen days of exhibition, that they must show a national short subject as part of each program of foreign films, that they purchase standardized tickets and box-office reporting sheets from Embrafilme at inflated prices, and that they keep national films in exhibition as long as total spectators (for two weeks or more) equal 60 percent of the previous year's average. In return, they have received nothing from the state. All of these items combined have caused a decline in income, which led to the closing of many theatres.[34]

Thus, while the filmmaker and one-time head of distribution at Embrafilme is right in observing that 'few moments in the history of cinematic production have had the freedom to produce as did Brazilian cinema during the Geisel government [1974–79]',[35] the high volume of production and viewing figures of the dictatorship period, and the failure to address the needs of the exhibition sector, came at a high price for the future of the industry.

4

CINEMA AND REDEMOCRATISATION (1984–2006)

Introduction

Just as the period of authoritarian rule in Brazil in the 1960s and 1970s coincided with a high point in terms of volume of film production, spectatorship for national films, and critical acclaim, the return to democracy in the 1980s heralded the darkest days of Brazil's cinematic history. For a start, inflation had been increasing at exponential rates since the bubble burst on the so-called economic miracle of the early 1970s, making film production unimaginably expensive in Brazil. And given the lack of importance traditionally paid to ancillary markets within the national industry, video as good as killed off Brazilian cinema in the 1980s, ghettoising it into the sordid world of hard-core porn, where audiences may well have been both unaware of and unconcerned about the nationality of the material on screen.[1] The truth is that the precipitous decline of the Brazilian film market began as early as 1975 with the consolidation of television and the introduction of VCR.

With the election of the neo-Liberal Fernando Collor de Mello in 1989 in the country's first direct presidential elections in nearly thirty years, the industry all but collapsed. Collor set to dissolving film institutions, described as an 'insane predatory act'[2] and 'obscurantist disaster',[3] beginning with Embrafilme in 1990. Collor's term of office was cut short after his impeachment in 1992 in the light of accusations of corruption, but the seeds of future audio-visual legislation were sown in his presidency. Nevertheless, the fact that Embrafilme was disbanded before new legislation for the film industry had been prepared meant that production practically ground to a halt in the first few years of the 1990s: only 36,000 spectators went to see the three feature films released in 1992,[4] for example, compared with 20 million spectators for (a relatively paltry) seventeen films in the last year of Embrafilme's existence.[5] Between 1992 and 1994 the city of Rio de Janeiro came to the rescue of the film industry, with Riofilme being practically the only company distributing national films.[6]

Retomada legislation

By far the most significant piece of legislation to appear since Embrafilme and its policy branch, CONCINE, were disbanded is the 1993 *Lei do Audiovisual* (Audio-visual Law), deemed responsible for the so-called *retomada* or rebirth of the film industry in Brazil in the mid-1990s. According to the law, businesses and individuals receive tax credits if they invest in cultural works of an audio-visual nature. The law also includes an article that encourages foreign distributors to invest in national production. The increase in foreign co-productions in Brazil is as a direct result of a tax incentive that permits foreign companies to forgo paying up to 70 per cent of tax due on products they distribute in Brazil (foreign films, in this case) in exchange for investing in the local industry (Brazilian films).

At first glance, the statistics, while nowhere near those of Embrafilme and the 1970s, are impressive. Between 1995 (by which time films benefiting from the Audio-visual Law began to be released) and 2000, 155 feature films had been made, along with 100 documentaries and 100 short films. During the same period, fifty-five new filmmakers had surfaced.[7] In 1999, more than 5.2 million people watched Brazilian films in the cinema, and in 2000 the number climbed to 7.2 million, twelve times more than the rest of the film market had grown in the country.[8]

José Álvaro Moisés, Brazil's Audio-visual Secretary from 1999 to 2002, observes that the *retomada*, after a period of euphoria, became discredited around 1998 with the media, investors and public authorities, when it was revealed that less than 15 per cent of audio-visual projects approved by the Ministry of Culture between 1994 and 1998 were completed.[9] Suspicion of the way cinema was now being financed, and of the film industry's overhyped return to glory, was further increased by Norma Benguel's *O Guarani* (The Guarani Indian, 1996), the most expensive film made, and a critical and commercial disaster. Questions were raised regarding the allocation of funds received via fiscal incentive laws on the film project, resulting in an on-going court case involving Benguel and her producers.

As a result of the *retomada* being called to account, some of the abuses of fiscal incentive laws began to be sorted out as early as 1999.[10] For example, filmmakers with poor completion records were less likely to secure funding, production companies were encouraged to have leaner portfolios, and projects that exceeded the time limit for fund-raising were shelved. In 2001 Embrafilme/CONCINE was finally replaced by the National Film Agency (ANCINE, renamed ANCINAV in 2004), charged with the task of regulating the industry. ANCINE's nationalist outlook can be seen in its continued push for compulsory fiscal contributions to be paid by producers and distributors of foreign films entering the country. The move has not been greeted favourably, needless to say, by the Motion Pictures Association of America (MPA), which argues that MPA companies are already (voluntarily) involved in co-producing and distributing the more successful Brazilian films, both at home and abroad, through the Audio-visual Law scheme.

Going global: cinema and television

In 1970 there were just under 5 million TV sets in Brazil, a figure that had risen by 1980 to over 18 million. Nowadays, with over 54 million sets, around 90 per cent of the Brazilian population has access to a television. Therefore, in Brazil, the cultural power of television, and the clear sector leader, TV Globo, should not be underestimated. The fact that the government in Brazil has never considered mediating the relationship between the two industries, and that TV stations have as a rule paid little attention to national cinema, has been a bone of contention since television's inception in the 1960s.

The relationship between television and cinema has, however, undergone a significant transformation since the late 1990s. For a start, with Globo's move into the satellite and cable market in the 1990s, it set up Canal Brasil, a channel that is dedicated to screening national films and programmes dealing with the national film industry. Globo's increased interest in national cinema can also be seen in its screening of spin-off series based on successful films. These include *Cidade dos homens* (*City of Men*), based on the national and international hit *Cidade de Deus* (*City of God*, 2002) and a first for Globo in that it is a national TV series not produced in-house, and *Carandiru: outras histórias* (Carandiru: Other Stories), a spin-off of Hector Babenco's blockbuster *Carandiru* (2003). Pedro Butcher also sees striking similarities in style between *Carlota Joaquina: Princesa do Brasil* (*Carlota Joaquina: Brazilian Princess*, 1995), the film that was said to have kick-started the renaissance of the Brazilian film industry in the 1990s, and the 2002 Globo mini-series *O quinto dos infernos.*[11]

More importantly, in terms of increasing the audience share for national films and influencing production values, is the creation of Globo Filmes, a branch of Organizações Globo, one of the world's largest and most powerful media empires. Globo Filmes was set up in 1998 with the express purpose of co-producing feature films for cinema. Globo Filmes does not directly finance films. Instead, it offers television advertising space for films: 'in this way, Globo has demonstrated considerable power to offer leverage to national films with regard to their greatest weakness compared to US products: intense investment in marketing'.[12]

Globo Filmes' website proudly declares that the films in which it has been involved have sold over 70 million cinema tickets since 1999, and include nine of the top ten highest-grossing films of the last ten years, among them *Dois filhos de Francisco* (*Two Sons of Francisco*, 2005), with over 5 million spectators, and *Cidade de Deus.*[13] 'Whether due to the hype of television marketing campaigns or their so-called "standard of quality" (a trademark of the network), Globo's films have attracted the closest thing to a mass audience for national products in recent years.'[14]

Perhaps inevitably, given Brazilian cinema's historical relationship with television, Globo's incursion into the film industry has been criticised. Some of this criticism is based on a long-held suspicion of both the autocratic way Globo is run and the dangerous influence it exerts over television audiences:

> The paradox of Brazilian television is that it is one of the best in the world and one of the most advanced in terms of technology and production values, but from an institutional point of view, it works along the lines of the old sugar mills of Brazil's North East, where a

> handful of feudal overlords decide the destiny of people's minds in private conversations on the veranda of their plantation houses.[15]

Furthermore, a number of industry observers are uneasy about the involvement of Globo in film production, because of the perceived 'aesthetic dumbing down' of the national films that will take place as a result. One of Globo's recent co-productions, *Olga* (Jayme Monjardim, 2004), provoked debate in the press because of its so-called TV aesthetic. This aesthetic can be seen in a number of successful films: the extent to which it has begun to infiltrate national cinema can be seen in the choice of *Dois filhos de Francisco*, with its evident Globo production values, to represent Brazil in 2005 at the race for Oscar nomination. Included in the target of eight to ten films per year that Globo Filmes sets itself are, as one might expect, a number of films based on its own successful TV series, such as *Casseta & Planeta urgente!*, which spawned *Casseta e Planeta: a taça do mundo é nossa* (Casseta and Planeta: The World Cup Is Ours, 2003), and *Seus problemas acabaram!!!* (Your Troubles Are Over!!!, 2006), the film version of the same name of *Os normais* (*So Normal*, 2003), and *A grande família – o filme* (Big Family – The Family, 2007).

Future prospects

The sheer volume of films being made in Brazil has put to rest rumours of the death of the industry that began to circulate, with good reason, in the early 1990s, and this volume to a great extent is a result of innovative international co-production and financing programmes. Brazil is increasingly looking beyond the US majors for sources of co-production financing. As well as the significant commercial achievements to date of Globo Filmes, Brazilian filmmakers have also been increasingly benefiting from European funding, first and foremost in the guise of Ibermedia. Ibermedia is an accord signed at the Ibero-American heads of state summit in 1997, which involves a sharing of audio-visual resources among member states. As a result of Brazil's participation, as well as a respectable number of co-productions arranged through Ibermedia, Brazilian filmmakers and producers now have closer links with other Latin American film industries than ever before, and Brazilian cinema audiences have access to an increased number of Spanish and Spanish-American films.[16]

Thus real strides have been made in terms of finding innovative ways of financing film production in Brazil, without returning to what would now be an outmoded funding policy: direct financial support by the State for what is a very costly art form. But for all the foreign and Globo co-productions that are being made, the required attendant changes in exhibition and distribution have not taken place.

Nominal attempts have been made to promote Brazilian film production abroad, mostly through Brazilian Cinema Promotion, a non-profit-making, non-governmental organisation set up in 2000 and dedicated exclusively to publicising Brazilian films overseas. In 2001 Brazil participated in twenty-six festivals and was present in twenty-five countries, while by 2003 these figures had risen to 122 festivals and forty-five countries. Brazilian embassies also appear to be taking a more positive interest in community and academic projects relating to cinema, recognising their importance in disseminating Brazilian cinema at a more 'grass-roots' level. But it has to be acknowledged that, at most film events (for example those tied in with the *Tropicalia* exhibition at the Barbican in London in 2006), audiences are limited to ex-pat Brazilians (there are 2 million of them scattered around the world), interspersed with a handful of students and academics.

While overall viewing figures (especially those of films co-produced by Globo) seem healthy, at least when compared to the first half of the 1990s, many of the most critically acclaimed films are not finding an audience:[17] films such as *O invasor* (*The Trespasser*, 2002), *Madame Satã* (2002) and *Ônibus 174* (*Bus 174*, 2002), all of which were distributed abroad. When *Crime delicado* (*Delicate Crime*, 2005), the fourth feature film by Beto Brant, considered to be one of the most talented Brazilian directors, can be seen by only 20,000 spectators in São Paulo (Brant's home town and the largest film market in the country), then commentators are right to express their deep concern for the state of the industry. Fewer than half a dozen of the 100-plus films produced in the 1990s attracted more than a million spectators, and, of the eighty films made and released in the market between 1995 and 1998, only ten roughly broke even or earned more than they cost to make.[18] Meanwhile, the Brazilian film industry is only making timid incursions into potentially lucrative ancillary markets such as DVDs, CD soundtracks and merchandising.[19]

Films are not screened for long enough to fulfil their income potential: exhibitors would rather run films for no longer than one week, in order to increase their general box-office income.[20] Screen quotas continue to exist, but governments continue to experience difficulties (both fiscal and in terms of the courage to do so) in enforcing these. While there are examples to be found of parallel circuits for screening national films, for example museums, cinémathèques and schools, these are not great enough in number and not widely enough distributed throughout the national territory to make a real difference. And although the number of film festivals is steadily growing all over Brazil, a film's successful appearance in a festival does not guarantee wider distribution.[21]

One result of the failure to address issues of distribution and exhibition is that the industry continues to be dogged by 'bottlenecks', whereby national films are forced into a queue to be released behind foreign films that benefit from more successful distribution strategies. As Randal Johnson remind us, 'It was precisely a governmental policy with a dual focus on supply and demand that led to the relative success of Brazilian cinema in the late 1970s.'[22]

Part II

DEFINING 'NATIONAL' CINEMA, 1896 TO 1960

5

THE PIONEERS

> Just think that to make a film here in Brazil the director has to fulfil the duties of more than twenty different professions! As well as controlling the film, the director has to deal with a thousand and one things. Sometimes, acquiring a simple object, a prop of minimal importance that must appear in the film, takes us hours and hours! If a piece of set is needed, it's the director who makes it; if a piece of furniture is required, it's the director who goes in search of it, going from door to door.[1]

This chapter will consider the contributions made to the development of early Brazilian sound cinema by four pioneering individuals, two men, Adhemar Gonzaga and Humberto Mauro, and two women, Carmen Santos and Gilda de Abreu, who played pivotal roles within the embryonic medium in the face of considerable practical constraints. In spite of their undeniable contributions against all odds, it is only Gonzaga and Mauro's careers that have merited extensive scholarly analysis. In contrast, only one slim volume has been published on Santos,[2] and Abreu is the subject of a handful of academic essays, in spite of the fact that she directed one of the most commercially successful Brazilian feature films of all time. Both Santos and Abreu were film actresses prior to their directorial debuts, moving from passive to active relationships with the camera in contravention of patriarchal norms. Both women were modest about their achievements but displayed a courageous determination to try their hand at directing. As Abreu stated in interview in 1978: 'It is funny, but I didn't understand anything about cinema. I liked it but didn't understand it. And I still don't understand it, even today. Cinema is very complex. So I just did it out of cheek.'[3]

Adhemar Gonzaga (1901–78)

Founder of the Cinédia film studio in Rio de Janeiro, producer and director, Adhemar Gonzaga equally made a lasting contribution to the formation of Brazilian cinema through his work as a film journalist, particularly for the influential *Cinearte* magazine (1926–42).[4] It was in the capacity of editor and film critic that he played a pivotal role in fostering a nascent expectation of a 'national cinema'. The magazine which he co-founded and was a driving force behind launched a self-styled 'Campaign for Brazilian Cinema', aimed at stimulating the interest of intellectuals, the general public and ideally the Brazilian State in domestic film production. Gonzaga's vision for Brazilian cinema centred on the veneration of Hollywood movies. It seems no coincidence that in his correspondence to his protégé, Humberto Mauro,[5] he jokingly referred to Cataguases in rural Minas Gerais, where Mauro's pioneering filmmaking took place, as 'Catawood'.[6] Gonzaga's Cinédia studio in Rio de Janeiro was the first in Brazil to seek to reproduce the Hollywood model. His vision for Brazil as a nation and for its cinema industry hinged on a modernising project that centred on the metropolis and on imported Hollywood paradigms.

Film critic and creator of Cinearte

Even as a child, Adhemar Gonzaga had a passion for cinema, going to see all the new releases in his home city of Rio de Janeiro, writing fan mail to his favourite stars, and beginning to compile his legendary archive of film ephemera. In an attempt to steer him towards more serious pursuits, his mother sent him to boarding school in 1914, but it was there that he met Pedro Lima and other enthusiasts for the fledgling medium.[7] In 1920 he made his first appearance on screen, in the short film *Convém martelar* (Keep Trying), an advertisement for a pharmaceutical product, and in the 1920s, in addition to developing his important film archive, he began to write regularly for the Rio press. In the early 1920s he wrote a column dedicated to cinema in the magazines *Palcos e Telas* and *Rio Jornal*, as well as writing frequent letters to *Para Todos* magazine (which later also employed him as a columnist), under the pseudonym of Senhorita Rio, pointing out the flaws in recent productions. In 1923 he and Mário Behring, director of the National Library, began writing the magazine's regular column on cinema. *Para Todos* provided a valuable learning environment for the young Gonzaga, with its team of correspondents who reported on cinematic initiatives taking place in far-flung regions of Brazil.[8] The magazine also inspired Gonzaga and Behring to launch their own publication, dedicated to cinema, and so *Cinearte* was born.

Cinearte's slogan was 'All Brazilian films must be seen', and the magazine played a key role in fomenting film production in Brazil. Its section on 'Amateur Cinema' was particularly important in encouraging new talent and, perhaps more importantly, in constructing a sense of a national film industry, however precarious, which focused on studio production and to which the creation of 'stars' was central. Hollywood provided the majority of material for the magazine, as evidenced by the fact that Gonzaga made four visits to the studios of Los Angeles between 1927 and 1935, as well as employing a permanent correspondent for his magazine in the city. This did not diminish, however, *Cinearte*'s commitment to championing Brazilian cinema. As Ismail Xavier writes:

> In the eyes of its creators, *Cinearte*'s stance was progressive and patriotic. Its oft-repeated slogan – 'a country's progress is gauged by the number of its cinema theatres' – highlights the idea that, striving for the development of the cinema industry, this magazine would be doing a great service to the nation.[9]

The magazine was instrumental in promoting Brazilian productions and creating film stars, tailoring its coverage to the tastes of its largely female readers by imitating the Hollywood star system, as discussed in more detail in Chapter 10. For Gonzaga, Brazilian cinema meant sophisticated, photogenic urban settings and characters, with a cosmopolitan gloss that projected Brazil as a modern, civilised nation, conveniently ignoring the realities of a predominantly agrarian, mixed-race society still dominated by backward-looking rural oligarchies.[10]

Directorial debut

Gonzaga made his first foray into film directing at the end of the 1920s. *Barro humano* (Human Mud, 1928) tells the tale of a young girl who decides to earn a living for herself outside the home, and thus meets with hostility and prejudice. The lead roles in this silent film were played by Eva Schnoor and Carlos Modesto, whose off-screen romance and subsequent marriage served to reinforce their status within the emerging star system, which certainly did not harm the popular appeal of the film. On the strength of its success at the box office, Gonzaga was able to convince his father, who had acquired considerable wealth in his work for the federal lottery, to provide his son with the funds to set up a film studio. *Barro humano* equally enjoyed critical acclaim, as the following review published in the Rio newspaper *Correio da manhã* attests:

> I believe that I am not mistaken when I state that it represents the most perfect work that has been produced in Brazil to date. Thanks to a group of courageous young men, cinema in Brazil is beginning to be a reality, when it once seemed to be an almost impossible dream.[11]

Fuelled by his initial directorial success, Gonzaga then took the ambitious step of travelling to Hollywood with Eva Schnoor and Carlos Modesto, where he hired a sound stage at United Artists studio for the sizeable sum of $500 per day.[12] His intention was to film scenes for a partial sound film entitled *Mulher* (Woman), the tale of two Brazilians who meet at a wedding in Hollywood. What would have been the first Portuguese-language sound film was guaranteed success back home, but Gonzaga was forced to abandon the project, allegedly owing to opposition from the family of its male lead, Modesto.

The Cinédia studio

Originally called the Cinearte studios, to tie in with Gonzaga's magazine, Cinédia was established in 1930 in Rio de Janeiro, and remained in continual operation until 1951. Gonzaga consciously modelled his studio on the Hollywood majors, employing technical staff and actors on a contract basis, importing the latest equipment, such as the first Mitchell camera to arrive in Brazil, Multiplex developing machines, Bell & Howell copiers, and Max Factor make-up from the United States, and constructing several sound stages to allow for simultaneous filming. It was at the Cinédia studio that the first recording of a fiction film using the Movietone process took place on Brazilian soil.[13] The contribution of Gonzaga's costly initiative, which ultimately drained his inherited wealth, to the development of the film industry in Brazil and individual talents and careers cannot be overstated.

It was at Cinédia that the *chanchada* tradition coalesced in the form of *Alô, alô, carnaval!* (Hello, Hello, Carnival!, 1936), directed by Gonzaga and starring Carmen Miranda, which definitively established the paradigms of Brazilian musical comedy.[14] This film is essential to understanding the origins of popular cinema in Brazil, and laid the foundations of the Atlântida *chanchada* of the 1940s and 1950s with its pioneering combination of carnival music and festivity, a backstage plot and a liberal dose of satire, particularly directed at foreign cultural forms. *Alô, alô, carnaval!* proved to be an unprecedented success at the box office in spite of its lack of sophistication in relation to imported Hollywood movies. In fact, Gonzaga's film celebrated the limitations of the Brazilian film industry to great comic effect, establishing a vein of self-deprecating humour and lack of pretension that would run through the *chanchada* tradition and guarantee its enduring popularity.

Popular genres became the mainstay of Cinédia's productions in the 1930s and 1940s, and included, in addition to carnival musicals, romantic comedies such as *Bonequinha de seda* (Little Silk Doll, 1936), starring Gilda de Abreu,[15] a hit at the box office, and *Maridinho de luxo* (Upmarket Hubbie, 1938). Gonzaga was astute enough to realise that these tried-and-trusted formulae were the key to the commercial viability of Cinédia. The profits, albeit limited, that such productions generated were periodically ploughed back into more high-brow projects, such as the historical epic *O descobrimento do Brasil* (The Discovery of Brazil, 1937, examined in more detail below), the semi-documentary *Aruanã* (made in 1938, and dealing with the Javahés indigenous tribe) and the literary adaptation *Pureza* (Purity, 1940).

In the 1940s Cinédia continued to concentrate its resources on popular genres, overwhelmingly musical comedies. These included *Samba em Berlim* (Samba in Berlin, 1943), directed by Luiz de Barros, which although critically panned served its commercial purpose.[16] Hitler was the butt of the joke in this film and in Cinédia's follow-up, *Berlim na batucada* (Berlin to the Samba Beat, 1944), also directed by Barros, who was equally candid about the financial motivation behind this production: 'it fulfilled its mission very well in provoking hearty laughter and making money'.[17] Cinédia thus made a major contribution not only to maintaining film production in Brazil during the 1940s but also to fostering the evolution of arguably the only true Brazilian cinematic genre, the *chanchada*. Ironically, however, it was the melodrama *O ébrio* (The Drunkard, 1946), co-produced by Cinédia and the film's director, Gilda de Abreu, and examined in more detail below, which was to prove to be the studio's most enduring commercial achievement. Gonzaga recognised the enormous potential offered by the eponymous play on which the film would be based, and invited Abreu, wife of the author of the play, to script and direct a screen adaptation.

Gonzaga as mentor

Adhemar Gonzaga must be given due credit for having nurtured the early career of Humberto Mauro, his most illustrious disciple.[18] On Mauro's arrival in Rio armed with a copy of his first feature-length film, *Na primavera da vida* (In the Springtime of Life, 1926), Gonzaga is reported to have given the self-taught director his first lesson in the artifice of filmmaking:

> When you want to say on screen that a man is a villain, you do not need to insert an intertitle saying: Jack the Baddie, the most feared, terrible and formidable criminal in the land. You just have to show him kicking a cat. The beauty of cinema is deducing or inferring the meaning, making people think, like that.[19]

Gonzaga's advice is clearly reflected in Mauro's film *Tesouro perdido* (Lost Treasure, 1927), in which the villain, played by Mauro himself, is introduced with the redundant intertitle 'Manoel Faca' (Mack the Knife), and promptly mistreats a passing cat.

In an interview with Alex Viany and David Neves on the event of his eightieth birthday, Mauro said that he considered Gonzaga's most important role within Brazilian cinema to be not that of producer but as an *animador* – an animator or motivator, who 'encouraged everyone'.[20] Elsewhere, Mauro acknowledged that Gonzaga alone was responsible for instructing him in the subtleties of film technique and their aesthetic uses.[21]

Humberto Mauro (1897–1983)

Throughout his filmmaking career, which spanned 1925 to 1974, Humberto Mauro always focused his lens on his homeland, and for this reason he is still widely considered to have been the most 'Brazilian' director that Brazil has ever produced.[22] He has thus become something of a metaphor for Brazil itself, not least in the eyes of subsequent filmmakers who have acknowledged the inspiration that he provided for their own work. Mauro's documentaries, particularly those set in rural areas in the state of Minas Gerais, have been seen as articulating national utopias and capturing an authentic vision of a rapidly disappearing version of the nation. He has consequently been seen by the *cinema novo* group as the most 'national' of all Brazilian filmmakers,[23] albeit heavily weighted in favour of bucolic Minas Gerais as centre of the nation. His ultimate return to an artisan style of filmmaking and rejection of industrialisation are also seen as part of some essential Brazilianness. He has thus become bound up in debates and reasoning about not only what Brazilian cinema is, but also who Brazilians are as a nation.

Pioneering initiatives in Minas Gerais

Humberto Mauro was born to an Italian father and Brazilian mother on 30 April 1897, near the small town of Cataguases in Minas Gerais. Electricity was only just making its way to such regions of Brazil's interior, and it was a young Mauro who pioneered the construction of radio receivers in his home town, having taught himself the necessary skills by dismantling a radio set. Passionate about photography, Mauro swapped his collection of rare stamps for a Kodak camera, but, since he married at the age of 23 and went on to have three children soon afterwards, he was forced to earn a living as an electrician, acting in a local amateur theatre group in his spare time. His initial contact with the cinema came via the only cinema theatre in Cataguases, the Recreio. Mauro is reported to have said to an Italian photographer friend, Pedro Comello: 'Can't we make films like these American ones? There is no secret to it.' With a borrowed Pathe Baby camera, the two of them made their first film, *Valadião, o Cratera* (Valadião, the Rogue, 1925), a tale of a young woman kidnapped by the villain of the piece, inspired by the Hollywood adventure films of Pearl White and Thomas Ince, and which featured a cast of family members, including Mauro's pet dog. In 1925 Mauro and Comello secured financial support from local businessmen to set up the Sul América Filme company, later renamed Phebo Brasil Film. Thus the so-called 'Cataguases Cycle' of regional cinema was born.

The team's determination made up for the lack of premises, actors, technical equipment and knowledge of the market or aesthetic theories. Their first attempt at a feature film, *Os dois irmãos* (The Two Brothers), was directed by Comello and starred Mauro as the leading man, but was never finished. The company's first completed full-length feature film, *Na primavera da vida* (In the Springtime of Life, 1926), was also Mauro's directorial debut.[24] Its subject matter was the illegal trade in *cachaça*, cheap firewater made from sugar cane, a topical issue in the region. From the pages of *Para Todos* magazine, Mauro soon became aware that he and his Cataguases group were not the only pioneering filmmakers in Brazil. Mauro explained in interview that he paid an intermediary a considerable sum of money in order to have an image from *Na primavera da vida* published in the magazine.[25] When the report failed to materialise, Mauro packed his bags and set off for the capital with a copy of the film, which he showed to the film columnist Adhemar Gonzaga, and thus their creative partnership was born.[26] Excited by the developments taking place in provincial Minas Gerais, Gonzaga promised to feature a report on the production in *Para Todos*.

The second film of the 'Cataguases Cycle', all of which were silent, was *Tesouro perdido* (Lost Treasure, 1927), a tale of a quest for buried riches loosely modelled on Hollywood westerns.[27] Paulo Perdigão argues that Mauro's direction on this film was influenced by German Expressionism, classic Hollywood cinema and the first French avant-garde film movement,[28] which he came into contact with during his stay in Rio.[29] Using considerable ingenuity, Mauro achieved the effects of a storm by using a humble watering can, and scratched the surface of the film stock to reproduce flashes of lightning. The plot was a simple tale of a young woman kidnapped by bandits, which clearly took its lead from the Hollywood adventure movies that Mauro had voraciously consumed in the cinema theatre in Cataguases. Mauro's family provided the main actors, with his wife in the starring role under the pseudonym of Lola Lys, and his brother, Bruno Mauro, as the leading man, Chiquinho. As well as appearing in the film himself as the ubiquitous villain, Humberto Mauro wrote the film's script. *Tesouro perdido* delighted local audiences, who enjoyed seeing their everyday surroundings on screen. Commercially successful and critically acclaimed, the film was awarded the first cinema prize ever offered in Brazil, the *Cinearte* medal for best Brazilian film, out of fourteen contenders. The magazine singled out Mauro's directorial skills for praise, comparing the film very favourably with other Brazilian productions. When shown in São Paulo, *Tesouro perdido* is said to have converted critic Octávio Gabus Mendes, who had previously only taken an interest in foreign productions, to national films.

Mauro's follow-up project was *Brasa dormida* (Dormant Embers, 1928), for which he also wrote the script, and which proved to be a major hit at the box office, being exhibited virtually all over Brazil, largely thanks to the efforts of the editors of *Cinearte*, who succeeded in bringing the film to the attention of Universal's distribution wing. The plot of Mauro's most expensive venture to date centred on the adventures of Luiz Soares, who after spending all his savings in Rio de Janeiro abandons his studies to earn his living in the interior. Organised into several narrative segments, *Brasa dormida* was noted for the melancholic tone and sensual mood of its love scenes featuring the film's star pairing, Nita Ney and Luiz Soroa, who had both been contracted during Mauro's time in Rio. A review of the film in *Cinearte* by Octávio Gabus Mendes described it as 'The best Brazilian film made to date', one of several very favourable reviews published in the press.[30]

Sangue mineiro (Blood of Minas Gerais, 1930), the melodramatic tale of the daughter of a millionaire from Minas Gerais who, suffering from a broken heart, tries to kill herself, signalled the director's transition from the 'Cataguases Cycle' to his work in Rio de Janeiro, initially at the Cinédia studio. The production of this film was made possible by the financial backing of Carmen Santos, who co-produced and starred in it.[31] The opening titles of *Sangue mineiro* underscore Mauro's belief in the patriotic value of filmmaking in Brazil, and the educational potential of the medium, pre-empting the rhetoric that would come to dominate the first Vargas regime's cultural policies:[32]

> We present to you today *Sangue mineiro* [Blood of Minas Gerais], Phebo's fourth cinematic work. What led us to call the film this, far

> from being a sense of parochialism, was, first and foremost, and principally, that vigorous breath of Brazilianness [*brasilidade*] that today revives and re-educates the new generation of Brazilians. Recording customs and aspects of the region of Minas Gerais, although in rapid details, we have attempted to capture, in some way, a little of the good and simple soul of our people.

Nevertheless, this declaration must also be seen in the context of the visit made to the Phebo Brasil Film studio during filming by the state governor of Minas Gerais, and his veiled promise of financial support from the government.[33]

Mauro in Rio: the Cinédia years

Recognising his prodigious talent, Adhemar Gonzaga helped ensure the exhibition of Mauro's work in the capital, and went on to invite him to work at Cinédia. Mauro directed two films for Gonzaga's studio, the first of which was *Lábios sem beijos* (Lips without Kisses, 1931). This silent comedy, written by Gonzaga, was labelled immoral by certain critics for its sensual images, such as close-ups of the legs and face of its star Lelita Rosa, and classified as 'unsuitable for children and ladies' by the censors.[34] Cinédia's first production, *Lábios sem beijos* has equally been described as 'a landmark in Brazilian comic film . . . a biting take on daily life, an ironic vision . . . that still makes us laugh today'.[35] The second production was *Ganga bruta* (Brutal Gang, 1933), Mauro's first experiment with sound. It was commenced as a silent project in 1931, but delays in production necessitated its incorporation of sound in order to keep pace with technical developments and audience expectations. Consequently the film relied on the Vitaphone system, which Gonzaga had familiarised himself with in Hollywood in 1929, by which the music, noises and occasional sections of dialogue were recorded on to discs that were played during the film's exhibition. With his move to the capital, a new element of urban sophistication was added to the purity and simplicity of Mauro's work.[36]

Ganga bruta has been seen as Mauro's finest work.[37] *Cinema novo*'s *enfant terrible*, Glauber Rocha, called it one of the twenty best films ever made,[38] but also 'a topsy-turvy classic', an Expressionist film for the opening five minutes, a realist documentary in the second part, then a Western 'in the style of John Ford' and a film which 'builds with the same strength as a work of classic Russian cinema'.[39] The only word uttered in this sound film is the forename Paulo, and Mauro explained his artistic choices as follows:

> I used, as in silent film, symbols and inferences, which earned me the nickname of the Freud of Cascadura [a district of Rio]. When Freud fever took hold, I read everything he wrote that I could get hold of. I tried to see what could be applied to the cinema. In *Ganga bruta* I wanted to see if I could create some Freudian effects, principally by

> means of the phallic symbols, like cranes, vertical camera movements, objects and composition of shots.[40]

Mauro's use of a hand-held camera and the resulting spontaneity achieved are widely recognised as having been ahead of their time and a major influence on the *cinema novo* generation. The film was, however, a box-office flop, and the majority of contemporary critics claimed not to understand it.[41] In 1934 Mauro's contract at Cinédia was abruptly terminated, and he went to work for Carmen Santos's Brasil Vita Filme studio.

Mauro and the Brasil Vita Filme studio

Humberto Mauro directed three feature-length films for Carmen Santos's studio, the most influential of which was *Favela dos meus amores* (Shantytown of my Loves, 1934), Mauro's personal favourite and his only film to enjoy widespread popular appeal.[42] The film incorporated two stories: one involving the love affair between a young man who wants to set up a night club in a shantytown and a young woman (played by Carmen Santos) who teaches in a school there, the other based on an Afro-Brazilian samba composer called Nhô-Nhô, modelled on the real-life figure Sinhô (José Barbosa da Silva, 1888–1930), known as the 'King of Samba'. In a review of the film, the writer Jorge Amado called it Mauro's masterpiece, adding: 'I can state that this is really a film worthy of all its praise, totally irrespective of the issue of it being a Brazilian film . . . It would be a good film even if it were American or German.'[43] As Mauro said of his film, 'I simply grabbed life in the *favelas* as it was. I documented it',[44] and the film's ground-breaking realism, achieved via the use of location shooting (almost two-thirds of the film was shot in the shantytown of Providência in Rio), non-professional actors who lived in the *favela*, and a soundtrack that featured the authentic percussion-based music of Rio's carnival parades, documentary footage of which was also incorporated into the film, doubtless contributed to its overwhelmingly positive reception among the public and the critics. The Portela samba school, with its 300 dancers, appeared in the film, which required the importing of expensive sound equipment.

Henrique Pongetti, author of the story line of *Favela dos meus amores*, vividly recounted his experiences of location shooting in the shantytown:

> I will never forget the days spent at the top of that hill, among the sordid shacks, in front of one of the most beautiful landscapes in the world, surrounded by criminals as sensitive about being well treated and understood as starving, beaten dogs. Their names were Moleque Dezenove, Baiano, Ananias. They had all committed serious crimes in the past, but were ready to behave honestly if they had proof that they would be treated humanely and honestly. Moleque Dezenove, with his soft, homicidal hands, rubbing manioc flour and alcohol on our backs blistered by the sun bouncing off the rock. Moleque Dezenove, who

> didn't steal any of Carmen Santos's large diamonds that she'd left on a table in our make-shift studio, set up in a samba school. Moleque Dezenove, a murderer and gentle![45]

Mauro's second film for Brasil Vita Filme was *Cidade mulher* (Woman City, 1936), a backstage tale that revolved around the staging of a revue show at Rio's Beira-Mar casino, and proved to be the director's one and only foray into the nascent *chanchada* tradition.[46] *Cidade mulher*'s show business setting provided the perfect excuse for the inclusion of songs composed especially for the film, for the first time ever in Brazilian cinema history, by popular songwriters Noel Rosa and Assis Valente. Mauro intended this film, like its predecessor, to be a musical tribute to the city of Rio de Janeiro. It failed, however, to repeat the critical or box-office success of *Favela dos meus amores*, perhaps owing, at least in part, to a series of technical failings linked to the sound quality.[47]

In 1940 Mauro took his innovative use of soundtrack a stage further, using incidental music by classical composers Heitor Villa-Lobos and Hekel Tavares in his film *Argila* (Clay),[48] the third film that he directed for Brasil Vita Filmes, and which starred Carmen Santos as a thoroughly modern woman, a patron of the arts, who sponsors and seduces a local ceramics artisan named Gilberto. In spite of its controversial eroticism, *Argila* clearly also bears the imprint of Mauro's contemporaneous documentary work for the INCE (*Instituto Nacional de Cinema Educativo* – National Institute of Educational Cinema), discussed at greater length in the section 'Mauro's documentaries for the INCE' below. The sequences that focus on the ceramic art of the inhabitants of the island of Marajó have a documentary quality and, although he refused to appear in the film, the voice of Roquette-Pinto, head of the INCE, can be heard during a scene at a conference on Marajó ceramics.[49] Under Roquette-Pinto's direction, the INCE commissioned two films on Marajó culture and ceramics, and Mauro's interest in the topic was clearly awoken by that of his friend and colleague. Schvarzman refers to *Argila* as an important reflection of the symbolic association made between more sophisticated elements of indigenous culture and national culture.[50]

The Discovery of Brazil

Finding himself unemployed in 1933, with seven children to raise and facing a crisis in film production in Brazil, Mauro readily accepted the invitation to become one of the founders of the INCE in 1936. This timely offer came when he was filming the historical epic *O descobrimento do Brasil* (The Discovery of Brazil, 1937), a fictional re-enactment of the arrival of the Portuguese in 1500, as documented in the letter sent by the scribe of the fleet, Pero Vaz de Caminha, to the king of Portugal.[51] This most lavish Brazilian production of the 1930s, and least representative of Mauro's work, was commissioned by the Cocoa Institute of Bahia, originally as part of a series of documentaries on the evolution of the cocoa trade in the state of Bahia that would begin with the 'discovery' of Brazil. Mauro, who replaced Luiz de Barros as director on the project, rejected the existing ultra-ambitious plans in favour of filming in Carmen Santos's studio in Rio, to which the replica of Cabral's sailing ship was transported from Rio de Janeiro's Guanabara Bay.

In *O descobrimento do Brasil*, Mauro's camera often appears to take the point of view of the official scribe and author of the famous letter to King Manuel of Portugal. Although this historical document is not acknowledged as the starting point of the film in the credits, its pivotal role is evident. As Schvarzman writes, 'Dialogue is substituted by the exhaustive work of the camera. The silence comes from Pero Vaz de Caminha, who observes and narrates. It is his gaze, mediated by the work of Mauro, which takes the film forward.'[52] This project, which took shape between October 1936 and November 1937, in the run-up to the creation of Vargas's authoritarian *Estado Novo* or New State, was depicted in the press as a powerful symbol of national pride. The newspaper *O Globo* called it a 'hymn to the Lusitanian [Portuguese] bravery of that century', claiming that it would demonstrate 'the possibility of recreating, in the cinema, the entire history of our land'.[53] The Vargas regime equally saw the film as a potential focus for national identity. In a letter to Humberto Mauro written in 1937, Lourival Fontes, head of the *Departamento de Propaganda e Difusão Cultural* (Department of Propaganda and Cultural Diffusion) between 1934 and 1938 (and subsequently of the *Departamento de Imprensa e Propaganda* – Press and Propaganda Department), stated: 'The filming of *O descobrimento do Brasil*, with its historical fidelity and technical orientation, represents an undeniable landmark in the evolution and improvement of Brazilian cinema.'[54] As the only celluloid re-enactment of the 'birth' of the Brazilian nation, *O descobrimento do Brasil*, with its insistence on a peaceful, 'natural' process of national foundation, clearly suited the regime's unifying zeal and rhetorical appeals to patriotism.

No efforts were spared on the attention to detail, with Mauro turning to Roquette-Pinto and Afonso de E. Taunay, then director of the National Library, for help with historical research. This intentionally didactic film has an epic quality, achieved via the anachronistic use of subtitles and intertitles, sparse dialogue, and extra-diegetic orchestral music by Heitor Villa-Lobos, to allude to a far-off time replete with mystery, and to avoid representing these heroes of the Brazilian nation as mere mortals who conversed in banal exchanges. No translations are given for the dialogues spoken in the Tupi language by the indigenous characters, again in an effort to recreate the experiences of the Portuguese navigators as vividly as possible. (Mauro learned to speak Tupi with the help of Roquette-Pinto, and these two enthusiasts of indigenous culture conversed in the language in their day-to-day dealings at the INCE.[55]) Extreme close-up shots of the arms and torsos of the Portuguese sailors, at the expense of shots of their faces, evoke their physical sacrifices and heroism, and navigational instruments such as the compass and astrolabe are shot in the extreme foreground, affording them the status of key players in the momentous event.[56]

The native Indians in the film are not in fact played by members of the indigenous community, but rather by white or mixed-race actors with painted faces and wigs.

Schvarzman observes that it is surprisingly these characters, and not the Portuguese explorers, who are troubled by insects and the tropical heat on screen, and who hop uneasily around what is effectively their land, in marked contrast to the confident, colonial gait of the Portuguese. The native inhabitants are depicted as detached from the land, thus justifying the imperial pretensions of the Portuguese crown.[57] The film was criticised by Mauro's intellectual, left-leaning contemporaries, such as the writers Graciliano Ramos and Oswald de Andrade, for its apparent apology for colonialism. Subsequently critics have remarked on Mauro's wholesale, uncritical adoption of the imperial ideologies of the Portuguese Crown in 1500, and his apparent willingness to endorse a foundational myth that complied with the view of Brazilian identity instilled by the Vargas regime, and to perpetuate the historical oppression of Brazil's indigenous peoples.[58]

Mauro screened his film at the Exhibition of Cinematic Art in Venice in 1938, which he attended as a special delegate.[59] It proved to be the most expensive Brazilian production until that dubious honour was passed to Carmen Santos's *Inconfidência mineira* and Gilda de Abreu's *Pinguinho de gente* some ten years later.[60] *O descobrimento do Brasil* proved to be a commercial failure, and was virtually only exhibited in Rio de Janeiro in the first few months of 1938, never making it to São Paulo or even to Bahia, the state which dreamed up and financed the original project.

Mauro's documentaries for the INCE

Although *O descobrimento do Brasil* was not commissioned by the INCE, the film bore the indelible hallmark of Roquette-Pinto, whom Schvarzman credits as responsible for 'intellectual collaboration' in the production,[61] and it effectively bridged the gap between Mauro's work on full-length fiction films and his subsequent documentary making for the INCE.[62] Having already made several documentaries, including *Sinfonia de Cataguases* (Symphony of Cataguases, 1929) about his home town, directly inspired by Walter Ruttmann's *Berlin, Symphony of a Great City*, and two shorts and one medium-length documentary for the Brasil Vita Filmes studio, Mauro now began to channel his talents into directing a total of 354 documentary films, the majority shot on 16-millimetre film, during the twenty-eight years that he remained at the INCE. This oeuvre embraced patriotic subjects and State events, in keeping with the New State's nationalistic fervour, such as *7 de Setembro de 1936 – Dia da Pátria* (7 September 1936 – Independence Day/Fatherland Day, 1936), a sound film that showed troops on parade in Rio and military fanfares. Mauro's documentaries for the INCE equally performed a didactic function, often implicitly praising the civilising advances introduced to Brazilian society by the Vargas regime. In addition, he directed educational documentaries on more artistic topics, such as the great Brazilian novelist Machado de Assis[63] and the influential writer Euclides da Cunha (*Euclydes da Cunha, 1866–1909*, made in 1944).[64] These celebrations of the lives of those who had contributed most to the development of Brazilian letters were imbued with national pride. In a radio broadcast made in 1944, Mauro outlined the latter film, describing da Cunha as 'the most Brazilian of Brazilian writers'.[65]

Mauro displayed nostalgia for rural life in his work, which was often characterised by its poetic, melancholy tone. The association drawn between traditional life in the countryside and the roots and core values of Brazilian national identity by the Vargas regime, and by extension the INCE, neatly complemented Mauro's own vision. A significant portion of his work at the INCE is dedicated to the recovery and valorisation of provincial culture and folkloric traditions, and many of these films were made after the demise of the first Vargas regime. This thematic strand of his work is best exemplified in the *Brasiliana* series of seven short films, made between 1945 and 1956, that give centre stage to various types of regional folk songs, but which also serve as a musical backdrop to depictions of aspects of rural life that faced extinction.[66] All, with one exception, were shot in or around Mauro's birthplace of Volta Grande, in Minas Gerais.

Carmen Santos (1904–52)

Naked ambition and film stardom

In 1919 a 15-year-old shop assistant in the Park Royal clothes store in Rio de Janeiro by the name of Maria do Carmo Santos entered a competition organised by the Omega Film studio, established in Rio de Janeiro by an American called William Jansen. With her slender build, dark brown hair and eyes, and contrasting pale complexion, Santos's rather androgynous beauty epitomised the thoroughly modern woman of the era, and she was duly chosen by the studio for the leading role of Marta in the film *Urutau* (1919).[67] Santos had arrived in Rio from her native Portugal at the age of 8 with her poor immigrant parents, but in spite of her humble background and very limited contact with the emerging medium (she claimed that the first film she ever saw was *Urutau*, in which she starred) Santos's debut performance and 'star quality' were praised in the press. The editor of the magazine *Palcos e Telas* described her as: 'a charming "mignonne" who is only seventeen years old and represents great promise for Brazilian cinema'.[68] Although *Urutau* was never shown commercially, owing to a lack of interest among exhibitors, who preferred foreign imports, Carmen, as she was now known, was undeterred. Determined to pursue her dream of stardom, and aided and abetted by the Brazilian film press, who as early as 1919 were hailing her as a future star, she became a consummate self-publicist. In 1920 she announced in the press her imminent departure for the United States to become a star in Hollywood:

> I want to go alone in order to learn English out of necessity. As soon as I can make myself understood I will walk into a studio, state my aim and what I want, and I will be accepted in any of them.[69]

Figure 5.1 Carmen Santos (courtesy of CTAv – Centro Técnico Audiovisual; reproduced with kind permission from Rosângela Sodré)

Three years later Santos resurfaced in Rio's film magazines, sending them innumerable provocative photographs of herself throughout the 1920s, wearing clothes and make-up which emphasised her sensuality and vampish, femme fatale qualities.[70] In 1924 she appeared in the controversial *A carne* (Flesh), an adaptation of Júlio Ribeiro's eponymous novel of 1888. The following year she starred in the equally risqué *Mademoiselle Cinema*, based on the 1922 novel of the same name by Benjamin Costallat. In both films she played a liberated, 'new' woman, in keeping with her emerging star text. *Mademoiselle Cinema* tapped into the moral outcry over the emergence of the very independent, modern woman that Santos's on-screen roles and off-screen star persona capitalised on. In both films the female protagonists that she played remain defiantly young, single and promiscuous, refusing to be 'saved' and returned to an ascribed, 'respectable' role within patriarchal society. Such new narrative possibilities undoubtedly complemented the star image that she cultivated.

Santos courted the press in order to promote both projects, and by 1925 she had become one of Brazil's most recognisable faces. She ensured that she enjoyed the same star status in the press as foreign leading actresses. *Cinearte* described her seductive star text as a mixture of 'nectar and poison', referring to her as a 'star who came down from heaven to adopt the form of a woman in order to fill humanity's senses with greed and sin' and as possessing a 'gentle tenderness that I do not call divine since she is diabolically a woman'.[71] Such descriptions suggest that such 'new' women could only be accepted in society if they toed the line between modernity and tradition, between independence and conformity to patriarchal norms. In spite of Santos's fame, the Brazilian public had never actually seen her on screen, since neither *A carne* nor *Mademoiselle Cinema* was ever exhibited. In September 1926 it was announced that an 'almost complete' version of *A carne* had been destroyed in a fire.[72] The official line was that *Mademoiselle Cinema* had met with an identical fate, but there is anecdotal evidence to suggest that Santos's boyfriend, Antônio Lartigaud Seabra, scion of a wealthy family of textile wholesalers, blocked their release to protect her, and by extension his, good name, recognising that both films blurred the distinction between the lascivious characters Santos played and the star herself.

Brimming with ambition, Santos had an impressive command of the nascent star discourse. As Ana Pessoa argues, she recreated

> the facts about her personal and professional life according to the ideals of the 1920s – of a free, daring, sporty young woman, who wants to fulfil her desires and aspirations of her own accord.[73] She hides her humble origins and adopts the habits and ways of a little rich girl.[74]

In an interview for the magazine *Palcos e Telas* entitled 'A Future Star: Carmen Santos', Santos declared:

> With the closure of the Omega studio I could not accept not being a star . . . I decided to go to the United States. I am going alone and I

have such determination to succeed that I firmly believe in my success . . . If I don't end up being a film star I'll be an aviator.[75]

A pioneering female producer

It was thanks to the financial support of Antônio Seabra that Santos was able to pursue her dream and take over the reins of her career, as only a few of her female contemporaries in Hollywood, such as Mary Pickford and Lillian Gish, were able to do. As well as choosing polemical film projects and adopting irreverent, seductive poses in the publicity photographs that were ubiquitous in the film press, in October 1924 she announced the creation of her own production company, FAB (*Film Artístico Brasileiro* – Brazilian Artistic Film), which completed the making of *A carne* after the collapse of the Guanabara Filmes studio, and went on to produce *Mademoiselle Cinema*. Santos shrewdly realised that the ultra 'now' title of *Mademoiselle Cinema* and the recent commercial success of and controversy surrounding the novel on which it was based would guarantee box-office appeal, an early sign of her entrepreneurial vision.[76] In the film press she was portrayed in a very sympathetic light, the delays in her films attributed to unscrupulous collaborators and unfair competition from Hollywood. She is repeatedly depicted as a helpless victim, in keeping with gender stereotypes, obliged to accept this patronising discourse in order to further her cause. An article by Pedro Lima in *Selecta* recounts:

> 'If only I were a man!' . . . She said to us with tears in her eyes, 'I would not always be as duped as I have been, and for sure I would have seen my efforts pay off by now! Unfortunately I'm a woman, and, to my great misfortune, I have almost only trusted people who absolutely do not deserve to be trusted.'[77]

All the evidence suggests, in fact, that Santos, like the characters she chose to play on screen, was a feisty trailblazer, who bore Seabra a child out of wedlock in 1928 in defiance of the rigid class hierarchy and Catholic moral code of contemporary Rio, both of which dictated that their union was deemed socially unacceptable.

Motherhood did not distract Santos from her chosen career, and she soon joined forces with the Cataguases regional film group, in provincial Minas Gerais, led by the talented, up-and-coming director Humberto Mauro. She co-produced and starred in *Sangue mineiro* (1930), made by Mauro's company Phebo Brasil Film. In a letter sent by Mauro to Adhemar Gonzaga, the former explains the financial arrangements agreed on with Santos, by which she invested heavily in the production in exchange for a starring role, but was also responsible for all the costs incurred in carrying out the role, including her travel and accommodation expenses whilst on location in Minas Gerais.[78] Santos employed her well-honed skills to promote both the production and her star status. During filming she was interviewed by the Belo Horizonte newspaper *Folha da Noite Mineira*, and the journalist reported how at the end of the interview she handed him a photograph of herself and took a red carnation from her outfit and attached it to the lapel of the editor in chief.[79]

Santos took it upon herself to campaign for greater publicity for this project even during filming. She wrote to the film's director, Mauro:

> We need to sort out the publicity! Pedro Lima [the editor of *Cinearte*] is showing no interest in us at all! I have sent him 40-odd stills and he hasn't published one of them, and then he goes and says he doesn't have any to print![80]

When *Sangue mineiro* was finally released, publicity for the film revolved around Santos, with the promotional poster featuring the image of the 'stolen kiss' between her character and that of Maury Bueno, in his first screen performance. The poster also gave greater prominence to her name than to the title of the film, giving ample evidence of her star status and box-office appeal.[81] In the annual publication *Cinearte-Album* of 1930, there is a full-page photograph of Santos, looking every inch an 'It girl',[82] and a photograph to promote *Sangue mineiro.*[83] She is portrayed as a dangerous femme fatale, with 'unsettling charms'.[84] In spite of critical acclaim, and the presence of Santos and the other darling of the Brazilian silent era, Nita Ney, *Sangue mineiro* did not fare well at the box office.

Undeterred, Santos was by the eve of the 1930s more determined than ever to play an active role within the emerging Brazilian film industry, which she saw as full of promise and possibility. She wrote to Humberto Mauro in June of 1929 expressing her desire to make a film with him and the acclaimed cinematographer Edgard Brasil. She concluded one of her letters as follows:

> But with all my heart I would prefer to work with you today, as I have total confidence in your work . . . I want you to be interested in me. I am certain that I will have a brilliant career if I am given the opportunity and am left in peace! Let them leave me in peace! I really need peace and quiet! . . . Your friend Carmen Santos.[85]

Her initiative resulted in the unfinished film *Lábios sem beijos* (Lips without Kisses), directed by Adhemar Gonzaga. Santos starred in the film as a flapper, and appeared in publicity stills in an ultra-modern dress made of a geometric fabric, and a cloche hat. Furthermore, she financed the film single-handedly.[86] As *Cinearte* reported: 'The company that Carmen Santos has just established is one of those which currently has the best film apparatus, which is currently at the disposal of Edgar Brasil.'[87] Early in 1930, however, in spite of all her promotional efforts and investments, Santos and Gonzaga parted company and he took on the project alone, claiming that her second pregnancy and ill health had prompted the move. Tellingly, however, Santos did not appear in Gonzaga's subsequent film, *Mulher* (Woman).[88] Resilient as ever, and astute in the contacts she made within the industry, such as Mauro and Brasil, Santos turned her attentions to the young director Mário Peixoto, offering him free use of the technical facilities in her home in exchange for writing a script that would turn her into a star.[89] Peixoto then gave her a small part in his celebrated film *Limite* (Limit, 1931), and went on to plan a new original screenplay inspired by Santos and designed to showcase her dramatic potential. Santos was happy to take on the role of sole producer, giving her greater freedom than she experienced at Phebo Brasil Film, and avoiding the pitfalls of her short-lived collaboration with Gonzaga at the Cinédia studio. Seabra was equally only too happy to support his common-law wife's most audacious project to date.[90]

Onde a terra acaba *and gender issues*

When news of Santos's creative and commercial partnership with Mário Peixoto first began to filter through to the film press in January 1931, she began to speak openly of her enthusiasm for the project, which resulted in the film *Onde a terra acaba* (The Ends of the Earth), and her optimism for the commercial viability of Brazilian cinema as a whole. She clearly had to deflect criticisms that were premised, at least in part, on her gender. As she stated in an interview published in the magazine *A Scena Muda*: 'I don't care if people call me mad or a maniac.'[91] Her determination and outspokenness seem to have presented problems for her male collaborators, and she declared that she would have liked to have been 'born a man, and been a doctor, with the sensitivity and the heart that I have'.[92]

It would appear that Santos's contemporaries found her assertiveness and passion for her career rather difficult to equate with her gender. In 1932 the journalist Afonso de Carvalho wrote a lengthy article about Santos the woman in which he concludes: 'when God created her he really had in his hands the most beautiful womanly form, but, at that moment, he was thinking of a man'.[93] Her professed love of scientific studies and classical literature rather than love stories, and her support of social causes and the underdog are seen as among her 'masculine' qualities. Above all it is her love of freedom and independence which the journalist finds most striking, his choice of psychoanalytical terminology betraying his value judgement of her flouting of the dominant patriarchal order:

> What weighs most heavily in her permanent revolutionary spirit is, above all, her *fetishistic* love of freedom . . . In Carmen Santos, freedom is a veritable *neurosis* . . . Her entire life is a continuous effort to conquer her freedom, her independence . . . To not depend on anyone, to not have to answer to anyone . . . To live off her work. Off her films. To be sincere. To be alone. Absolutely alone![94]

The role that Peixoto created for Santos in *Onde a terra acaba* was that of a mysterious urbane novelist, Eva, who embittered yet determined flees the city to set up home on an island to write her next novel, where she has an intense relationship with a solitary island dweller. The location was the island of Marambaia, off the coast of Rio de Janeiro, to which a large quantity of technical equipment had to be transported at considerable effort and expense. During filming, relations between Santos and Peixoto became increasingly tense and eventually the production ground to a halt. The press discreetly attributed the difficulties to her poor health, a veiled allusion to her apparent depression, a further indication of the industry's equation of her gender with frailty: 'Carmen Santos, the much loved star . . . has been working very hard in recent times and has striven so much that her doctor has recommended a brief period of rest away from the camera.'[95]

With her characteristic determination, Santos approached Adhemar Gonzaga to assist in completing *Onde a terra acaba*. Under Cinédia's roof, and under the direction of Octávio Gabus Mendes, Peixoto's script was abandoned and a new plot was adapted from José de Alencar's novel *Senhora* (Lady). As Pessoa observes, in the first half of 1932 the press focused on Santos the star, rather than on the film in question, with photographs of her appearing alongside those of Hollywood stars and illustrating an article on the fashion for smoking among women.[96] (The stills she supplied to the press often showed her with a cigarette in her hand or in the corner of her mouth, a useful prop for her seductive, ultra-modern poses.) In January 1933 she appeared on the front cover of the magazines *Cine-Luz* and *A Scena Muda*.[97] *Onde a terra acaba* premiered in October 1933 to a mixed reception, remaining in exhibition for just one week. The majority of the reviews in the press, however, were full of praise for 'a different Carmen Santos, beautiful and full of "it"',[98] with her 'simply marvellous' close-ups[99] and her dedication to raising the capital for the production.[100]

The arrival of sound and Brasil Vita Filme

In spite of the commercial failure of *Onde a terra acaba*, Santos persevered, drawing on the advice of Humberto Mauro in planning the establishment of her own studio for the production of sound films. In 1933, with Seabra's financial support, Santos founded the Brasil Fox Filmes studio, obliged by Hollywood's Fox studio to change its name to Brasil Vita Filme from 1935, by which time it had become the second largest film studio in Brazil. Santos's company also became a distributor in 1936.

Santos tirelessly campaigned for Brazilian cinema, and on 6 January 1932 she was the only producer to speak out at the first National Film Industry Convention, organised by the exhibition sector via the Brazilian Filmmaking Association (*Associação Brasileira Cinematográfica* – ABC). She delivered an impassioned speech about the difficulties involved in making films in Brazil and the sacrifices made by the nation's pioneering filmmakers, drawing attention to the cinema's patriotic aspect. She expressed her interest in making educational films for children and the possibilities opened up by the arrival of the talking cinema in Brazil.[101] She also attended a meeting with President Getúlio Vargas in 1934 organised by the ABC, following the government's introduction in May of that year of compulsory exhibition of Brazilian films in national film theatres. Santos was spurred on by this official backing for the emerging industry. As early as 1934 she was referred to in the press as a female pioneer.

Cinearte was generous in its praise and support for Santos's endeavours. In 1935, she featured in every edition of the fortnightly publication, usually in the form of large close-up photographs and reports on her forthcoming productions. She evidently continued to supply the magazine with her own promotional material, and a photograph of her as a child, dressed in her confirmation outfit, was published in *Cinearte* number 428, on 1 December 1935. Her star status is reflected in the numerous letters from fans published in the magazine, and confirmed by a photograph of the Alhambra cinema in Rio de Janeiro, where Santos's name in neon lights is even more prominent than the title of the film in which she was starring, *Cidade mulher*.[102]

Cinearte was not alone in extolling Santos's contribution to Brazilian cinema. The magazine *A Scena Muda* described her as possessing 'an unbreakable will power', adding:

> Having produced *Favela dos meus amores* Carmen Santos gave us our first real talking film, with beginning, middle and end, and showed us that the Brazilian people already had a great desire for a national cinema made with good taste and honesty.[103]

Alice Gonzaga Assaf recounts how Santos ploughed back all the profits from the box-office returns of *Cidade mulher* into a cinema school to improve both the technical and the artistic standards of the industry in Brazil.[104]

Inconfidência mineira

The historical epic *Inconfidência mineira* (Conspiracy in Minas Gerais, 1948) was Santos's next and undoubtedly her boldest venture, and a project with high production values which took almost ten years to complete, drained the dwindling Seabra fortune and took a drastic toll on Santos's health.[105] She began making plans for the film in 1937, but only commenced production in 1941. It was not until 22 April 1948 that the film premiered. She starred in the film and was to eventually become the director, making her only the second woman to direct a full-length feature film in Brazil.[106] The project became her life's work, and she spared no expense or attention to detail in re-creating the costumes and props of the colonial era. She employed the acclaimed architect and director of the prestigious National School of Fine Arts in Rio, Lucio Costa, to advise her on the finer points of colonial architecture when constructing the set of an eighteenth-century street in the Brasil Vita Filme studio. She also enlisted the support of the director of the National Institute of Educational Cinema (INCE),[107] Roquette-Pinto, who, like Santos herself, saw the didactic and patriotic merits of the film. She made numerous research visits to the colonial towns of Minas Gerais and filmed incessantly between 1945 and 1948 in spite of considerable difficulties.

Relentlessly proactive in forming contacts with the emerging key players in the Brazilian film industry, Santos did not hesitate to approach the very highest authorities to gain support for this film about the failed independence plot of 1789, which she saw as having great nationalistic appeal. A letter from Gustavo Capanema, head of the Ministry of Education and Health, to President Getúlio Vargas, dated 20 June 1939, begins:

> The actress Carmen Santos, who is also a film producer, wishes to speak to you about a film about the Inconfidência Mineira, which she is making with great effort and sacrifice.
>
> She wishes to know if the making of this work would go against the wishes of the Government. Of course it would not, since the Inconfidência constitutes one of the most beautiful pages of Brazilian history, and any attempt to make an artistic and educational work based on it is praiseworthy.
>
> Furthermore, this Ministry, through the National Institute of Educational Cinema, is already offering her the necessary collaboration, having examined and corrected, in the presence of the historian Afonso de E. Taunay, the film's scenario.
>
> Mrs Carmen Santos also requests the introduction of laws to support and give value to Brazilian cinema . . . She does not enter into details that would allow us to better consider the matter.[108]

In a letter addressed directly to President Vargas, thought to have been written in 1939, Santos explains that she has gone as far as to pawn her jewellery in order to pursue the project, and she seeks assurance that the film has the full approval of the government. In the concluding paragraph she expresses her desire to be taken more seriously and as more than just a photogenic movie star, stating:

> I would be profoundly hurt if, within Brazilian cinema, I were given the title of 'star' – I have a brain[109] and I work tirelessly from 8 a.m. to midnight, fighting for a more organised film industry in our country with the utmost sincerity, and for this reason, almost always single-handedly. If the government should need the Brasil Vita Filme studio, it is at your disposal, at no charge whatsoever. What I want is to work, to create conscientious films, films in our own language featuring entirely Brazilian habits, environments, techniques – absolutely, essentially Brazilian.[110]

Carmen Santos never gave up on her dream, and in the last few weeks of her life, when she had lost her voice, she wrote to her friends asking them to continue her work at Brasil Vita Filme, and begging them not to allow the studio to be used for other purposes.[111]

Gilda de Abreu (1904–79)

From stage to screen

Gilda de Abreu was born into a wealthy family at a time when her parents, a doctor from the south of Brazil and a successful opera singer, Nícia Silva, were both working in Paris. The family returned to Brazil just before the outbreak of the First World War, settling in Rio de Janeiro. Following in the footsteps of her mother, the young Abreu studied at the National Music Institute, graduating in 1926 with the institution's highest accolade. The death of her father plunged the family into financial difficulties, which inspired Abreu to use her talents to support the household. At the age of 28 she began her career as a professional singer, performing in the comedy stage musical *A canção brasileira* (Brazilian Song). Through the theatrical world she met and married the well-known tenor Vicente Celestino (1894–1968), and they went on to set up a travelling operetta company that performed all over Brazil. Multi-talented, Abreu wrote her own light operas, several of which were adapted for the radio, and went on to manage her husband's career and to write plays based on his hit compositions, a novel that was adapted for radio and film scripts.

Her screen debut came in 1936 in *Bonequinha de seda*, a musical cum romantic comedy directed by Oduvaldo Vianna and produced by the Cinédia studio. She recounted how she was in Buenos Aires with Celestino when the invitation came to star in her first film. 'If it had been the theatre, I wouldn't have thought twice, but the cinema terrified me', she admitted.[112] She went on, however, to give an accomplished performance in the lead role of Marilda, a beautiful young woman who pretends to be French and recently arrived in Brazil in order to gain a place in Rio's high society. Her refined manners and style are deemed to be proof that she cannot be Brazilian, in an implicit critique of the relative status afforded European culture among the Brazilian elite. As well as being the lead actress, Abreu was responsible for her costumes, collaborated in the direction of several musical numbers, drawing on her extensive experience of staging light operas, and composed the music for the film's signature waltz. *Bonequinha de seda*, frequently referred to as Brazil's first superproduction,[113] premiered on 26 October 1936 at the Palácio Teatro cinema in Rio and proved to be a huge success story (as far afield as Buenos Aires), remaining in exhibition for five weeks. In a role originally designed for Carmen Miranda, Abreu was able to draw on her talent as a singer to great acclaim, consolidating the star status that she had already enjoyed on the stage. In recognition of her performance she was crowned the 'Queen of Actresses' in the carnival of 1937.

The film was warmly received by *Cinearte* magazine, with one reviewer even going as far as saying that the audience, usually scathing about Brazilian productions, soon forgot that they were not watching a foreign film and at the end of the screening brimmed over with national pride.[114] Several commentators recognised Abreu's long-term star potential. *Cinearte* published a double-page spread entitled

'A bonequinha de seda', accompanied by a large close-up photograph of Abreu, her beautiful face half covered by a fan, and three smaller stills from the film. It featured a long 'special' report on the star, which began:

> Those who know this artist and know the significance of her name in the entertainment world understand the value of her presence in a Brazilian film. Gilda de Abreu is not a mere artist – she is a vocation polished through lengthy study, she is all the inspiration of a legitimate artistic ideal. A soprano with impeccable singing training, a very fine comedian, a special personality, an intelligent and cultured creature, a young and pretty figure – she is a complete artist, who has the power to captivate us, intensely reflecting the emotion of a role on our sensibilities.[115]

The article continues by describing Abreu's musical and theatrical pedigree, as well as making clear her elite family background, surrounding her in star discourse with references to her 'malleable talent' and her 'film star' aspect, and even calling her 'Gilda-star'.[116]

O ébrio *(The Drunkard)*

In spite of the popularity she enjoyed as a star of stage and screen, Abreu's greatest achievement was as the first female director to complete a full-length talkie in Brazil. At the invitation of Adhemar Gonzaga she agreed to direct the film *O ébrio* (The Drunkard, 1946), based on a play written by her husband, in turn inspired by a song that he wrote and recorded on 7 August 1936 at RCA, which proved to be an immediate and long-standing hit. The play proved to be equally successful when performed at Rio's Carlos Gomes theatre, and this prompted Gonzaga to invite Gilda de Abreu to adapt, script and direct a screen version of it. This tale of a well-respected doctor, Dr Gilberto Silva, played by Vicente Celestino, who turns to drink after being apparently betrayed by his wife, was an unprecedented commercial success. It was shown throughout Brazil and has continued to appeal to wide audiences ever since. João Luiz Vieira calls it 'Cinédia's most well-known film and one of the greatest successes of Brazilian cinema' and the quintessential Brazilian moralistic melodrama.[117] *O ébrio* was equally well received by the critics, but, as Vieira wrote in the late 1980s, 'the film's consecration stems from the public, who watched this melodrama time and again in the state capitals and throughout the countryside until very recently'.[118] It continues to be a favourite with film clubs in Brazil.

Adhemar Gonzaga must have anticipated the success of *O ébrio*, arranging for it to premiere on 26 August 1946 in a total of five movie theatres, a rare occurrence in those days. According to conservative estimates, 4 million Brazilians saw the film in the four years immediately following its premiere, almost 10 per cent of Brazil's entire population in 1946.[119] Luiz Zanin Oricchio puts this figure nearer

8 million, arguing that the huge appeal of the film lay in its unusual mix of melodrama with occasional comic touches.[120] Alice Gonzaga, Adhemar's daughter, explains that her father used to re-release the film whenever he found himself in financial difficulties.[121] When it was first released 530 copies were distributed throughout Brazil, at a time when even the biggest foreign films only commanded a maximum of twenty copies.

The runaway success of *O ébrio*, particularly among the popular classes in both rural and urban Brazil, must be attributed in large part to the star status of its charismatic leading man, Vicente Celestino, and to the popularity of his hit song of the same name, well known throughout Brazil, which he performs at the climax of the film. (In turn, the song enjoyed a second wave of success after the release of the film in 1946.) Only known to his fans from his voice and publicity photographs, it was not surprising that this extraordinarily popular singer's appearance on cinema screens should arouse widespread curiosity all over Brazil. This explanation is backed up by ample anecdotal evidence that audiences sometimes insisted that the projectionist replay the song sequences after the film had ended.[122] Alice Gonzaga recounts how:

> In the centre and poor suburbs of Rio, the public demanded that the film remain in exhibition for months, and the same happened in many other towns and cities, principally in the rural interior . . . There were even cases when the projectionist was obliged to show over and over again the scene in which Vicente Celestino sings the title-song of the film, running the risk of getting a good hiding if he didn't do as he was told.[123]

In the run-up to the film's release the excitement among the general public was such that, when US distributors attempted to delay it in order to show *Gilda* (1946), starring Rita Hayworth, as well as raising the entrance fee, violent protests by students broke out in the Cinelândia area of downtown Rio. Of the five cinema theatres in which the film premiered, it was those located in the city centre and poorer suburbs of the north of Rio in which audiences demanded *O ébrio* remain in exhibition for up to three months.[124]

This unabashed melodrama clearly appealed to popular audiences more than to a self-consciously discerning elite. Alice Gonzaga recalls attending screenings in the rural interior of Brazil where members of the audience openly burst into tears during the final scene.[125] In contrast, she says, audience members in Rio's upmarket *Zona Sul* (the city's 'South Zone' alongside the coast) laughed out loud.[126] The popular appeal of *O ébrio* continued throughout the ensuing decades, meriting a considerable investment on the part of the State agency, Rio Filme and the Cinédia studios to restore it in the 1990s, and the decision to premiere the new print at the prestigious Gramado film festival in Brazil.

It is interesting to note that critics were all too ready to dismiss perceived weaknesses in *O ébrio* as a consequence of Abreu's lack of directorial experience and, implicitly, her gender. When the film was restored and remastered in 1998, missing sections of it were found at the Cinédia studio. These had been edited out of the original version by the studio, which had deemed the film to be too long, and thus these sequences, such as the scene when Gilberto proposes to his future wife, had never previously been seen. In total they added twenty-five minutes to the 1998 version and remedied many of the 'errors' and continuity slips attributed to Abreu. As the film's restorer, Hernani Heffner, explained: 'The truth is that, during all those years, Gilda took the blame for a "crime" that was not of her doing',[127] adding that her place within Brazilian film history now deserves to be re-evaluated.[128] The critic Helena Salem agrees that the restored version of the film reveals that Abreu was much more concerned with the fluency of the narrative than was previously believed, and had created a more carefully crafted work.[129]

Abreu acknowledged the particular difficulties that she faced as a female director in the 1940s:

> Nobody believed that a story like that could give rise to a hit film. And there was also the issue of me being a woman, a female director, at a time when that role was only entrusted to men and, in Brazilian cinema, only Carmen Santos had tried to direct, no other women [*sic*]. However, Vicente believed in me, as did my mother.[130]

Abreu evidently encountered sexism, with film technicians doubting her ability and reluctantly taking her orders. In interview, she recounted how she would turn up at the set of *O ébrio* wearing trousers in an effort to make them feel less demeaned, and yet they constantly questioned her artistic decisions.[131] Even the overwhelming success of this film did not prevent similar prejudices when she directed her second film. In another article published on the occasion of her death, Abreu is quoted as saying in relation to the making of *O ébrio*:

> It was difficult to direct Vicente. He was always a very unstable person. After we spent hours preparing a scene, and when I, with all the difficulties that a woman faces, and with men not really accepting being directed by me, was getting everything ready and telling everyone to begin, Vicente was no longer in his place. He had gone to smoke a cigarette outside.[132]

Further directorial projects

Spurred on by the critical acclaim and popular reception of *O ébrio*, Abreu proceeded to script and direct her second film, *Pinguinho de gente* (Tiny Tot, 1949), another tale of adultery, which starred Anselmo Duarte in his first lead role. Abreu was not afraid to take on controversial projects, and this film touched on the prejudices that women suffered in the patriarchal society of the 1940s. Perhaps for this reason, *Pinguinho de gente* was not well received in the press. Having previously only worked as a director in collaboration with Adhemar Gonzaga, in 1951 Abreu decided to go it alone, setting up her own production company, Pro-Arte, in order to make the romantic comedy *Coração materno* (Maternal Heart, 1951), based on a song of the same name by Vicente Celestino. Such was her commitment to this project, which she produced and scripted, that in interview Abreu referred to the nervous exhaustion that she suffered as a result.[133] Both films failed to capture the imaginations of the audience or the attention of the critics to the same extent as her directorial debut. In all three of the feature-length films that she directed, Abreu chose her husband as the male lead, but to her credit she managed not to succumb to his artistic influence. In some ways, directing her husband, a well-respected artist many years her senior, only made her achievements all the more remarkable. Only much later, in 1977, did Abreu resume her career as a director, making the short film *Canção de amor* (Love Song, 1977), dedicated to her late husband.[134]

The pioneers and the nation

Adhemar Gonzaga's vision for Brazilian cinema was clearly based on industrial (Hollywood) lines, whereas Humberto Mauro saw filmmaking as primarily a way of expressing a particular vision of Brazilian identity. The self-consciously Brazilian film *Lábios sem beijos* (1931) provides an illuminating insight into the designs both men had for Brazilian cinema. Written and produced by Gonzaga and directed by Mauro, the former's desire to emulate the sophistication and glamour of Hollywood is evident in the lavish sets and costumes, and the cosmopolitan young characters. Gonzaga's influence dominates that of Mauro in this film, and for that reason it is something of a stylistic anomaly in Mauro's oeuvre, and the film that he was least happy with. Schvarzman argues, however, that the director ironically subverts some of the Hollywood conventions imposed on him by Gonzaga, such as the traditional happy ending. Although the leading man and leading lady are romantically united in the final scene in a rural idyll, their final kiss is rudely interrupted by a passing ox, a symbol of rural, backward Brazil par excellence.[135] Although less widely known than those of Gonzaga and Mauro, the contributions made by Carmen Santos and Gilda de Abreu to the evolution of early sound cinema are perhaps all the more remarkable. Both women tackled the difficulties inherent in dominant discourses of femininity in order to succeed in the male bastion of the film industry. Carmen Santos clearly saw her *magnum opus*, *Inconfidência mineira*, as a grand narrative of national foundation, as evidenced in her correspondence to the highest echelons of the Vargas administration. Her enthusiastic courting of the film press in her earlier career revealed her intuitive understanding of the inner workings of the burgeoning star system, and of the vital contribution of the latter to the formation of a national cinema. The multi-talented Gilda de Abreu's finest achievement was undoubtedly her directorial debut, the melodrama *O ébrio*, a film that clearly spoke to large swathes of the Brazilian population. As the landslide popularity of *O ébrio* proved, the talking cinema was now poised to take over from the radio as the main medium through which Brazilians from the four corners of the nation could imagine a wider community in the 1950s, as examined in the following chapter.

6

THE *CHANCHADA*, THE ONLY BRAZILIAN GENRE?

Carnival films

The roots of the *chanchada* musical comedies that came to dominate film production in Brazil during the 1940s and 1950s, and which constitute arguably the only truly Brazilian genre, lie in a tradition of documentary films about Rio de Janeiro's famous carnival. Even during the silent era, carnival was the focus of great interest amongst Brazilian filmmakers. It has been estimated that between 1906 and the arrival of the talkies in the early 1930s around fifty shorts were produced using footage from the annual celebrations in the city of Rio de Janeiro.[1] The year 1918 saw the release of the first so-called 'singing film' (*filme cantante*) on the theme of carnival, for which a team of actors sang along with the images from behind the cinema screen. Gradually sound technology gathered pace and culminated in the first sound documentary on this theme, *O carnaval cantado de 1933 no Rio de Janeiro* (The 1933 Rio de Janeiro Carnival in Song), with the sound recorded on disc using the Vitaphone method. *A voz do carnaval* (The Voice of Carnival, 1933) from Rio de Janeiro's Cinédia studio,[2] which combined real-life footage of carnival balls and processions with a fictitious story line filmed in the studio, reproduced the sound directly. Both of the musical genres synonymous with carnival, the samba and the *marcha carnavalesca* or *marchinha* (carnival march), were to feature prominently in the early musical comedies. Plot was subordinate to the promotion of popular songs and of both established and up-and-coming singers and musicians. Well-known popular songwriters such as Noel Rosa, Ari Barroso, Braguinha and Lamartine Babo wrote sambas and *marchinhas* for carnival throughout the 1930s, and often competed with each other in the official music contests that the Vargas administration (1930–45) introduced. The performance of their hits in musical films was a major attraction for Brazilians of all social classes, and thus the song titles and names of the performers featured heavily on publicity material for these movies. Household names from the world of radio, such as Carmen Miranda and Mário Reis, now found themselves in front of the cameras, performing the hit songs that were on everyone's lips in the run-up to carnival.[3] The links between the radio, popular carnival music and film in the 1930s were instrumental in ensuring the success of the latter in the face of the might of Hollywood. As Bastos argues, 'Radio supported and was supported by the myth of the cinema. The two media in conjunction were used to propagate the nationalist and centralizing ideas of the first Vargas period.'[4]

The *chanchada* is born

From the early sound films that hinged on the promotion of carnival music and revolved around a frequently flimsy plot, the *chanchada* was born in the mid-1930s. *Alô, alô, Brasil!* (Hello, Hello, Brazil!, 1935) featured a roll-call of radio presenters, comedians and singers, including Carmen Miranda and her sister Aurora. In addition to this veritable 'who's who' of radio stars, the plot centred on an avid radio fan who falls in love with a radio singer. The sequel, *Alô, alô, Carnaval!* (Hello, Hello, Carnival!, 1936), which also premiered in the run-up to the carnival celebrations, was inspired by the first musicals from Metro-Goldwyn-Mayer and was constructed around a rather static, almost theatrical, stage show that combined comedians trained in the *teatro de revista*, Brazil's answer to vaudeville or music hall, and popular musicians and singers, such as the Miranda sisters. *Alô, alô, Carnaval!* proved to be an overwhelming box-office and critical success, and with its release 'the paradigms of the *chanchada* tradition were definitively established'.[5]

Although initially a pejorative term, often used by journalists to refer with contempt to the low-budget musical comedy films produced in Brazil in the 1930s, the label *chanchada* gradually lost its implications of poor quality and worthlessness, and came to be the accepted way of referring to this emerging tradition. Various directors and producers turned their hand to this successful format, bowing to commercial pressure and turning a blind eye to the scathing reviews of the critics. *Samba em Berlim* (Samba in Berlin, 1943), written and directed by Luiz de Barros for the Cinédia studio, and made in just twenty-five days, was a typical example. The film, which starred the radio comedian Silvino Neto, was fiercely attacked in the press but the public adored its mix of carnival music and irreverent humour, which poked fun at Hitler and Nazi Germany. As the film's director candidly wrote in his memoirs, 'Those [films] that I made at carnival time, when those films generated the most money, were produced out of absolute commercial necessity, given that they were a great source of income.'[6]

It was with the founding of the Atlântida Cinematográfica studio in Rio de Janeiro in 1941 that the *chanchada* came into its own. Despite its ambitious and patriotic mission statement in which it promised to create cinema that provided 'indisputable services to national greatness',[7] and initial investment in feature-length dramas that dealt with serious social themes, Atlântida soon turned its attentions to carnival musicals, developing the comedic dimension of the tried-and-trusted formula.

The Atlântida studio, Rio de Janeiro

Modest in its aspirations, Atlântida catered to an unsophisticated audience, many of whom were recent migrants to Brazil's big cities, who could see aspects of their own lives portrayed on screen, and thus identified with the underdog characters played by the likes of Oscarito and Grande Otelo, the studio's most famous comic double act.[8] Atlântida looked to the Hollywood studios for inspiration when it came to creating home-grown stars with box-office appeal. In addition to familiar faces from the worlds of the *teatro de revista*, the radio and the travelling circus, it constructed a team of contract stars, such as Eliana Macedo and Cyl Farney, who did not have established careers in other areas of the entertainment world. Atlântida also exploited the popular press to the full in an effort to foster a large fan base, as discussed more extensively in Chapter 10. This helped to ensure that the appeal of the *chanchada* was not solely an urban phenomenon, and the tradition's stars made the most of their widespread fame by touring the interior with their own stage shows, often in the wake of the release of the studio's latest film. As Renato Ortiz argues, Atlântida set out to conquer the Brazilian market at a time when the country had scarcely begun to unite as a nation, and in order to do so it was necessary to develop a formula for success, namely the *chanchada*, which appealed to both middle-class and popular audiences.[9] Between 1941 and 1962 the studio produced more than seventy films, and during the 1950s its output attained industrial proportions, largely owing to the involvement of Luís Severiano Ribeiro, owner of one of the biggest exhibition circuits in Brazil at the time, who became a major shareholder in the studio in 1947. 'The formula adopted by Ribeiro was relatively simple: ensure the studio was constantly in use, keep operational costs to a minimum and invest in distribution.'[10]

The Atlântida *chanchada Os dois ladrões* (The Two Thieves, 1960), directed by Carlos Manga, is paradigmatic of this cinematic tradition. Its opening credits reveal Oscarito to be the star attraction, whose name precedes even the title of the film. His co-star is the broad-shouldered, would-be 'all American guy' Cyl Farney. The opening credits lead us to expect a slick crime thriller, but we are soon transported to the carnivalesque realm of the *chanchada* in which the motif of inversion or *troca* (exchange) constantly resurfaces, whether in the form of irreverent overturning of social hierarchies, dramatic changes of identity or the simple exchange of one object for another, characteristically via a dishonest ruse. Oscarito's character, Jonjoca, for example, a lowly thief who lives in a discarded drainage pipe with other down-and-outs, convincingly catapults himself up the social ladder by disguising himself as a French gentleman, who sports a dapper blazer, white slacks, grey wig and false beard and moustache, in order to distract a wealthy lady. Meanwhile Mão Leve ('Light-fingered', played by Cyl Farney), a gentleman thief, steals her jewels and replaces them with top-quality fakes.

In this film Oscarito appears no less than four times in drag, impersonating women as diverse as a socialite, an old lady, a nun and a mixed-race nanny. Ample visual humour is provided by Jonjoca's cross-dressing, whether as the sassy Afro-Brazilian pushing a baby's pram,[11] who flirts with Mão Leve, or when he impersonates the wealthy Mme Gaby, complete with a sexy wiggle which attracts the unwanted advances of a married man. As Jonjoca squeezes his feet into his high-heeled shoes he complains: 'We women suffer so much!', and in a later scene appears in a woman's undergarments when shaving his legs. Such slapstick comedy is typical of the *chanchada*, a form of family entertainment that nevertheless appealed to adult men by providing gratuitous flesh shots – in the case of this film we are treated to scenes of young women being massaged in a beauty salon and wearing swimsuits on a hotel's sun terrace. Similarly, no *chanchada* would be complete without a fight sequence, and *Os dois ladrões* is no exception, featuring a brawl in which Jonjoca, dressed in drag as an elderly woman, hits several hoodlums over the head with his handbag. The physical humour is accompanied by risqué comments directed at the adults in the audience, such as when Jonjoca, in drag, tells an attractive female masseuse that she is in for a surprise when 'she' (Jonjoca, Oscarito's character) strips off.

This film, like countless others produced by Atlântida, showcases the modernity and urban splendour of Rio de Janeiro, with lingering establishing shots of the swanky Hotel Glória (and the equally upmarket Quitandinha hotel and casino in the state of Rio de Janeiro), traffic speeding down wide avenues past the iconic Sugar Loaf Mountain and beaches, and highways linking the city to other parts of the state, backed by towering electricity pylons, soft-top sports cars, location shots of Rio's Santos Dumont airport, and high-rise apartment blocks. The latter, however, are drawn in sharp contrast to the wasteland where Jonjoca lives in his make-shift 'home'. In spite of such poverty, there is true camaraderie among this community of vagrants, and this film is typical of the *chanchada* in its ultimate assertion of the 'nobility' of the poor and, conversely, the vanity, pretentiousness and futility of society's elite. The counter-cultural ethos of *malandragem*[12] underpins the plot, as we see the two thieves steal from the very rich in order to help less fortunate members of society.

As the 1950s wore on, Atlântida's *chanchadas* developed a parodic element in relation to Hollywood movies, a further twist to the tradition's fondness for debunking established hierarchies and irreverent humour. In 1954 the studio released *Nem Sansão, nem Dalila* (Neither Samson nor Delilah), which poked fun at Cecil B. de Mille's Biblical epic *Samson and Delilah* (1949), and starred Oscarito as an unlikely Samson, whose strength resides in an ill-fitting wig.[13] The same year saw the premiere of Atlântida's most sophisticated attempt at film parody, *Matar ou correr* (Kill or Run Away), a spoof of the highly respected western *High Noon* (1952), which had been released in Brazil with the title *Matar ou morrer* (Kill or Die). In Brazil's response to the macho posturing and WASP supremacy of the classic western, Oscarito and Grande Otelo star as the cowardly sheriff and his equally useless black sidekick.[14] In spite of these attempts to introduce innovations into the *chanchada* tradition, Atlântida's productions still met with the scorn of critics and filmmakers with a more 'high-brow' agenda.

The São Paulo backlash: the Vera Cruz studio

In the late 1940s a group of bourgeois intellectuals in the industrial city of São Paulo, 'inspired by the commercial success of the *chanchadas* but scorning what it saw as that genre's "vulgarity"',[15] founded the Vera Cruz film company. Although the studio system was by then in decline in Hollywood, Vera Cruz looked to the MGM studios for inspiration with regard to its structure, employing contract stars and directors on generous salaries, in spite of the absence of any sound economic infrastructure. 'In a Third World country economically dominated by American multinationals, the company's slogan, "From the Plateau de Piratininga to the Screens of the World!", reflected Vera Cruz's ideological imitation of the increasingly globalised Hollywood studios.'[16] In spite of the undeniable influence of the Hollywood studio system, 'Vera Cruz was Euro-international in spirit and in personnel', and employed the English light technician Chick Fowle, the Italian director Adolfo Celi, and an Austrian editor, Oswald Haffenrichter.[17] The studio appointed the director Alberto Cavalcânti, who, although Brazilian, had worked for many years in Europe, and chose not to employ any established or up-and-coming local talent.

Vera Cruz has become synonymous with foolhardy commercial judgements,[18] but equally with high production values and 'quality' feature films. There is little doubt that the company did raise the bar within Brazilian cinema when it came to the technical aspects of filmmaking, such as camera work, montage, musical scores and lighting. However, the accepted wisdom that Vera Cruz rejected with distaste the popular comedy format favoured by the Atlântida studio in Rio seems ripe for questioning. Vera Cruz ostensibly developed as a self-conscious reaction to the *chanchada*, which it saw as 'low-brow Rio-based, argot-ridden, entertainment',[19] and it is thus perhaps surprising, and often overlooked, that several productions from the studio displayed many *chanchada*-inspired elements, seemingly taking their lead from Atlântida's successful formula. Vera Cruz's *Sai da frente* (Get Out of My Way, 1952), the first film to showcase the talents of the comedian Amácio Mazzaropi, for example, features musical interludes, acrobatic sequences, comic intertextual allusions to Hollywood movies,[20] and the theme of the hillbilly in the big city, combining them with aspects of melodrama. The *chanchada*'s predilection for poking fun at authority and undermining the Brazilian State and the nation's social elite also permeates this film. Playing the archetypal *caipira* or hick, Mazzaropi visits various government offices, where he is told to join 'the queue to join the queue to fill in the forms', under the watchful eye of a prominent portrait of President Getúlio Vargas. Later, a passer-by who takes charge at the scene of a traffic accident performs a blatant comic impersonation of Brazil's president, repeating Vargas's well-known slogans and mimicking his speech patterns.

In the same vein, in Vera Cruz's *Uma pulga na balança* (Eany, meany, miny, mo, 1953), the thief protagonist's pet dog, a scruffy mongrel, is named Barnabé, the slang term used to refer to the plethora of overpaid and underworked civil servants who personified the unwieldy bureaucracy synonymous with the Vargas regime. This light-hearted tale centres on a likeable thief who embodies *malandragem*, a theme so central to the *chanchada*. Twice in the opening minutes of the film this character declares that he will pull off an act of *jeitinho*, another term that refers to the evasion of the law or authority so characteristic of the *malandro* hustler. In the film the thief succeeds in overturning the hierarchical rules and norms of society by earning a place of prestige and power inside a prison where he is ostensibly held captive and yet respectfully addressed by the prison warder as Dr Dorival, in a classic case of *troca* and *jeitinho* worthy of the streetwise characters played by Oscarito at Atlântida. *Uma pulga na balança* appears to borrow various other stock motifs from the *chanchada*, in spite of its rather unexpected and ill-fitting melodramatic denouement. These include slapstick comedy and fight scenes, jokes at the expense of the pretentious and insincere elite, and visual celebrations of modernity in the form of establishing shots of São Paulo's traffic-filled avenues, in addition to the recurrent motif of carnivalesque inversion of the rules of social interaction.

The musical melodrama *Tico-Tico no fubá* (Tico-Tico Bird in the Corn Meal, 1952), directed by Adolfo Celi, was based on the life story of the popular composer Zequinha de Abreu. Once again this Vera Cruz production bears the clear imprint of established popular cinematic traditions, not least in its protracted circus sequence, with its typical comic aspects, such as a clown who bears more than a passing resemblance to Oscarito. Like the Atlântida *chanchadas*, this film contains frequent musical interludes, perhaps not surprisingly given its subject matter. Most striking are the final scenes in which Zequinha de Abreu's most famous tune, 'Tico-Tico no fubá', is performed to an up-tempo samba rhythm, prompting a festive carnival atmosphere at an elite party in São Paulo. This is followed by establishing shots of the city, and then those of its perennial rival, Rio de Janeiro, including documentary footage of the carnival parade, complete with Afro-Brazilian women in *baiana* costume,[21] extravagantly decorated floats and delirious revellers.

This celebration of the city of Rio and the archetypal *chanchada* ending are totally unexpected in a Vera Cruz production, and particularly in a melodrama in which the central character has just died of a heart attack on screen. *Tico-Tico no fubá* stars Anselmo Duarte in the leading role, in his first film for Vera Cruz, after working under contract at Atlântida for four years and appearing in countless *chanchadas* as the handsome romantic lead, often opposite Eliana Macedo,[22] a baton that he passed on to Cyl Farney. The stock flesh shots characteristic of the *chanchada* are provided by the shapely legs of Tônia Carrero, one of Vera Cruz's biggest stars, who plays a circus performer who falls for Zequinha. She is aptly named Branca (White), a pale-skinned, fair-haired beauty, who, in spite of her grace and rather aristocratic airs, is cast as a member of a travelling circus troupe. Other tropes omnipresent in the *chanchada* surface in this Vera Cruz production, namely the conflict between the big city and the countryside, and their respective inhabitants, the presence of a good-hearted local villain, slapstick visual comedy (such as a portly, unattractive older woman catching the bride's bouquet at a wedding party) and a comic swipe at authority figures (Zequinha's humorous father adapts one of Vargas's well-known political slogans to encourage the local brass band to strike up: 'Santa Rita hopes that each of you will do your duty').

Out of a total of sixteen feature films made by Vera Cruz, three are low-brow comedies starring Mazzaropi, namely *Sai da frente* (1952), *Nadando em dinheiro*

(Rolling in Money, 1952) and *Candinho* (Little Candide, 1953),[23] in addition to the comic social satire *Uma pulga na balança*, the humorous tale of a wayward civil servant, *A família Lero-Lero* (The Lero-Lero Family, 1953) and the clearly Hollywood-inspired romantic comedy *É proibido beijar* (Kissing Is Forbidden, 1954), in many ways primarily a vehicle for the photogenic star Tônia Carrero. Vera Cruz's *boletim de divulgação* or mission statement stated that the company was committed to producing 'eminently popular comedies', so it is surprising that the studio has become associated primarily with big-budget dramas. This is undoubtedly a consequence of the critical acclaim garnered by the historical epic *O cangaceiro* (*The Bandit*, 1953), a double prize-winner at the 1953 Cannes film festival. Furthermore, both *O cangaceiro* and *Sinhá moça* (The Plantation Owner's Daughter, 1953) – the latter a costume drama set in the time just prior to the abolition of slavery in 1888 – were major successes at the box office in Brazil. However, Vera Cruz's outspoken critique of the Rio de Janeiro-based film industry, and the legendary rivalry between the two cities have perhaps also contributed to the consecration of the São Paulo studio as purveyor of 'quality' Brazilian cinema.

Despite the commercial failure of Vera Cruz, which forced the company into bankruptcy in 1954, other smaller-scale São Paulo studios, such as Maristela and Multifilmes, sprang up in its wake, adopting the same policy of high production values and 'international style',[24] but ultimately they too bowed to commercial pressure and turned their hand to more popular styles.[25] In 1955, for example, Maristela released the *chanchada Carnaval em lá maior* (Carnival in A Major), featuring Renata Fronzi, the star of several Atlântida productions, the samba composer Ataúlfo Alves and the popular singer Araci de Almeida. Stam concludes that 'the [São Paulo] films of this period reveal an immense effort to demonstrate technical proficiency and to avoid what the filmmakers regarded as the sloppiness of the *chanchada*', but he dismisses this notion of 'high quality' as a fantasy fuelled by the prestige of Hollywood movies.[26] It would seem that Vera Cruz loudly vaunted its superior production values and 'serious' subject matter in preference to taking pride in the popular appeal of almost a third of the studio's feature-length productions.

The *chanchada* as national genre

João Luiz Vieira traces the roots of the *chanchada* to the silent film *Paz e amor* (Peace and Love, 1910), which combined popular music, parody and carnivalesque elements.[27] He cites the magazine *Careta*, which described the film as the first example of a genre that combined music and dance with comic characters and familiar situations from everyday life.[28] Without doubt similar cinematic traditions or genres emerged in other national contexts, such as tango films in Argentina, *fado* films in Portugal, and the *ranchera* musical comedies in Mexico,[29] each with its own particular relationship to Hollywood paradigms, so can it, in fact, be argued that the *chanchada* had culturally specific elements that differentiated it from these foreign cousins? Vieira argues that the Portuguese language, used in the songs performed in these films and more importantly in the dialogue, was largely responsible for the immense popularity of the *chanchada* and central to understanding these films as the embodiment of some kind of inescapable 'Brazilianness'. He writes, 'The spoken Brazilian language became a means of survival for Brazilian cinema, which came into existence because of its music and language.'[30] Other Brazilian critics situate the *chanchada*'s cultural specificity in its particular brand of humour, which relies heavily on self-deprecation. Audiences were continually invited to laugh at their own inadequacies as a nation, drawn in stark opposition to the supposed sophistication of foreigners.[31] Bastos argues that *chanchada* audiences were left in no doubt that the only way to deal with everyday difficulties in Brazil was to laugh them off, approaching adversity with the quick wit and relaxed attitude of the *malandro*.[32]

Most *chanchadas* undoubtedly qualify as genre films in terms of their repetitive format and cumulative effect, their predictability being precisely the key to their popularity among mass audiences.[33] As Altman writes:

> the pleasure of the faithful genre film fan is thus not so much a question of novelty as it is one of reaffirmation. People go to the genre films to renew contact with old friends, to hear old stories, to participate in events which somehow seem familiar.[34]

Brazilian audiences acquired particular expectations about films produced by studios such as Atlântida, expectations that were endorsed by publicity material, such as posters and magazine advertisements, featuring well-known comic stars. As Andrew Tudor has argued, the use of the generic label by critics and journalists reinforces audience expectations and, 'once such conventions develop, they can in turn affect a filmmaker's conception of what he or she is doing', leading the studios to actively use the generic tag to boost a film's commercial potential.[35] If we follow Tudor's lead and think of genre less as a way in which critics classify films and more in the looser way in which audiences classify films,[36] focusing on the processes of reception and consumption, we can argue that, by seeing the *chanchada* as an intrinsically national film style of which they could be proud, in spite of the disdain of high-brow journalists, audiences were drawn into an imagined community.

Perhaps the last word on the subject should be given to respected critic Paulo Emílio Salles Gomes, who was responsible for the radical re-evaluation of the *chanchada* among Brazilian film critics in the 1980s:

> The young, popular audience that guaranteed the success of these films found in them re-elaborated and rejuvenated models which, although not without links to broad Western traditions, also emanated directly from a tenacious Brazilian heritage. To these relatively stable values, the films added ephemeral *carioca* [Rio] features in the form of jokes and speech mannerisms, thought and behaviour.[37]

Part III

DEFINING 'NATIONAL' CINEMA SINCE 1960

7

CINEMA NOVO

Introduction

The *cinema novo* movement[1] lies at the heart of any discussion on national culture in Brazil, because it was conceived specifically to create a 'Brazilian cinema' in Brazil,[2] to reveal the country's true face and to contribute to its transformation. *Cinema novo* was unlike other new cinemas around the world, in that its objective was not to work in the margins of the established industry, but to *be* the Brazilian film industry. *Cinema novo* was arguably the only real cinema movement in Brazil. While there have been a number of clearly defined styles, epochs and popular genres or sub-genres (the *chanchada*, *pornochanchada* and *retomada*, for example), *cinema novo* represents the only occasion on which a relatively cohesive group of intellectuals, filmmakers and producers with a common ideology strove towards a set of common cultural and artistic goals.[3] Furthermore, as witnessed in Chapter 8, over forty years later *cinema novo* continues to be held up as a benchmark against which all 'quality' Brazilian films are judged.

Cinema novo literally means New Cinema, and thus the movement's intention to break with the past and ring the changes is made explicit even in its title.[4] It was born out of a reaction to the failure of the Vera Cruz project, a dissatisfaction with the 'alienating' *chanchada*, and frustration at US domination of the Brazilian box office. It is often regarded as Latin America's answer to Italian neo-realism and the French Nouvelle Vague (and reductively read as nothing more than some kind of tropical version of European post-war avant-garde filmmaking), but while these were strong influences, seen for example in the preference for small production teams, location shooting, non-professional actors, and collaborative financing strategies, the proponents of the movement did not share a common aesthetics, unlike the Italian neo-realists, and unlike the Nouvelle Vague they were not initially brought together and inspired by a desire to modernise domestic production or the film industry. They sought most of their inspiration at home, such as from Brazilian literary modernism, the changing socio-political landscape, and the work of pioneer filmmakers Humberto Mauro[5] and Nelson Pereira dos Santos.

The desire for rupture expressed by the so-called *cinemanovistas* was typical of the late 1950s and early 1960s and the spirit of ambitious developmentalism witnessed, for example, in the building of the new capital, Brasília, in the 'frontier' territory of Goiás, in the growth of labour movements and a politically informed and pseudo-revolutionary middle-class intelligentsia, and in an increasing interest in new cultural forms (Bossa Nova in music, for example), including a long overdue re-evaluation of Brazilian popular culture. Around this time the Brazilian National Union of Students (UNE) was created, reflecting the strongly held belief at the time that young people really could make a difference and could bring about the long-overdue revolution. Such developmentalist and revolutionary fervour went hand in hand with a certain amount of cultural and economic nationalism, which ostensibly manifested itself as anti-Americanism. It is also clear to see the influence on the *cinema novo* movement of the Instituto Superior de Estudos Brasileiros (ISEB), the Higher Institute of Brazilian Studies, founded in 1955 by Juscelino Kubitschek, with the express purpose of formulating a national ideology of development.[6]

The *cinemanovistas* were at the centre of debates in the early 1960s on the one hand on the alienating quality and, on the other, on the representative power of popular culture in Brazilian society. What is considered to be one of the first *cinema novo* films, the episodic *Cinco Vezes Favela* (*Favela X Five*) was produced in 1961 by the newly formed Centro Popular de Cultura (the Popular Culture Centre, with branches in a number of Brazilian cities), which was organised by the UNE with a view to rethinking what popular culture was and how it could be expressed and channelled for revolutionary purposes.

The filmmakers of the *cinema novo* movement sought to transform society by applying a new, critical and modernist vision of the nation, and to find a new cinematic language that better reflected Brazilian reality, as a challenge to what they considered the vacuous, derivative and industrially produced *chanchada* films that had dominated film production since the 1930s. At first, unsurprisingly, given the moniker 'New Cinema', any innovative film or filmmakers who were producing work that broke the cinematic mould in one way or another were associated with the movement, until Glauber Rocha and Nelson Pereira dos Santos took the lead and defined the group as the only defender of a cinema capable of expressing the transformation of Brazilian society.[7] With the creation in 1965 of Difilm, a production and distribution company almost exclusively aimed at promoting *cinema novo* films, the movement became better organised and was specifically made up of eleven directors and producers linked to Luis Carlos Barreto.[8] While the *cinema novo* group comprised as many as thirty members at the height of its production,[9] there are six directors whose names are most strongly associated with the movement and upon whom studies and retrospectives tend to concentrate: Glauber Rocha (1938–1981), Nelson Pereira dos Santos (b. 1928), Carlos Diegues (b. 1940), Leon Hirzsman (1937–87), Joaquim Pedro de Andrade (1932–88) and Ruy Guerra (b. 1931).[10] Randal Johnson's *Cinema Novo X Five: Masters of Contemporary Brazilian Film* provides a very useful and balanced overview in English of the development of the *cinema novo* movement, the work and views of the chief protagonists listed above, and the aesthetic and thematic features that they shared.

Cinema novo at its best: *Vidas secas* and Glauber Rocha

Nelson Pereira dos Santos is considered by many to be the godfather of the *cinema novo* movement, given that already in the mid-1950s he had voiced criticism of the *chanchada* and the 'studio system', and that two of his so-called 'neo-realist' films led the way in terms of producing a break with Brazil's cinematic past, both in style and in production methods, and setting up a dialogue with the nation's popular classes.[11] His early feature film, *Vidas secas* (*Barren Lives*, 1963) is rightly held up as being one of *cinema novo*'s (and world cinema's) finest moments, and it serves as an illustration of many of the stylistic features, innovative qualities and cinematic power of *cinema novo*, not least because of its capacity to 'turn scarcity into a signifier', as Ismail Xavier famously put it.[12]

Dos Santos, originally from São Paulo and based in Rio de Janeiro, visited the North-East of Brazil in 1958 during one of the worst droughts in living memory: it was this experience that inspired him to adapt for the screen *Vidas secas*, Graciliano Ramos's 1938 neo-realist novel of the same name about the plight of a North-Eastern family in the barren *sertão*.[13] Dos Santos, despite severing links with the Communist Party in 1956 in a disagreement over the role of filmmaking in pre-revolutionary society, made his continued socialist sympathies clear in choosing to adapt fellow communist Ramos's scathing indictment of social injustice in Brazil's North-East,[14] in a clear attempt to make a contribution to the contemporary debate on the need for urgent land reform.

One of the most arresting and innovative features of the film version of *Vidas secas*, which has become one of the most recognisable features of *cinema novo*, is the photography, for which Luis Carlos Barreto fashioned a new 'overexposed' style by rejecting the use of filters, described at times as *lente nua* (literally naked lens) and at others as *luz nacional* (national lighting), in order to capture the overpowering natural light of the North-East[15] and to convey the oppressive heat of the *sertão* (and all that this comes to symbolise). The precarious conditions in which films are made in Brazil are flagged up in the shaky hand-held camera shots, the simplicity of the mise-en-scène, and the limited use of indoor sets. The film has practically no script or complicated plot, which fits with both the theme and the message of the film, and the goal of the *cinema novo* movement: to produce films that reflect, not only thematically but aesthetically also, the experience of the majority of the population of one of the world's largest Third World countries.

While *Vidas secas* stands out as the most representative film of the *cinema novo* movement, there is no denying that, in terms of a body of work, the movement is most closely associated with the oeuvre of Glauber Rocha, so much so that descriptions of the evolution of the movement mirror developments in Rocha's work.[16] The exceptionally talented Rocha was a larger-than-life character, seemingly as complex and at times impossible to decipher as his own films. He made a series of overtly stylised, visually dazzling, complex, but often hermetic and indulgent films between 1960 and his death in 1981. Born in Vitória da Conquista in the North-Eastern state of Bahia, he began his career in the film industry as a critic while

Figure 7.1 Othon Bastos as the notorious *cangaceiro* Corisco in Glauber Rocha's *Deus e o diabo na terra do sol* (*Black God, White Devil*, 1964) (courtesy of Tempo Glauber, Rio de Janeiro)

still very young and living in Salvador. In 1956 with other friends he founded Yemanjá Filmes. While travelling south in search of financial support, he met filmmakers Nelson Pereira dos Santos and Alex Viany. He moved permanently to Rio in 1962, helping to root and consolidate the fledgling *cinema novo* group.

In his feature films Rocha displayed a less realist and more lyrical and baroque storytelling style than that in early films by the other main *cinemanovistas.*[17] He did not produce any literary adaptations,[18] but he was very clearly inspired by *literatura de cordel*, the cheaply produced chapbooks popular in the North-East of Brazil. Rocha peopled his films with the mythical/historical figures that featured in *cordel* literature, such as the *cangaceiro* (the North-Eastern social bandit)[19] and the messianic religious leader, in the style of Antonio Conselheiro. With this in mind, Rocha's seminal *Deus e o diabo na terra do sol* (*Black God, White Devil*, 1964) can

Figure 7.2 Glauber Rocha behind the camera (courtesy of Tempo Glauber, Rio de Janeiro)

be read as a '*cordel* film'.[20] Rocha followed this up with *Terra em transe* (*Land in Anguish*, 1967),[21] a more political film and the first to reflect on the aftermath of dictatorship, to return once again to the *sertão* in *O dragão da maldade contra o santo guerreiro* (*Antônio das Mortes*, 1968), in which he resurrected the character Antônio das Mortes, the infamous slayer of *cangaceiros*.[22] These three films constitute the most screened and most highly regarded of Rocha's oeuvre, which also includes a number of films produced abroad in the first half of the 1970s.[23] All three are complex, Brechtian-inflected and, in retrospect, politically ambiguous films.

Rocha's own political stance was ambiguous, to say the least, throughout the dictatorship. In the 1960s he was one of the most persecuted filmmakers. He was arrested and detained for a week in 1965 in Rio de Janeiro along with Joaquim Pedro de Andrade and six others for demonstrating outside the Hotel Glória in Rio where a meeting of the Organization of American States was being held.[24] Such was the suspicion on the part of the authorities of Rocha, his movements and his filmmaking that during the heady days of the dictatorship he famously booked flights in his middle name (Andrade) to avoid being spotted, he was reduced to smuggling his films out of Brazil in order to screen them abroad and, eventually, in 1971, he was forced into self-imposed exile in Europe, where he made a number of films until his less-than-glorious return to Brazil after *abertura* in 1976.

Rocha's political ambiguity (and his seeming delight in courting controversy and playing devil's advocate) led him to support the military dictatorship in light of the Generals' assurances of a gradual return to democracy in the 1970s. Such was the level of disbelief that someone in Rocha's position could support the Generals that a number of commentators, literally, questioned his sanity. His presumed mental illness both affected the reception of his later films in his homeland and sparked rumours about the cause of his premature death from an unknown cause in 1981. His cultural legacy has been recuperated since then,[25] but at the time reaction to him on the part of the press and critics in obituaries, for example, was at best ambivalent and at worst cold and dismissive.

The international dimension of *cinema novo*

Writing in 1975, Julianne Burton observed:

> First World critics have a fascination with the Brazilian Cinema Novo. In both Europe and the U.S., the amount of critical material on the Brazilian film cycle rivals that which can be found on all other Latin American national film movements combined.[26]

The link between the critical success and development of *cinema novo* and the European critics and art-house audiences is one that is not widely accepted in Brazil, perhaps understandably, given the spirit of challenge to neo-imperialism that inspired the movement. Yet it has to be acknowledged that the European market was clearly important to *cinema novo* directors, not only in terms of sales and the promotion of films, but also strategically to help them deal with the dictatorship.[27] With the international praise of *cinema novo*, it was difficult for the dictatorship, with its 'business as usual' posturing, at least up until 1968, to deny Brazilians the right to view the films at home.[28] At the same time, there is no denying that at least part of the interest generated in the *cinema novo* in Europe derived from the notion that *cinemanovistas* were, through their films, actively combating an authoritarian regime.[29]

In his detailed study of the reception of *cinema novo* in France, Alexandre Figueirôa states that Brazilian films in the 1960s were popular in France (and other cinephile nations in Europe, one imagines) because their release coincided with a time when both *auteur* cinema and 'sociological' films were particularly popular.[30] Paulo Cesar Saraceni's *Arraial do Cabo* (1960), a documentary on a North-Eastern fishing community, was shown in the Museum of Mankind in France under the initiative of documentary maker Jean Rouch, himself a major influence on the *cinema novo* directors.[31] The film was considered to be the first international success of *cinema novo*. From 1965 cineclub journals in France were beginning to take notice of Brazilian cinema, and two of the most influential film journals, *Positif* and *Cahiers du cinéma*, wrote about *cinema novo* in 1966.[32] The *cinemanovistas*, and Glauber Rocha in particular, were regular contributors to film and culture journals and magazines in Europe, and it was in magazines in France in the beginning of the 1970s, rather than at home, that both Rocha and Carlos Diegues declared the death of the *cinema novo* movement.

A large number of European filmmakers and critics visited Brazil in the late 1950s and early 1960s, such as Roberto Rossellini, François Truffaut, John Grierson and Arne Sucksdorff. *Cinema novo* filmmakers likewise made regular trips to Europe, where they were received in film festivals such as Cannes and Pesaro, like heroes. The two most fêted *cinema novo* directors in Europe were Glauber Rocha and Ruy Guerra. They made a number of films abroad (Guerra made co-productions, films in his native Mozambique, and a number of adaptations of the work of Colombian author Gabriel García Márquez) and forged links with the proponents of the European new wave. And both starred in 'new wave' films: Rocha in Jean-Luc Godard's *Vent L'est* (*East Wind*, 1970) and Guerra in Werner Herzog's *Aguirre, Der Zorn Gottes* (*Aguirre, Wrath of God*, 1972).

Cinema novo also served the purpose in Europe of educating audiences, hungry for knowledge of other cultures, about Brazil.[33] In France, for example, when Brazilian films were screened in cineclubs, they were accompanied by detailed handouts, lest the audiences should misconstrue the complex socio-political context portrayed on screen.[34] Glauber Rocha, for one, was acutely aware of the way Brazilian films were often consumed in Europe, and of Europeans' habit of turning to the culture of the underdeveloped world to satisfy their nostalgia for primitivism.[35]

Cinema novo: a failed project?

While the *cinema novo* undoubtedly left behind an aesthetically innovative, contextually rich and internationally acclaimed body of work, its contribution to national cinema has to be qualified by the (perhaps inevitable) failure of its revolutionary project, and its ultimate failure to engage with the Brazilian public. In Brazil it is understood that it is the role of the elite to attempt to comprehend a country it does not fully understand, and sometimes has never seen. In the late nineteenth century, Euclides da Cunha had revealed a whole new world to his Southern readers through his documenting of the infamous Canudos massacre (1897) and his description of rural life in the North-East. And Mario de Andrade and the Modernists of the 1920s and 1930s set themselves the task of discovering the 'true Brazil' through incursions to the North-East and the rural interior. In this sense, the *cinemanovistas* were merely the next in a long line of (mostly Southern, mostly urban and almost exclusively privileged) adventurers to head into the culturally uncharted interior, on a kind of cultural mission whose purpose was to explain the 'problem of Brazil'.[36] The young *cinema novo* directors' understanding of the North-East was predicated on these 'adventures', and information gleaned from the regionalist writers they had read, rather than a lived experience of the *sertão*.

Even Paulo Emílio Salles Gomes, one of the great defenders of *cinema novo*, recognised the movement's shortcomings: 'it remained to the end an accurate barometer of young people aspiring to interpret the will of the colonized'.[37] Put bluntly:

> The people involved in the production and, to a large extent, in the consumption of Cinema Novo were young people who disassociated themselves from their origins as colonizers . . . They saw themselves as representatives of the colonized, charged with a mediating function in the reaching of social equilibrium. In reality they were speaking and acting primarily for themselves.[38]

We have argued in Chapter 3 that Embrafilme was able to maintain a considerable amount of decision-making freedom, and so *cinema novo*'s relationship with the State-run production and distribution agency was not as controversial as it might at first appear. But *cinema novo* in the 1960s received funds from other, more questionable sources. Before the coup d'état of 1964, the main source of funding for *cinema novo* films came from banks. Alexandre Figueirôa suggests that these films were by and large set in the North-East as depictions of underdevelopment in cities could have presented problems for their investors.[39] José de Magalhães Pinto, of the National Bank of Minas Gerais, financed *Vidas secas*, *Deus e o diabo na terra do sol* and *Os fuzis*. Magalhães Pinto was one of the civilian conspirators of the coup of 1964. And the fiercely conservative and ultra-controversial Carlos Lacerda, state governor of Guanabara (Rio) 1960–65 and defender of the military coup d'état of 1964, set up a film aid commission (CAIC), which became a major early source of funding for *cinema novo*.[40]

Furthermore, according to Randal Johnson, *cinema novo* filmmakers made no real attempt to create alternative or parallel exhibition circuits,[41] and instead released their films in established commercial circuits. While the key *cinema novo* directors who survived into the 1980s continued through their filmmaking, with occasional moments of brilliance, the important debate of the role of popular culture in Brazilian society, the project of political consciousness raising was effectively abandoned. It is interesting to note that, as relatively inexpensive video equipment became available in the mid-1970s, it was non-professionals from within social movements who began to make use of it, rather than *cinema novo* directors,[42] resulting in community video groups taking over from the *cinema novo* the goal of politically organising the *povo* or people.[43]

Going underground: *cinema marginal*

In the late 1960s, as the *cinemanovistas* ostensibly sought new directions in what could be perceived as a move away from the precepts of the 'Aesthetics of Hunger' manifesto, a younger group of cineastes, this time based in São Paulo, challenged the hegemony of *cinema novo* in the realm of alternative cinema. *Cinema marginal* has been given a number of labels over the years: underground or *udigrudi* (a deliberate mispronunciation of the English term), experimental cinema, *cinema maldito* (literally, damned or cursed cinema) and *cinema do lixo/cinema da boca*, the final two labels referring to the centre of production of these films.[44] Described by Fernão Ramos as 'the bastard relative, still not quite of a stature with its cousin',[45] *cinema marginal* did not herald a definitive break with *cinema novo*, but rather a radicalisation of the original purpose of *cinema novo*, in light of a perceived 'selling out' towards the end of the 1960s (with glossy colour productions like Leon Hirzsman's *Garota de Ipanema* (*Girl from Ipanema*, 1967), Glauber Rocha's *O dragão da maldade contra o santo guerreiro* (1968) and Joaquim Pedro de Andrade's *Macunaíma* (1969). Fernão Ramos points to the prophetic nature of Rocha's 'aesthetics of hunger' in relation to *cinema marginal*, with its references to the aesthetics of horror, violence and the need for *cinema novo* to marginalise itself from commercial cinematic production.[46]

While *cinema novo* created a mythical universe made up of the impoverished interior, urban slums, lower-class suburbs, fishing villages, dance halls and the soccer stadium,[47] marginal cineastes dealt with drug abuse; promiscuity; lack of respect for traditional values such as the family, property and professional development; an anti-work ethic and celebration of laziness; a lack of respect for 'normal' behaviour, manifested in scruffy attire, dirty appearance and a slovenly way of walking;[48] a celebration of an alternative lifestyle; and an empathy with traditionally marginalised groups such as blacks, homosexuals, indigenous populations and women.[49] As Robert Stam puts it, 'Just as Cinema Novo decided to reach out for a popular audience, the Underground opted to slap that audience in its face.'[50]

Paulo Emílio Salles Gomes defines marginal cinema as lasting for three years and consisting of around twenty films,[51] while Fernão Ramos, in the most complete study to date of the movement, dates it from 1968 to 1973 and lists fifty-six films,[52] including Glauber Rocha's experimental *Câncer* (1972), a number of *pornochanchadas* and the Zé do Caixão films.[53]

> A heterogeneous conglomerate of nervous artists, the *Lixo* movement proposes an anarchistic culture and tends to transform the populace into rabble, the colonized into trash. This degraded subworld, traversed by grotesque processions, condemned to the absurd, mutilated by crime, sex and exploitation, hopeless and fallacious, is, however, animated and redeemed by its inarticulate wrath.[54]

As a number of chapters in this book testify, this trashy, self-deprecating and anarchic aesthetic, creating a sense of pointlessness and unworthiness, has more echoes in national cinema production, past and future, than the high-art seriousness of *cinema novo*.

8

THE *PORNOCHANCHADA*

Introduction

Pornochanchada is a catch-all term used to determine a large group of films with popular appeal that were produced in Brazil in the 1970s and 1980s, which, given a certain move towards more liberal social codes, took as their main focus the subject of sex and sexuality. Although strictly speaking the *pornochanchada* refers to soft-core sex comedies (and comedy provides the main link with *chanchada*), the term is often extended to include all popular films with an erotic content (including films depicting quite graphic sexual violence from the late 1970s and early 1980s, for example), as well as the logical heir to the *pornochanchada*: hard-core porn. *Pornochanchada*, like many popular film genres, has been condemned to the dustbin of Brazilian cinema, given its supposed lack of aesthetic qualities and its connection, in the minds of left-wing critics, with the dictatorship (1964–84).

The *pornochanchada* is closely associated with film production in São Paulo's Boca do Lixo district: around 700 *pornochanchada*s were produced in the Boca during the genre's lifetime. During the 1970s and early 1980s, the Boca do Lixo was responsible for around sixty of the ninety Brazilian films produced annually.[1] Hard-core sex films, as opposed to straight-to-video or DVD sex films, the market for which continues to be buoyant in Brazil, dominated Brazilian screens to such an extent in the 1980s that it is no exaggeration to state that national cinema became synonymous with hard-core at that time. For example, of the top-grossing 100 Brazilian films in 1988, only twenty were *not* pornographic.[2]

The *pornochanchada* rose in popularity in the 1970s as a result of the introduction of compulsory screen quotas, which resulted in exhibition groups producing their own films, the outcome being cheap, mass-produced soft-core porn films (Brazil's own 'quota quickies'). In 1971 a group of exhibitors joined forces to produce films to meet the requirements of the compulsory exhibition law. Independent producers then began to make *pornochanchadas*, which flooded the reserve market in 1972 and 1973, forcing out, as a result, other more 'culturally worthy' films.[3] A large number of directors associated with other 'genres' turned their hand to making *pornochanchadas* in an attempt to stay afloat financially. In the 1970s erstwhile horror maestro José Mojica Marins (aka Zé do Caixão or Coffin Joe), under the pseudonym of J. Avelar, also made incursions into the world of the *pornochanchada*, for example A *virgem e o machão* (The Virgin and the Macho Man, 1974), and later hard-core.[4] After the death of popular comic actor and producer Mazzaropi in 1981, cinematographer Pio Zamuner, who had directed twelve Mazzaropi films, turned his attention to *pornochanchada* and then hard-core porn, making films with the likes of Jose Miziara (*Sem vaselina* (Without Vaseline, 1985)) and Rafaele Rossi (*Gemidos e sussurros* (Moans and Whispers, 1987)). But it was not just penniless directors and producers who jumped on the bandwagon of *pornochanchada*: it seemed that anyone with suitable connections with the Boca, regardless of filmmaking experience, could make money from the genre. Paris Filmes, for example, a film importer and distributor (and therefore with little or no filmmaking experience), set up a production side to its business in 1976, aiming to produce six films per year, as a result of the raising of the annual quota for national films to 112 days.[5] In the early 1980s a *pornochanchada* film could be made for less than one-sixth of the cost of the average co-production by Embrafilme, the State production and distribution agency.[6]

As witnessed in many national cinemas in the 1970s (British and French cinema, for example), the *pornochanchada* can be seen as a natural development in popular film. For a start, much of the success of popular theatre in Brazil (the origins of popular film) was predicated on its sauciness, its use of innuendo, and jokes of a sexual nature. As Paulo Emílio Salles Gomes pointed out, 'Within the *pornochanchada* we find all the traditions of popular Brazilian entertainment, and people who are shocked by such things have no idea of what went on in a certain area of our popular culture.'[7] As the name suggests, the *pornochanchada* comprised a number of the established characteristics of the *chanchada* (humour, plots commonly reliant on a clash between the archaic and modern in society and on mistaken identity, the glamorisation of Brazil's urban spaces, and so on), with added spice. But it is worth bearing in mind that the *chanchadas* in the late 1950s and early 1960s were already coming under fire for their saucy titles and inclusion of strip-tease scenes. *Pornochanchadas* were pre-hard-core films that relied on suggestion rather than on sexual explicitness. The occasional breast shot and distant glimpse of women's bodies in showers was usually the most that (early) *pornochanchada* fans could expect. That does not mean to say that nudity was non-existent in Brazilian cinema: a number of adaptations of the controversial work of playwright and author Nelson Rodrigues, for example, shocked the public and censors alike in the 1960s for their discussions of sexuality,[8] and the *cinema novo* was not averse to displays of nudity on screen. As we shall see, however, it was not in the commercial interests of 'quota quickies' to have problems with the censor, and thus nudity was, at least in the first half of the 1970s, kept to a minimum, and the smutty plotlines were frequently balanced out by a suitably moral message at the end of films.

The *pornochanchada* was influenced by the episodic Italian sex comedies, such as those starring Lando Buzzanca, which were commercially successful (and thus an interesting genre to imitate) both in Europe and in Brazil at the time. The episodic nature of these Italian films (i.e. three short films edited together to produce a feature-length film), copied in most cases in their Brazilian counterparts, made them cheaper and quicker to produce than feature-length films with a single plotline, and narratively less challenging for inexperienced writers. In the early days of the *pornochanchada*, these Italian films were copied wholesale, such as Dino Risi's *Sessomatto* (*How Funny Can Sex Be?*, 1973), which was transformed in Brazil into *Com as calças na mão* (With His Pants in His Hands, 1975). Given the *pornochanchada*'s origins in São Paulo's Boca do Lixo district, there are also very clear influences of Japanese cinema, and in particular the so-called *pink eiga* or pink films (soft-core comedies), which filled cinema screens in São Paulo in the 1960s and 1970s.

Sex and the Generals

For José Carlos Avellar, ironically the *pornochanchada* came into being as a result of censorship.[9] Avellar believes that it is more than a coincidence that censorship and the *pornochanchada* both appeared in the first few months of 1969. Censorship, for Avellar, also influenced the style of the *pornochanchada*: 'Censorship, the violent language of power, could do nothing against those who used the same methods. Censorship did not alter a language that in its own conception was censored and disarticulated.'[10]

Evidence of the self-censorship to which Avellar refers above (a kind of *coitus interruptus*, in the words of Randal Johnson and Robert Stam[11]) and disarticulation can be found in the fact that films rarely delivered on the promise of sex and nudity, and in the omission of rude words from the film soundtrack but which can clearly be read on the lips of actors. For example, in the provocatively titled *As secretárias . . . que fazem de tudo* (Secretaries . . . Who Do It All, 1975), in point of fact, the said secretaries do next to nothing, other than wiggle their bottoms, and they even get married at the end of the film. Self-censorship can also be seen in the large number of euphemisms and double entendres in the film scripts and film titles. For example, the verb *dar* literally means 'to give' in Portuguese, but it can also suggest penetration, 'giving it out' or offering sex. The innuendo frequently crops up in the titles of *pornochanchadas*, for example *Cada um dá o que tem* and *Eu dou o que ela gosta* (I Give Her What She Likes, 1975). The word *boa*, the feminine form of the adjective 'good', also implies both good-looking and good in bed, as suggested in the 1973 film *Como é boa nossa empregada*. Many titles feature a form of self-censorship: nouns are often omitted, while the meaning remains clear. The 1985 film *Senta no meu que eu entro na sua* (which roughly translates as 'Sit on mine and I'll put it in yours') provides the best example of the phenomenon. The omission of words and replacement with ellipses was particularly common in hard-core: for example Geraldo Dominó's *A b . . . profunda* (Deep A[ss], 1984).[12]

Avellar saw in the *pornochanchada* audience a carnivalesque defiance in the light of the dictatorship. He argued that:

> The spectator . . . would go to the cinema to take part in a kind of plot, to conspire against the established order, to conspire against

> conversations in broad daylight, made up of irrelevant subjects, or using words that he could not even understand.[13]

In the darkness of the cinema, the established order, as depicted by the government propaganda films that preceded all feature films at the time, could be freely derided. These advertisements for the dictatorship were shot frequently in soft focus, with smooth, paternalistic voiceovers, echoing messages such as 'Meu Brasil, eu amo você' (My Brazil, I love you), and they dealt with themes like hygiene, health and work, with the objective of improving living conditions and galvanising the work force. Also, they sought to strengthen 'the national character with regard to love for work and patriotism, and to maintain the support and patience of the masses'.[14] *Pornochanchadas*, by contrast, were bad-mannered, sluttish and utterly stupid, and promoted individualism and a rejection of the work ethic.[15] Avellar thus concludes that it is possible that audiences started going to see these films because they knew they were bad – when you cannot deal rationally with your own reality, you (in good Bakhtinian fashion) turn to the absurd.[16] Avellar cites as an example of this Mozael Silveira's 1975 film *Secas e molhadas* (Dried Up and Moist).[17] The critic explains that the film is shoddily produced and plays on its poor quality to attract the public. Perhaps, he argues, it is an unconscious act of revenge on the official publicity that depicted Brazil as a super-nation, with, among other jewels in the crown, the Trans-Amazonian Highway, Maracanã, the largest football stadium in the world,

> and other such things, equally gigantic, but far removed from the experience of the spectator of *pornochanchada*. The film is badly made: if this has been done deliberately or if it is as a result of lack of money and the creative incapacity of the director is of no consequence. What is for certain is that the *pornochanchada* plays with this idea.[18]

The *pornochanchada* audience enjoyed a secret intimacy with the films they watched, similar to the experience of regular viewers of the *chanchada*. As José Carlos Avellar has put it:

> There is an easy complicity between the spectator and the irreverent world [of the *pornochanchada*], very probably because he finds relief from the tensions of day-to-day life in this special reality: [in the cinema] he has no material problems, no duty to the person beside him or with society, nor anyone to tell him how to behave.[19]

With its co-production of films with titles such as *Um soutien para papai* (A Bra for Daddy, 1975), it is hardly surprising that Embrafilme came under fire. Nelson Pereira dos Santos, the 'godfather' of *cinema novo*, observed on the subject: 'We had . . . "the Ministry of Education and Culture presents *The Virgin Widow* or *The Woman Who Does I Don't Know What* . . . ": this was a violent contradiction within the moralism of the Brazilian military, with the government financing shit.'[20] The widely held belief that *pornochanchadas* were government sanctioned caused a federal senator, amid a media frenzy, to denounce Embrafilme for producing pornographic films. His denunciation led President João Figueiredo to make an uninformed statement against such practices, which in reality never existed.[21]

Randal Johnson argues that the link which is regularly made between the *pornochanchada* and the military government has been overplayed.[22] Granted, Embrafilme, the State film production and distribution agency, did finance films under its loan programme by Victor di Mello, Pedro Rovai and Aníbal Massaini Neto, for example, three of the most prolific producer/directors in *pornochanchada*. But Embrafilme possessed a remarkable autonomy during the dictatorship, and, while some of the organisation's financial initiatives were 'quality-driven', others rewarded popular appeal and volume of production. Johnson states that such a contradiction, which ironically went some way to proving the impartiality of Embrafilme, led to the reformulation of Embrafilme's policy of production financing. It is also worth bearing in mind that, while Embrafilme did not censor the *pornochanchada* (it would not have possessed the powers to do so anyway), it did make it its main target during the 1970s and was constantly seeking ways to limit its financial support.

No sex please, we're Brazilian!

While it is true to say that many national cinemas produced soft-core sex comedies in the 1970s, *pornochanchadas* are worth examining as they reflected on changing sexual mores at a crucial period of Brazilian history. Paulo Emílio Salles Gomes wrote of the *pornochanchada*: 'The eroticism of these films, despite their hurried, inefficient vulgarity, their self-destructive obsession with breasts and buttocks, is, in fact, what is most truthful about them.'[23] Going against stereotypical views of Brazil held throughout the twentieth century by much of the international community as a nation of both hypersexual and oversexed beings, the *pornochanchada* suggests that the population, in the 1970s, was sexually frustrated, deeply repressed and ultimately confused.

The *pornochanchada* typically dealt, in a good-humoured way, with the issue of sex (and in particular how to get some), using stock characters, many of whom were familiar to audiences from bawdier examples of the *teatro de revista* and the circus. These types included the womaniser, the virgin (male and female), the homosexual, the impotent old man, the old prostitute, the frustrated widow, the randy maid, the repressed secretary and so on. The early films marked a return of the tradition of popular urban comedies (these had practically disappeared with the growth of television) and gave expression to a new wave of permissiveness in (sophisticated, urban) Brazilian society.

As José Carlos Avellar summed up succinctly in an article entitled 'Gross National Product', the goal of the *pornochanchada* was not to be erotic or pornographic, but lewd, smutty and dirty.[24] He cites as an example of this a scene from *Cada um dá o que tem* (Each One Gives Whatever He Can, 1975), in which a short-sighted seminary student sniffs the bed sheets to see if a woman had been in his bed, or if it was a wet dream. A further example of this is the overuse in *pornochanchada* titles and plots of *bacalhau* or codfish: the word *bacalhau* in Brazil is pejoratively associated, through its strong smell, with aroused sexuality in women.[25]

When the first *pornochanchada* film, *Os paqueras* (The Flirts, 1969), was released to popular acclaim, it stood out with critics and the audience, because of the film's irreverence in dealing with social relationships. The two main characters in the film are an older, wealthy womaniser and his young follower, a work-shy, middle-class dropout. An example of the irreverent treatment afforded marital relationships in the film can be found in a seminal scene in which the womaniser is caught in the act with another woman by her husband and the police. En route to the police station, the husband is booed by gathering crowds while the old seducer is carried through the streets by a rejoicing throng. As a result of the success of the film, the word *paquera* (flirting) started to be used almost indiscriminately in film titles, and helped to crystallise one of the principal elements of the *pornochanchada*, which itself suggests sexual frustration: the element of voyeurism.

This voyeurism is often articulated literally in these films, with the act of peering through telescopes or spy-holes, over walls and round corners, all carried out, on behalf of eager audiences, by the camera itself. For example, in the episodic *Como é boa nossa empregada* (How Good Our Maid Is, 1973) the plotline of the first part of the film revolves around a young lad's attempt to spy on his maid, using a series of contraptions that supply the film's humour. His attempts to see her naked during the course of the film are ultimately frustrated. In *A superfêmea* (Superwoman, 1973), during a test for a photo shoot involving a large number of women, an advertising executive inspects one of them, tellingly and for no good reason, through a telescope. And in the *Jaws* (1975) parody *Bacalhau* (Codfish, 1975) a policeman using a monocular to search for a deadly beast that is terrorising the coastline shouts 'Que monstruosidade!' (What a monstrosity!), while the camera, peering as if through the monocular, reveals he is in fact checking out a young woman's backside. Snatched glances are typical of the furtive kind of behaviour displayed by male characters in many *pornochanchadas*. Such furtiveness is often alluded to only in film titles: for example, in the 1975 film *O roubo das calcinhas* (The Theft of the Panties) the supposed subject hardly enters the film.

As the bulk of the *pornochanchada* audience was made up of men, it was to men that the films were ultimately addressed: hence the allusions to male sexual concerns and peccadilloes. Many of the features that are highly characteristic of Brazilian sexual life are dealt with in the *pornochanchada*, for example the complex relationship that white, middle-class men have with maids and other subaltern females, commonly of mixed race, such as secretaries and nannies. Although nowadays maids are considered a luxury, given their increased wages and fairer working hours, in the 1970s even most lower-middle-class families could afford a live-in (and frequently exploited) maid, the majority of whom were mixed-race or black migrant workers. According to urban mythology, it was common practice for young men to 'lose their virginity' to and experiment sexually with such women, very much in the tradition of master–slave relations and the stereotype of the seductive charms of the *mulata* described, for example, by sociologist Gilberto Freyre.[26] The maid usually represents a different race and class to her boss, and thus the whole notion of furtive, naughty sex, one of the lynchpins of the *pornochanchada*, could successfully be explored through her. Sex with maids was naughty because the inappropriateness of such relationships was taken as read.

Another feature of Brazilian sexual life that is dealt with, albeit in a more veiled way, is the issue of sodomy. Although sodomy is a more openly popular sexual practice in Brazil than, say, in some Anglo-Saxon societies, where it is strongly associated with homosexuality, in the *pornochanchada* the threat of homosexual, rather than heterosexual, sodomy often appears in the form of a visual gag. Camera positions (which eventually pull back to reveal innocent scenarios) frequently hint at anal penetration. We clearly get the impression of homosexual activity in one scene involving the psychologist and the teenager in *Como é boa nossa empregada*, and on at least three occasions the camera hints at it again, in *Nos tempos da vaselina* (In the Days of Vaseline, 1979). For example, in one scene, the protagonist is lying face down on the bed and, in a common enough visual joke involving heterosexual couples, his cousin can be seen moving behind him in what looks like a penetrating motion. When the camera pulls back we discover that the cousin is merely putting cream on the other's sunburned back.[27] As these scenes have no bearing on the plot of the films in question, they seem to be merely an opportunity to include some near-the-knuckle depictions of sexuality without the censors picking up on them (after all, how many examples of bad editing must the censors have sat through when assessing these films?). Sodomy, like sex with subaltern females and homosexual desire, is equated in early *pornochanchadas* with dirtiness and smut.[28]

The socio-political context of the time (dictatorship, rural exodus to cities and the attendant loss of cultural identity, tentative growth of women's movements, and so on) arguably produced a crisis of masculinity, and Jean-Claude Bernardet has argued that many of the sexual themes of the *pornochanchada* spoke to the Brazilian male psyche in crisis, such as machismo and fear of castration: hence the presence of the homosexual character in these films; laughing at these modern-day court jesters proved the audience's masculinity and exorcised their sexual insecurity and fear of impotence.[29] A number of *pornochanchada*s portray parents living in fear of having a homosexual son: see for example the second part of *Como é boa nossa empregada*. Related to the issue of sexual confusion is the reflection in the *pornochanchada* of the growing interest displayed by the urban middle classes in psychology and psychotherapy, which by the 1990s had been transformed into a veritable national obsession. Sexual therapy is the subject of a number of films, including *Banana mecânica* (Clockwork Banana, 1974) and *Terapia do sexo* (Sexual Therapy, 1978). In the second episode of *Como é boa nossa empregada*, a teenage lad is taken to a psychologist (a particularly randy character in such films) because of his fixation for maids.

The new wave of permissiveness of the 1960s and 1970s inevitably brought with it clashes between different generations in Brazilian urban society, and the issue of the generation gap is dealt with in many *pornochanchadas*. *Os paqueras* itself pitches the young anti-hero against his stuffy, bourgeois family. In the third part of *Como é boa nossa empregada* an aggressive, authoritarian father dominates his family, and is seen as being out of place in the chilled-out seventies. In *Essa gostosa brincadeira a dois* (This Tasty Game for Two, 1974) a young couple are thwarted by their elders in their plan to move in together. What tends to happen in films that deal with the generation gap is that the older generation are happily indulging in all sorts of peccadilloes while chastising their offspring for their liberal take on relationships. Such hypocrisy is one of the comedic staples of the *pornochanchada*, as is the younger family members' use of *malandragem* or streetwise trickery to outwit their parents or take their revenge.

Since the purpose of the *pornochanchada* was first and foremost to titillate male viewers, the changing role of women is dealt with only superficially and only to the extent that it does not interfere with the ultimate goal of female objectification. Take, for example, *A superfêmea*, a film that notionally deals with the issues of contraception and feminism, but which merely succeeds in ridiculing both. In Fauzi Mansur's *Sexo às avessas* (Sex the Other Way Round, 1981), social roles are swapped over, with the lead actor playing a stay-at-home husband and the actress a promiscuous 'executive' wife, but in the film the inversion of hierarchies, in the tradition of the *teatro de revista* and the *chanchada*, is played purely for laughs.

The *pornochanchada* documented the significant demographic shifts taking place in Brazil's large cities, and in particular São Paulo. As in the *chanchada* before it and in, for example, British and French soft-core porn films of the same period, pivotal characters in the *pornochanchada* were often ingenues from the interior, and new to the big city. For example, in *Cada um dá o que tem*, the protagonist arrives in the city having just worked for six months on the Trans-Amazonian Highway. In *Nos tempos da vaselina*, the young protagonist arrives at Rio's busy bus station from a small town upstate (the suggestively titled Macacú[30]) and immediately has his luggage stolen. Film producers' fascination with places in the interior of the states of Rio and São Paulo continued throughout the life of the *pornochanchada*. In *Bem-dotado: o homem de Itu* (Well-Endowed: The Man from Itu, 1977), a young lad from the interior is invited to work in the home of a rich woman in the city. The town of Itu is renowned in Brazil for containing bigger-than-average flora and fauna. Needless to say, the rich hostess soon finds out that nature has blessed her houseguest in a similar way.

In another typical storyline, in *Como é boa nossa empregada*, an innocent young girl from Campos (also in the interior of the state of Rio de Janeiro) arrives in Rio city looking for work as a maid in a decent home, and quickly becomes the object of lust of the men of the house. In the *pornochanchada*, characters from the sticks, like the stock *chanchada* heroes, are portrayed as gullible and naive alongside their *carioca* and *paulista* counterparts, but by the end of the film they have usually 'come of age' through an (admittedly superficial) exploration of their repressed sexuality. Japanese characters (and East Asians in general), who before had been absent from Brazilian cinema despite the growing number of Japanese and *nikkei* in the South of Brazil, and especially São Paulo, crop up frequently in *pornochanchadas*: conforming to stereotype, the men are portrayed as sexless and the women as available and kinky.[31]

There has been a consensus of opinion over the years that the depiction of sexuality in the *pornochanchada* was unmistakably conservative and sexist. The *pornochanchada* is conservative in that sexually liberated characters are usually either punished or, more frequently, married off by the end of the film. According to Salles Gomes, while the *chanchada* mocked conventional social relations, the *pornochanchada* endorsed them.[32] Likewise, the only mocking going on in the *pornochanchada*, in Jean-Claude Bernardet's view, was of elderly, ugly and gay people who wanted a sex life like anyone else.[33] What critics fail to take into account is that, while porn is undoubtedly a conservative genre, such moralising may well have been present in order to avoid trouble with the censor, as if supplying a conservative ending could make up for sexual daring earlier on in the films. It is worth bearing in mind that sexuality, no matter how conservative, repressed and commodified, had never been systematically discussed on screen in Brazil before then. And besides, any kind of confirmation of the status quo was never going to be tolerated by a left-wing press during a military dictatorship, so the *pornochanchada* was doomed to be either condemned or ignored by critics at the time.

By the mid-1970s, occasionally actors and directors associated with mainstream cinema and television would wander into the territory of erotic comedy, usually in an attempt to tap into the huge commercial success that the *pornochanchada* was enjoying at the time. With their big budgets, famous actresses and catwalk models, and high production values, films such as *Xica da Silva* (*Xica*, 1976), *Dona Flor e seus dois maridos* (Dona Flor and Her Two Husbands, 1976) and *A dama do lotação* (Lady on the Bus, 1978) created a cleaned-up version of the *pornochanchada*, as Jean-Claude Bernardet has put it.[34] According to the soft and later hard-core porn producer and actor David Cardoso, the *pornochanchada*, despite the almost unanimous suspicion it generated in both cultural and political circles at the time, was responsible for forming the audience that put *Dona Flor* in the record books for the most viewed film of all time.[35]

In the late 1970s and early 1980s, partly as a result of the loosening of censorship regulations, a number of 'serious' films with a graphic sexual content appeared, which were frequently lumped in together with the *pornochanchada*. A number of these films sought to challenge the *pornochanchada* head on by appropriating the genre in order to produce a counter-argument to its conservatism and sexism. Many of these films were made by filmmakers associated with *cinema marginal*.[36] These include João Callegaro's timely attempt at a serious discussion of what pornography means in *O pornógrafo* (The Pornographer, 1970), and Carlos Reichenbach's *O império do desejo* (In the Realm of Desire, 1980), a more grown-up discussion of sexuality clearly inspired by Nagisa Oshima's *Ai no corrida* (In the Realm of the Senses, 1976).[37] *Cinemanovista* veteran Joaquim Pedro de Andrade's short film *Vereda tropical* (Tropical Paths, 1980) is a deliberate send-up of the *pornochanchada*. In the film the subject of the male protagonist's affections, rather than the usual attractive female, is a watermelon. Thus, the film 'answers the male voyeur's implicit request for female sex object by offering an ironically reified, vegetative exemplar of alterity'.[38] Despite the film's refusal to meet the demands for female nudity, *Vereda tropical* was banned by the military government, which 'tolerated the much more explicit *pornochanchadas* that [the film] so acerbically mocked'.[39]

The arrival of hard-core

Following patterns to be found in many other countries, the passage in Brazilian cinema from light-hearted sex romps to hard-core was a relatively rapid one. There was a period of no more than a couple of years at the beginning of the 1980s when (still simulated) sex scenes took over from furtive glances of 'tits and bums'. By 1985, pornographic films accounted for almost three-quarters of film production in Brazil.[40]

Many downtown cinemas, in order to stay open during the recession-hit 1980s, converted into porn theatres, which in turn became notorious haunts for picking up prostitutes, with its concomitant associations with sleaze, disease, drugs, crime and violence.[41] These included erstwhile 'family' cinemas, such as the Art Palácio in São Paulo, where popular screen performer Mazzaropi premiered all his films in the 1960s and 1970s.[42] In February 1985, of the fifty-three cinema halls in the centre of São Paulo, forty-four were showing explicit sex films.[43] The downtown area of Rio de Janeiro known as Cinelândia, where smart cinema halls existed comfortably alongside the more highbrow Municipal Theatre, National Library and Fine Arts Museum, was practically transformed into a second red-light district by the number of cinemas showing hard-core films in the 1980s.

Most hard-core porn films were (and still are) screened in 'specialist' film theatres, which only permitted entry to over-18s and which made it clear that films being screened contained *sexo explícito* or scenes of an explicit (i.e. unsimulated) nature. Adding to the horror of seeing the words *sexo explícito* appearing in lights above cinemas and on billboards all over town, the films' names also caused moral outrage. For example, on the poster for Roberto Fedegoso's (pseudonym for David Cardoso) *Viciado em C . . .* (Addicted to A . . . , 1985), the missing noun (*cu* or ass) is supplied by a drawing of a woman's curvy buttocks. The tagline read: 'There's never been anything like it! Animals, men, women and queers in a real orgy!'

Thus, to the understandable chagrin of cinephiles, within national cinema it is the *pornochanchada* and hard-core porn that has had the greatest social impact on Brazil, shifting whole communities out of erstwhile respectable city-centre neighbourhoods, feeding the demand for out-of-town leisure complexes and new neighbourhoods, alienating mainstream audiences and, for many observers, merely adding to the moral and sexual confusion of the times. Within the industry itself the family atmosphere that, according to *pornochanchada* stars, existed in the Boca do Lixo in the 1970s was replaced by one of seediness and exploitation, as many actresses were forced to give up their careers and were replaced by prostitutes, who earned for one film what they would be paid for an overnight trick.[44]

Although underground hard-core filmmaking had existed in Brazil since the early days of cinema, it was not until 1982 that the first Brazilian hard-core film was given an exhibition certificate: the film in question was Italian-born director Rafaele Rossi's *Coisas eróticas* (Erotic Things, 1982). This move took place as a result of the Board of Censors approving, in 1981, the setting up of special theatres for showing more explicit material, and two art-house films in particular, Nagisa Oshima's *In the Realm of the Senses* and Tinto Brass and Bob Guccione's *Caligula* (1979). A blanket ban on international box-office hits (and art-house films to boot) was, after all, difficult to reconcile with the dictatorship's assurances of a more politically open society post-1976.

Coisas eróticas, which took three weeks to make and was produced as cheaply as possible with the intention of securing a release in these same special theatres, was unexpectedly granted a certificate for general release. It remains unclear (and the source of much speculation and amusement) as to how this came about: allegations include bribery of the Board of Censors on the part of the producer, and human error (the wrong certificate was issued). As a result of its general release, the film was seen by over 4 million people.

With the release of *Coisas eróticas* the floodgates opened and by 1983, of the sixty-one films produced in São Paulo, around half were sexually explicit. By the end of the decade some 500 hard-core films had been produced in Brazil, which fought for space usually in downtown cinemas alongside US hard-core. Hard-core's domination of the national film market was intensive, arguably destructive on a number of levels, but relatively short-lived. By the end of the 1980s film production in the Boca do Lixo had ceased. Economic crisis, the constant struggles with the censor and local government, and competition from hard-core video from the USA meant that even the production of cheap hard-core films was no longer viable.

9

THE NATION IN CONTEMPORARY CINEMA

Brazilian cinema since the so-called *retomada* or renaissance of the mid-1990s has been characterised by its thematic and stylistic diversity.[1] As various critics have pointed out, recent production has included animation, children's films, historical dramas, historical farces, comedies of manners, romantic comedies, urban dramas, literary adaptations, neo-*cangaceiro* (bandit) films (the Brazilian equivalent of the Hollywood western), political thrillers, neo-noir detective films, documentaries and experimental films.[2] Nonetheless, within this wide range of themes and approaches, there has been a discernible tendency for filmmakers to seek to locate the nation and map its inherent contradictions, representing both urban and rural life from the perspective of the disenfranchised, marginalised fringes of society. The binary tension between the city and the countryside has been a constant thematic concern of Brazilian cinema since its inception, often represented in a simplistic, dichotomous way by the arrival of a naive hick in an urban jungle in the films of Mazzaropi and the Atlântida *chanchadas* of the 1950s.[3] The *sertão* (arid hinterland of Brazil's North-East) and the *favela* (urban slum) were the settings of landmark films made in Brazil in the 1950s and early 1960s, such as *Rio, 40 graus* (*Rio, 40 Degrees*, 1955), *Rio, Zona Norte* (*Rio, Northern Zone*, 1957) and *Vidas secas* (*Barren Lives*, 1963), all directed by Nelson Pereira dos Santos, *Deus e o diabo na terra do sol* (*Black God, White Devil*, Glauber Rocha, 1964) and *A grande cidade* (*The Big City*, Carlos Diegues, 1966). Both real and symbolic, these two locations and their inhabitants resurface in films of the *retomada*, but with a radically different tone and significance.[4]

Dystopian cityscapes

A notable trend within post-1995 film production in Brazil has been the portrayal of contemporary life in the *favelas* of the big cities, particularly Rio de Janeiro. The fiction films *O primeiro dia* (*Midnight*, Walter Salles and Daniela Thomas, 1999) and *Cidade de Deus* (*City of God*, Fernando Meirelles, 2002) and the documentary *Notícias de uma guerra particular* (*News of a Private War*, João Moreira Salles, 1998), for example, contrast the grim realities of the gang warfare that dominates shantytown life today with the relatively utopian days before the arrival of guns.

Orfeu (*Orpheus*, Carlos Diegues, 1999), a critical reworking of French director Marcel Camus's *Orfeu negro* (*Black Orpheus*, France/Italy, 1958), relies on a realistic dialogue rich in Rio *favela* slang,[5] and depicts the complexities of today's *favela* population, which embraces blacks and North-Eastern migrants.

The representation of Brazil's underbelly extends from the shantytowns to other run-down, crime-ridden quarters of the nation's major cities. José Henrique Fonseca's *O homem do ano* (*The Man of the Year*, 2003), for example, based on the novel *O matador* (*The Killer*) by Patrícia Melo, tells the story of Máiquel, a young, male inhabitant of Rio's deprived northern outskirts who murders a local thug for merely branding him a 'queer', and becomes an unwitting local hero and contract killer, who is even congratulated by the police. Fonseca's film highlights the paranoia that the city's violent crime rate has bred among all classes of the population, and which has given rise to a culture of vigilantes who operate with impunity in poorer areas, and hi-tech security systems for the wealthier. As the professional hit man's main client, an ostensibly respectable dentist comments, when reading the newspaper clippings of his latest killings: 'That's how you build a decent nation.'

Life in Brazil's urban slums has also provided inspiration for critically acclaimed documentary films, such as the work of influential filmmaker Eduardo Coutinho, discussed in more detail below, and *Fala tu* (*Living Rap in Rio*, Guilherme Coelho, 2003), which deals with the daily struggle of three aspiring rap artists. The vibrant contemporary music scene chiefly associated with *favela* communities is showcased in another documentary, *O rap do pequeno príncipe contras as almas sebosas* (*The Little Prince's Rap against the Wicked Souls*, Paulo Caldas and Marcelo Luna, 2000), set in the slums of Recife, and in several fiction films, including *O invasor* (*The Trespasser*, Beto Brant, 2002), set in São Paulo, and *Orpheus*, set in Rio. Other important films of the *retomada* have focused on the lives of the urban underclass in the North-East of Brazil, such as *Cidade baixa* (*Lower City*, Sérgio Machado, 2004), which exposes the realities of low-rent prostitution in the port of Salvador, Bahia, and *Amarelo manga* (*Mango Yellow*, Cláudio Assis, 2002). Set in the city of Recife, *Mango Yellow* centres on the motley characters who reside in a down-market hotel that is little more than a dosshouse. The film provides a disquieting and often shocking vision of life for the urban poor of the North-East, making effective use of documentary elements. It incorporates real-life scenes shot in the mean streets and poor areas of Recife that feature the ubiquitous street vendors of the informal sector scratching a living, reinforcing the central theme of social exclusion. *Carandiru* (Hector Babenco, 2003), a bleak portrayal of human deprivation in the eponymous São Paulo penitentiary, returns the focus to the megalopolis of the South-East, more specifically to its impoverished periphery, from which the film's central characters hail. Based on Dráuzio Varella's best-selling book *Estação Carandiru* (*Carandiru Station*, 1999), a non-fiction work based on his experiences as the prison doctor, Babenco's film broke the box-office records set by *City of God*, attracting more than 4.5 million spectators in its first two months of exhibition in Brazil.[6]

City of God

City of God, directed by Fernando Meirelles, former independent producer of documentaries and director of TV advertisements, with the collaboration of Kátia Lund, deals in very graphic terms with the history of a poor community on the outskirts of Rio de Janeiro during the 1960s, 1970s and 1980s, and its descent into drug trafficking and gang warfare. With a cast of predominantly non-professional actors,[7] the film exceeded all expectations, attracting more than 3 million spectators in Brazil alone, securing distribution around the world, and becoming the third most successful foreign film in Britain, after *Crouching Tiger, Hidden Dragon* (Ang Lee, 2000) and *Amélie* (Jean-Pierre Jeunet, 2001). The film also provoked controversy, sparking a series of debates and polemics concerning its representation of violence. Ivana Bentes, for example, takes issue with *City of God* for its depiction of violence as pure spectacle for voyeuristic, middle-class audiences.[8] She accuses the film of reproducing the empty clichés traditionally reserved for the exoticised 'foreigner's eye view' of Brazil, and more specifically its racial stereotypes.[9] As Johnson notes, however, 'numerous critics disagreed, and the ensuing polemic almost certainly contributed in some way to the film's success'.[10]

Nagib analyses the film's striking degree of realism from the starting point of the language of the novel by Paulo Lins, on which it was based, and how this is transferred to the script, written by Bráulio Mantovani, but, more innovatively, into cinematic techniques. 'The frenetic rhythm of the novel', she argues, 'is translated into the quick-fire cuts of the digital editing, in the style of an advertisement or music video.'[11] The cinematic potential of Lins's earth-shattering depiction of violence and social exclusion was recognised by the film's producer, Walter Salles, who stated, 'For the first time in Brazil, someone had described from within the social "apartheid" in a *favela*. It was not the work of sociologists, but a more organic, penetrative vision.'[12]

The performances of the cast, which are often shocking and uncomfortable to watch, such is their degree of realism, were achieved at tremendous physical and financial cost. Casting took an entire year to complete, involving 400 children and teenagers in theatre workshops that centred on improvisation exercises, and from which the film's cast of sixty main actors and supporting cast of 150 were selected by the directors and their team.[13] Fernando Meirelles explained in interview how he noted down bits of dialogue improvised by the film's cast, who essentially devised their own characters, which he would then email to Mantovani so that they could be incorporated into redrafts of the script. There was always a camera present during the improvisation workshops, although it was not always switched on. Nearly all the participants had a chance to operate the camera, thus gaining valuable awareness of acting technique.[14]

This tale of progressive social exclusion and examination of the inner workings of gangland culture, filmed on location in three different Rio *favelas*,[15] was clearly intended to make middle-class Brazilians aware of the realities of life on their doorsteps. As the director has commented, 'when I read the novel I was horrified to see how life is organised in poor communities in Brazil. My interest was more anthropological. I made the film in order to get to know my country better.'[16] The film's intended realism, however, was not deemed incompatible by its creators with 'the language of the MTV, rap and disco cultures familiar to young people of the same age as its protagonists'.[17] Ismail Xavier adds that the film's 'neorealism is combined with a sense of the image as artifice, the narrative as a fast-moving train of emotions conveyed through elaborate fast edits and computer-created effects', commenting that it is no coincidence that Meirelles's background is as a director of television commercials. *City of God*'s combination of documentary elements with music video montage polarised the opinions of critics. As Beatriz Jaguaribe writes, '[the film] has been allegorically read as a synecdoche of the nation while being upheld as an example of realism. Conversely, it has been denounced as a spectacularized Americanized action film devoid of realism.'[18]

The eclectic soundtrack of *City of God*, which combines soul, funk and samba, and the uses made of extra-diegetic and diegetic music, are similarly part and parcel of the film's attempts to recreate an epoch and environment with verisimilitude, rather than an incongruous aesthetic embellishment. The soundtrack is a mixture of music especially composed for the film by Antonio Pinto and Ed Cortes and a selection of music (both Brazilian and international) that represents each decade dealt with in the film. As David Treece writes:

> One of the interesting features of Fernando Meirelles's *Cidade de Deus* – and perhaps a contributing factor in its success internationally – is a

Figure 9.1 A scene from *Cidade de Deus* (*City of God*, 2002) featuring the character of Rocket (photograph by César Charlone; courtesy of Fernando Meirelles, 02 Filmes)

> soundtrack which, while including some familiar 'Brazilian' sounds, also challenges audiences' expectations about the musical loyalties of young, urban working-class blacks in today's Brazil. The film's chronological span encompasses two moments [. . .] when the hegemony of samba, as the symbol of an optimistic, one-nation populist consensus rooted in the idea of an integrated *mestiço* culture, has been challenged by a self-conscious and militant identification with non-local, diasporic black musical idioms.[19]

Treece goes on to argue that the dominance of Brazilian funk in the film's soundtrack reinforces, musically and linguistically, the theme of social exclusion and the sense of difference that divides the city of Rio from itself.[20] In its creative use of popular music *City of God* has much in common with Beto Brant's feature film *The Trespasser*.

The Trespasser

Based on a fictional idea by novelist Marçal de Aquino, *The Trespasser* was the winner of the Best Latin American Film award at the Sundance Film Festival in 2002. The film's central themes are the relationship between economic power, politics and corruption, prostitution and crime, and the systematic practice of public and private violence, also depicted as the ills of contemporary Brazilian reality in Brant's striking first feature film *Os matadores* (*Belly Up*, 1997), the tale of two hit men waiting for their victim on the border between Brazil and Paraguay.[21] The plot of *The Trespasser* involves two successful São Paulo businessmen, partners in a lucrative construction business, who hire a hit man to kill their third partner. The professional killer, Anísio, played by Paulo Miklos (singer in the popular rock band *Os Titãs* – The Titans), then blackmails his way up the social ladder, corrupting the unwitting teenage daughter of his victim en route. He is thus the trespasser of the film's title, a slum dweller who challenges traditional social boundaries, a member of Brazil's excluded underclass who simply wants to gain entry into the hedonistic world of nightclubs and drugs, fast cars and luxury houses. In her evocatively titled article 'Is This Really Brazil? The Dystopian City of *The Trespasser*', Lúcia Nagib begins by citing a phrase from Neusa Barbosa's essay in the press release for the film: '*The Trespasser* is . . . the portrait . . . of Brazil trapped in a moral and social cul-de-sac.'[22] Barbosa continues, 'São Paulo, as a peripheral, chaotic metropolis, typical of late capitalism, provides the ideal material for the updating of the crime thriller, with its typical mixture of blackmail, conspiracy, greed, murder and general pessimism.'[23] The film depicts an amoral city characterised by capitalist greed, white-collar corruption, widespread hard drug abuse, prostitution and casual sex, where violence permeates all levels of the social structure and functions as a kind of currency. There are no positive characters, no heroes or anti-heroes.

São Paulo takes centre stage in several long takes in the film, as the characters move about the city, back and forth between the commercial centre, the upmarket residential districts and the poor periphery, drawing attention to the social fragmentation of the metropolis. Just as Anísio cuts across unspoken social boundaries, the film 'attempts to photograph the city as a whole, making a surgical incision in the social pyramid from which it is composed. It produces a scale model of Brazilian society as a whole.'[24] Beto Brant's intention, however, is not to suggest that social mobility is possible, but rather that the class structure remains intransigent and the city brutally divided.[25]

The soundtrack of *The Trespasser* includes rap, rock and hip hop music by local musicians Paulo Miklos, Sabotage, Pavilhão 9 and Tolerância Zero. The hip hop artist Sabotage appears in a cameo role in the film, performing an impromptu rap at Anísio's request in the incongruous setting of the offices of the construction company.[26] As well as contributing to the authentication of the temporal and geographic setting, the choice of diegetic and extra-diegetic music is often intended to underline the film's dominant themes. The fact that at key points in the narrative the lyrics of songs are translated in the subtitles of the DVD version of the film is a clear reflection of Brant's deliberate choice of songs that reflect the action on screen. To take one example, when the bodies of the hit man's two victims are discovered, over-loud extra-diegetic thrash metal suddenly erupts, with the repeated lyrics 'welcome to the nightmare of reality'. This deafening music continues into the next scene, at the victims' funeral, where the inappropriateness of the musical genre coupled with the shaky hand-held camera adds to the surreal, edgy mood. The same song continues, uninterrupted, as the camera's eye enters the office of the construction business. It then stops abruptly when the identity of the point of view is revealed – it is that of Anísio, the hit man, who is 'trespassing' on a territory to which he does not belong in the highly stratified social hierarchy.

Documentary and Bus 174

Within documentary film, which has enjoyed something of an unexpected renaissance since the mid-1990s, the urban slum and its inhabitants have similarly provided a rich vein to be mined, most notably in the work of Eduardo Coutinho, who since 1979 'has devoted himself exclusively to the documentary genre and has come to be considered Brazil's greatest documentary filmmaker'.[27] Two of his recent works, *Santo forte* (*Strong Saint*, 1999) and *Babilônia 2000* (2000), along with the earlier *Santa Marta – duas semanas no morro* (*Santa Marta – Two Weeks on the Hill*, 1987), were filmed in the hillside shantytowns of Rio de Janeiro, but approach the topic from a fresh perspective, representing 'not only the vision of this outsider [Coutinho] who went up the hill, but the image of the *favela* inhabitants as they would like to be seen'.[28]

Coutinho structures his documentaries around interviews with the shantytown residents, rejecting voiceovers or other interpreting voices, and explicitly including himself, his team and their filmmaking apparatus in the frame. He chooses not to edit out extraneous diegetic noise or redundancy and lapses in the dialogue, giving the impression that the viewer is witnessing a film in the making, and thus 'the effect of reality is rendered by the exhibition of the conditions of the filmic fabrication'.[29] Coutinho's chosen medium is increasingly digital video, which increases the mobility of the camera and reduces the number of interruptions. He does not involve himself at all in the pre-production phase, with his interviewees meeting him for the first time when they are captured by the lens, which further contributes to the sense of spontaneity and realism.

João Moreira Salles's documentary on the drug trade in Rio de Janeiro, *Notícias de uma guerra particular* (*News from a Private War*, 1999), combines filming in the shantytown of Santa Marta with scenes shot in institutions for juvenile delinquents and police headquarters. The startling interviews with teenage drug dealers reveal their obsession with consumer goods, particularly clothes, and their adoption of a self-conscious gangster posturing for the camera.[30] Another documentary maker who has turned her attention to social disenfranchisement and deprivation is Maria Ramos, whose critically acclaimed *Justiça* (*Justice*, 2004) was awarded the Golden Wave for best film at the Bordeaux International Festival of Women in Cinema in 2004. This incisive film exposes the inflexible and punitive nature of Brazil's penal system, characterised by inhumanely overcrowded detention centres, police corruption and brutality.

The most provocative documentary to come out of Brazil and reach international audiences in recent years is *Ônibus 174* (*Bus 174*, José Padilha, 2002). Constructed around TV news footage of a real-life hold-up of a bus that took place in Rio de Janeiro on 12 June 2000 and was broadcast live for four long hours, *Bus 174* uses these archive images, interviews and official documents to construct two separate narratives, one the actual hold-up, the other the life story of its perpetrator, Sandro, a former street kid. In interview, the film's co-director, Felipe Lacerda, stated that the aim was to achieve an impartial, balanced representation of events and of the film's 'protagonist', Sandro.[31] *Bus 174* thus avoids showing any of the interviewees in visible distress, and for the most part rejects the exploitative, manipulative techniques favoured by the plethora of sensationalist news/reality TV shows in Brazil, such as emotive extra-diegetic soundtracks. The film includes scenes shot inside one of Rio's jails, showing inmates desperately screaming for someone to listen to them. As Lacerda commented in interview, they clearly wanted attention more than anything else, and their violence is simply a way of trying to achieve this.[32]

Bus 174 succeeds in humanising Sandro, in direct contrast to Brazilian television's blatant tendency to demonise black and mixed-race youth. As Lorraine Leu argues, one of the film's main concerns 'is to make Sandro's life real and his death grievable'.[33] It recounts his tragic childhood, when he witnessed the murder of his mother, his survival of the notorious massacre of street children by off-duty policemen on the steps of the Candelária church in Rio's city centre in 1993, and his spells in inhumanely overcrowded juvenile detention centres and 'Dantesque prison cells'.[34] The film pieces together the life story of this otherwise faceless *favelado* (*favela* inhabitant), repeatedly branded a ruthless, violent, drug-crazed *bandido* (criminal) in television news coverage and in the press, even after his own violent death at the hands of the police, which is captured on the news footage shown in the film. The media's manipulation of the stereotype of the young black men who live in Rio's slums is exposed in the film, and the director seeks to redress the invisibility of men like Sandro, treated by society as an anonymous, criminal scourge, by uncovering details of his life, and including interviews with those who knew him. A sociologist is interviewed on screen, and analyses the racial and social marginalisation of young men like Sandro, but this 'expert' opinion merely serves to reinforce the objectification of the urban poor by the educated elite, adding to the former's alienation. The corrupting power of the media is further illustrated when we learn from the interviews with some of those passengers taken hostage on the bus that Sandro, aware of his 'audience', told them to go along with his simulated death threats by pretending to be afraid and behaving as if he had killed one of their fellow passengers. At one point we even hear Sandro shout to the police: 'This isn't an action film. It's serious', and later: 'Hey, officer, haven't you seen that movie where the guy throws the girl out of the plane?' before he pretends to shoot the first hostage, again articulating his actions in cinematic terms.

Padilha's documentary, like those of Eduardo Coutinho referred to above, calls into question the dividing line between fact and fiction, and acknowledges the performativity inherent in the genre. In contrast to Coutinho's work, however, it incorporates aesthetic choices that traditionally belong to fiction films, such as slow-motion sequences, the repetition of certain scenes, music video-style editing, sound and colour effects, extra-diegetic music, and the manipulation of real and diegetic time. In doing so, *Bus 174* draws attention to and denounces the media's sensationalist distortions of real-life events, the 'spectacularization of daily life' that makes it virtually impossible to experience facts without media mediation.[35] By including Sandro's own words, 'This isn't an action film. It's serious', the film reminds us of its intentions, thus narrowly avoiding its own descent into the kind of tasteless voyeuristic spectacle that Brazilian television's coverage of the event epitomised.

Bus 174 struck a chord with urban audiences in Brazil, particularly in Rio, where armed hold-ups and muggings are not uncommon on public transport and many motorists live in fear of being held up at gun or knife point in their own cars at certain traffic lights or junctions. Padilha's film provocatively goes against the Brazilian media's dominant discourse on urban crime by portraying the perpetrator as himself a victim of social injustice, potentially alienating large swathes of city dwellers who experience the sensation of being under siege on a daily basis. More problematically for some, the real victims of this incident who are interviewed in the film are themselves also representatives of Rio's poor, thus largely denied a voice in the media themselves and consequently more deserving 'victims' than Sandro.

Utopian landscapes

Brazil's arid North-Eastern interior, or *sertão*, and its predominantly impoverished inhabitants have provided considerable inspiration for Brazilian filmmakers since the mid-1990s. The *sertão* reappears in the 1990s in films such as *Sertão das memórias* (*Landscapes of Memory*, José Araujo, 1997), *Baile perfumado* (*Perfumed Ball*, Paulo Caldas and Lírio Ferreira, 1997), *Guerra de Canudos* (*Battle of Canudos*, Sérgio Rezende, 1997), *O cangaceiro* (*The Cangaceiro*, Aníbal Massaini Neto, 1997) and *Central do Brasil* (*Central Station*, Walter Salles, 1998). Subsequent additions to this list include *Eu, tu, eles* (*Me, You, Them*, Andrucha Waddington, 2000) and *Abril despedaçado* (*Behind the Sun*, Walter Salles, 2002). These recent films about the *sertão*, in contrast to the politically committed *cinema novo* films of the 1960s, value the beauty and good quality of the filmic image, and employ conventional narrative techniques. As Bentes says, 'the goal is a "popular" and "globalized" film industry, dealing with local, historic and traditional subjects wrapped in an "international" aesthetics'.[36] Waldemar Lima, photographer on Glauber Rocha's emblematic *Black God, White Devil*, has criticised the way lighting is used in these recent films,[37] stating: 'They want to use a Hollywood lighting for stories that take place in the *sertão* and this looks strange. The light of the *sertão* is harsh, with strong shadows not soft ones. What they are doing is not convincing.'[38]

Central Station

Central do Brasil (*Central Station*, Walter Salles, 1998) brings the 'two Brazils' – the urban and the rural – together, and, as the film's director has made clear, it is an allegory of the Brazilian nation:

> *Central Station* is a microcosm of what is happening in Brazil. That is why the film opens in the railway station, to show a country without its make-up on, with its veil removed, with all its blemishes on show. As soon as the film takes to the road, in search of lost innocence, Brazil ceases to be the one seen in that station, and there is a possibility of redemption and change.[39]

The film enjoyed great commercial success in Brazil, pulling in an audience of more than 1.5 million people. It was equally acclaimed by the critics, winning a Golden Bear for best film at the Berlin Film Festival and a BAFTA for best non-English-language film, amongst other accolades.

Salles's film deals with the relationship that develops between a young boy, Josué, orphaned and alone in Rio de Janeiro, and the middle-aged, world-weary former schoolteacher, Dora, who first encounters Josué in the city's main railway station, the name of which gives the film its title. It is there that Dora earns her living by writing letters on behalf of the illiterate migrant workers from all over Brazil who converge on the station. Before her untimely death on the chaotic, traffic-filled streets outside the station, Josué's mother pays Dora to write to her estranged husband back in her native Ceará, at the insistence of Josué. The hard-faced Dora, who rarely actually posts such letters, simply pocketing the cash of Brazil's poorest, gradually lets down her emotional guard (not before selling the boy to organ traffickers but subsequently repenting and rescuing him) and agrees to help the now orphaned Josué to find his father. Thus begins a momentous road trip to the interior of Brazil's North-East by two unlikely travelling companions, one played by the famous, much lauded actress Fernanda Montenegro, the other by the unknown Vinícius de Oliveira, discovered by Salles in an airport in Rio shining the patrons' shoes.

The film opens with a series of arresting close-ups of real-life illiterate migrants who use the station, lending a distinct documentary quality to these first scenes.[40] Dictating their letters to Dora, they represent in their faces the gamut of racial mixtures found in the Brazilian population. The film's title in Portuguese can be interpreted as a reference to the centre or heartland of Brazil as a nation, the rural North-East, to which this road movie ultimately takes the viewer. Life in Rio de Janeiro as depicted in the film is characterised by isolation and alienation, illiteracy and poverty, noise and dirt, violence and crime, ranging from petty theft to organ trafficking. As the film's two protagonists set off in search of Josué's father, their arduous physical journey also becomes one of self-discovery for the cynical, embittered Dora. As she moves further and further away from the dehumanising city of Rio, she gradually begins to feel emotion again, and begins to acknowledge her own feelings about the father who abandoned her as a child. As the unknown landscapes of the arid, sparsely populated interior of Brazil's North-East open up before her eyes, she returns to both the heart of her country and the essence of her own being. *Central Station* is ultimately a search for both the father and the fatherland. As Walter Salles has said in interview: '*Central* [*Station*] looks for a solution in the heart of the country. The film deals with the search for distinctly Brazilian roots . . . The character of Josué . . . rewrites his own future by taking action.'[41] The film proposes the search for a lost nation, or at least the notion of the Brazilian population reconnecting with its core values.

The urban/rural dichotomy is emphasised by lighting techniques; Rio is characterised by darkness and low-key artificial lighting, as exemplified in the scene when Dora first takes Josué to her gloomy apartment, in marked contrast to the use of natural light or candle light in the setting of the *sertão*, which is repeatedly shot at sunrise or sundown. As Dora and Josué travel in the direction of this interior land, so close-up shots are replaced by stunning panoramas, captured by the lens of acclaimed cinematographer Walter Carvalho. As Paulo Passos de Oliveira has argued, the North-East becomes a protagonist of the film itself.[42] The *sertão* is a site of reconciliation for both Dora and Josué.

Central Station depicts the migratory journey of *Barren Lives* in reverse, from the city to the countryside, and replaces the bleak mood of that *cinema novo* classic, which became synonymous with the 'aesthetics of hunger', with a sense of optimism and possibility for the inhabitants of the long-neglected North-East. Drought and poverty are presented in the film as aspects of local colour rather than serious impediments to a better life. As Nagib succinctly puts it, the search for the father, in the diegesis, corresponds, on a metalinguistic level, to the quest for the North-Eastern fatherland lost in the past of *cinema novo*, destined to offer historical affiliation to contemporary filmmakers.[43]

Me, You, Them

Me, You, Them is based on a true story, reported on Brazilian television, of a poor woman from Brazil's *sertão* who was living with her three male partners in the 1990s. Directed by Andrucha Waddington, who learned his trade making TV advertisements, this celebration of female autonomy is set in the rural interior of the North-Eastern state of Ceará, a part of Brazil where even today there is no electricity and drought continues to blight the lives of the effectively indentured peasant farmers. The film stars the homely Regina Casé, a household name in Brazil for her work on light-hearted TV reality shows,[44] as Darlene.

In spite of this barren setting and the somewhat unusual choice of leading lady, the film uses safe, TV Globo soap-opera actors (Lima Duarte and Stênio Garcia in the roles of 'husbands' number one and two) and the ubiquitous North-Eastern pin-up Luís Carlos Vasconcelos as husband number three. As the director Andrucha Waddington said in interview:

> I never set out to make a propaganda film. *Vidas secas* already deals with man and social conflict [in the North-East]. *Cinema novo* had that aspect of showing the beauty of Brazil, but in precarious technical conditions. Brazilian cinema was badly thought of by the public because of its [technical] finish and the latest crop of films is correcting this image.[45]

Me, You, Them was shot entirely on location near the interior town of Juazeiro, in the North-Eastern state of Bahia, an area scarred by cyclic droughts. The cast were thus in close contact with the local inhabitants, some of whom were incorporated into the film as extras and who also lent their worn-in clothes to the professional actors, all of which was intended to contribute to the realism of the finished product.[46] The film's realistic aspects are combined with stunning cinematography of the arid, sun-drenched landscape. Beautiful shots of dawn or sunset permeate the film, such as in one of the opening scenes when a pregnant Darlene, wearing a simple bridal outfit, sets off from her mother's ramshackle home in the early hours of the morning on the back of a donkey. The impoverished nature of her surroundings and her precarious social situation are reinforced by her mother's suggestion that Darlene should not bother ever returning there, and her prayer that her grandchild not be born a girl. The natural beauty of the dawn, however, coupled with the diegetic crowing of a cockerel, lend an idyllic quality to the scene, a reflection of Darlene's indomitable spirit and determination to change her fate.

Various shots capture her in silhouette against an exquisite sunset, with the photography attenuating the harshness of the lifestyle and landscape. Yet these visually breathtaking shots equally underscore the pathos of the narrative, such as when Darlene returns on foot and grief-stricken from having given her eldest son away to the local *coronel* or political boss, presumably the child's biological father who abandoned her at the altar at the start of the film. Waddington's film thus successfully marries realism with aesthetic pleasure.

Me, You, Them also benefits from an upbeat and commercially appealing soundtrack, which earned it an award at the 2000 Havana Film Festival, consisting largely of the local folk music called *forró*. Gilberto Gil, former *enfant terrible* of the Tropicália movement in Brazilian popular music in the late 1960s, and now Minister of Culture in the Lula government, re-recorded classic examples of this musical genre by legendary North-Eastern singer Luiz Gonzaga for the film's soundtrack, which proved to be a tremendous commercial success in its own right. The film was equally well received both at film festivals, such as Cannes and Brazil's own Gramado festival, and among the general public at home and abroad. One hundred copies of the film were exhibited in Brazil, and it allegedly paid for itself with overseas sales alone, irrespective of box-office receipts.

Behind the Sun

Behind the Sun, directed by Walter Salles, is a tale of two feuding families set in 1910 again in Brazil's North-Eastern *sertão*.[47] The main characters are the two sons of the Breves family, dirt-poor and dogged by the moral obligation to avenge the murder of their brother. The continuing conflict over land, fired by the strict honour code of this backward region, results in brutal violence and death for various members of each family. Salles has stated that the physical geography of the setting is central to the nature and behaviour of the film's characters, and thus he chose to shoot his film on location 800 kilometres from the city of Salvador in the north-west of the state of Bahia, and 100 kilometres from the nearest hotel. He obliged the central actors to live the life of the protagonists, carrying out hard manual labour in 40-degree heat to process sugar cane using archaic methods for an entire month.[48] The tragedies inherent in the story line and the barren geographical setting are made more palatable by the stunning vistas captured by the acclaimed cinematographer Walter Carvalho, who had previously worked on Salles's *Central Station*. The audience's visual pleasure is similarly enhanced via a painterly mise-en-scène, in which low-key lighting evokes the constant presence of death.

Criticisms could be levelled at Salles's film for inappropriate casting decisions that owe more to commercial considerations than the desire for authenticity and verisimilitude. The elder son, Tonho, is played by the strikingly handsome former TV actor Rodrigo Santoro,[49] whose 'Mediterranean' movie star good looks provide welcome relief from the arid landscape, the material poverty in which the characters live, the repetitive and doomed nature of their existence, and the tragic plot. Unlike Wagner Moura, another good-looking young actor well known to TV and film audiences in Brazil, who plays the rather gauche, bespectacled offspring of the rival Ferreira clan, Santoro does not have his physical charms toned down for this role, and they form a marked contrast with those of the other members of the Breves family. His younger brother, Pacu, is played by Ravi Ramos Lacerda, originally a street-theatre performer and non-professional actor from an amateur theatre group, whose features and skin tone suggest a mixed racial heritage. Santoro had come to the director's attention not via his TV work but in the lead role of the film *Bicho de sete cabeças* (*Brainstorm*, 2000), for which he won the Best Actor award at the Brasília and the Recife film festivals in 2000. He was chosen for his proven acting skills, and his presence in *Behind the Sun* clearly contributed to the film's box-office appeal, as his star billing in the trailers confirmed.

José Carlos Avellar has remarked on the similarities between the character traits of Tonho's family and those of the protagonists of Nelson Pereira dos Santos's *Barren Lives*, not least the monosyllabic father. The feud between the two families in *Behind the Sun* is mirrored by the stifled conflict that exists within Tonho's home, where his younger brother defies the order imposed by his authoritarian, stubborn-minded father.[50] Salles's film also evocatively draws on the imagery of Glauber Rocha's *Black God, White Devil*, more specifically the well-known line 'the *sertão* will become the sea, and the sea will become the *sertão*'. At the close of *Behind the Sun*, and after the needless death of his younger brother, Pacu, who himself also daydreamed about tales of the sea, Tonho makes the migratory journey from the hinterland to the coast.[51] But in contrast to the long sequence shots of the *cinema novo* classics mentioned above, which served to accentuate spatial continuity and the real physical effort required, a series of short takes sees Tonho walking calmly across the parched interior, soon emerging, thanks to the power of editing, in sand dunes on the coast.[52] *Behind the Sun* presents a pre-capitalist *sertão*, frozen in time, with a very different ideological perspective to that of the region's treatment by *cinema novo* filmmakers. The images of the sea at the end of the film are poetic ones that represent the victory of the individual over the societal restraints traditionally imposed on his freedom, in contrast to the restless sea in the closing scenes of *Black God, White Devil*, which suggest the time for revolutionary action has arrived.[53]

Conclusion

Many filmmakers of the *retomada* have sought to portray the locus of contemporary Brazil and to debate the feasibility of the nation by turning their minds back to the central thematic binary of the *cinema novo* movement: the drought-stricken North-East and the *favelas* of the South-East. In marked contrast to the 'aesthetics of hunger' and 'violence' that characterised *cinema novo*, in films of the *retomada* 'conventional language and cinematography turn the *sertão* into a garden or a museum of exoticism, thus "rescuing" it through spectacle'. Bentes continues:

> It is a move from the 'aesthetics' to the 'cosmetics' of hunger, from the 'camera-in-hand and idea-in-mind' (a hand-to-hand battle with reality)

> to the steadicam, a camera that surfs on reality, a narrative that values beauty and the good quality of the image, and is often dominated by conventional techniques and narratives.[54]

The treatment of the *sertão* since the mid-1990s has combined the unavoidable presence of material scarcity and deprivation, provoked by both the area's climate and social injustices, with an embracing of high production values and the provision of visually pleasing entertainment for a mainstream audience raised on a diet of predominantly Hollywood fare.

In contrast to the *sertão* and its contemporary screen representations, the *favelas* and poor peripheries of Brazil's big cities, which were 'always the site for idealized dreams of a beautiful and dignified poverty' in Brazilian films from the 1950s and 1960s,[55] have been given a brutally realistic treatment in recent productions. As Arnaldo Jabor writes in relation to *The Trespasser*, *Carandiru*, *City of God* and *The Man of the Year*, 'the four films depict this new world that is growing like a cancer around us and which we only want to be distanced from and protected against'.[56] But it is precisely this gritty vision of urban Brazil that has increasingly caught the attentions and imaginations of both domestic and international audiences, as the box-office statistics for *City of God* and *Carandiru* attest. As Randal Johnson quite rightly argues,

> It makes little sense in the early 21st century, to expect Brazilian cinema to conform to the political idealism or the film aesthetics of the 1960s. Brazilian society has changed since then, as has Brazilian cinema. The one thing that has remained constant is the foreign occupation of the domestic market, with all of its implications.[57]

Cinematic portrayals of the underbelly of Brazil's urban realm have drawn on a kind of new realism that sees no conflict between Hollywood- and MTV-inspired camera work, stylistic techniques and soundtracks, and attempts to denounce an actuality of poverty, injustice and social exclusion that is aggravated by the corrosive effects of a mass media-fuelled desire for material consumption and social status. In this thematic context the distinction between works of fiction and documentary films is becoming increasingly blurred as 'real people' enact their own life experiences on screen, and non-fiction films incorporate cinematic techniques traditionally exclusive to fictional narratives. In both cases, and from opposite directions, each type of film is seeking to 'enforce the tangibility of the "real", essential to the realist experience in media cultures saturated with images, hyper-stimulations, spectacularized events and technological reinventions of nature'.[58]

Part IV

BRAZILIAN IDENTITIES ON SCREEN

Stars

10

THE STARS OF THE *CHANCHADAS*, 1933–60

This chapter will focus on four major stars, two female and two male, who came to prominence in the *chanchada* musical comedies that dominated film production in Brazil between 1930 and 1960. It will focus in particular on their star texts from the perspective of 'national' identities, whether based on race, class or gender. Carmen Miranda was a green-eyed, white-skinned woman of southern European descent, who became the respectable face of a pan-Latino identity in Hollywood during the 'Good Neighbour Policy' of the late 1930s and 1940s, and yet she self-consciously based her stage persona and performances on intrinsically African elements of Brazilian culture. Eliana (Macedo) became Brazil's home-grown screen sweetheart in the late 1940s and 1950s, the wholesome, fresh-faced, pale-skinned girl-next-door of the Atlântida *chanchadas*, whose screen persona owed more than a little to Hollywood stars such as Debbie Reynolds. Her star text was complicated further by her frequent reworking on screen of the racially marked *baiana* figure, made famous by Miranda in Hollywood. Oscarito and Grande Otelo are the most famous comic double act in Brazilian cinematic history, and starred together in thirteen of Atlântida's musical comedies (see Figure 10.4). It has been argued that the 'Brazilianness' of the *chanchada* lay in the tradition's comic elements, and chiefly the comedy roles played by Oscarito and Grande Otelo. They are both synonymous with exaggerated physical characteristics: Oscarito's puny body and facial features, namely his bulbous nose, full cheeks and odd-shaped mouth, that have been likened to a clown's mask,[1] and Grande Otelo's very black skin, thick lips and bulging eyes, which are conducive to an interpretation of his physicality as a caricature of Afro-Brazilianness.

Nationhood and ethnicity

Until the coup of 1930 Brazilian nationhood had largely been a white construction. Racial democracy was a widely accepted myth, propagated by members of the white elite, apologists who had benefited from the slavocracy that only came to an end in 1888. Perhaps the most well-known defender of Brazil's history of racial harmony was Gilberto Freyre, although, well before the publication in 1933 of his pseudo-sociological study *Casa grande e senzala* (*The Masters and the Slaves*), the abolitionist politician Joaquim Nabuco had already compared Brazil to other slave economies in the most favourable terms. The realities of post-Abolition Brazil, however, were deep-rooted prejudice and discrimination against Afro-Brazilians, whose labour was replaced with that of idealised white European immigrant workers, and widespread fear of the black, polluting menace, whipped up by a racist press. With the installation of the first Vargas regime (1930–45) nationalism was placed firmly at the top of the political agenda, with the aim of fostering a sense of belonging, known in the rhetoric as *brasilidade* or 'Brazilianness', to the explicit detriment of racial, ethnic or class identifications. The nationalisation of Afro-Brazilian culture, not least samba music, meant the emergence and promotion of white-skinned performers (the utilisation of white masks, to quote from Franz Fanon's work[2]), such as Carmen Miranda, whose image and face could be applauded by the upper, middle and popular classes.[3]

Creating a star system in Brazil

From the early 1920s, Brazilian film magazines were instrumental in fostering a sense of a fledgling film industry to which the creation of home-grown stars was central. They were thus responsible for creating film stardom in Brazil at a time when the so-called Brazilian stars rarely appeared on screen, thanks to the domination of the Brazilian market by Hollywood. These popular publications included *Para Todos* (1924–26), *Selecta* (1924–30), *Cinearte* (1926–42), *A Scena Muda* (1922–55) and *Cinelândia* (1952–64). It has been estimated that in its heyday *Cinearte* was read by 100,000 people from all over Brazil and therefore played an unprecedented role in shaping the public's perceptions and expectations in relation to screen icons.[4] Magazines of this type became the key vehicles for disseminating standards of feminine beauty, modernity and fashion. *Cinearte* in particular reflected the fact that Hollywood had taken over from Paris in dictating the clothes that women should wear and the hairstyles they should copy.[5] These magazines established a homogenised aesthetic of female beauty and photogeneity that was imported wholesale from Hollywood, even incorporating the English terms for classifying the acceptable types of screen actress, who had 'it', 'sex-appeal' or 'spleen', for example, who covered the whole gamut of roles from 'vamp' to 'ingenue'.[6] Concessions were made to Brazil's patriarchal traditions and Catholic conservatism, with the press toning down the risqué connotations of the 'star texts' of actresses who played vamps on screen in their reporting, as the following item reveals:

> Lying on a divan with a distracted air, a cigarette in her hand and with lively, intense eyes like those of Clara Bow . . . She had 'it'! . . .
>
> But when Lia Jardim was introduced to me I was able to see just how photographs can be deceiving . . .
>
> . . .
>
> Of medium height, on the short side, with short hair, she looked more like an inoffensive 'flapper', just nervous, simply sweet, considerate, good-natured and easy-going.[7]

The Aryan model of white skin was adopted in Brazil for both female and male screen stars, and actively promoted in *Cinearte*.[8] In the magazine, 'there was only space for one image, one Brazil'.[9] Its editors dictated that quality films had to be photogenic, in line with ideals of beauty linked to hygiene, luxury and youthfulness. The critic Ismail Xavier has analysed an article published in the magazine, attributed to a psychiatrist by the name of Dr Louis Bisch, an eminent 'scientific authority', on the subject of sex appeal, which stated that quality cinema involved showing beautiful people on screen, in beautiful photogenic landscapes or sumptuous settings.[10] The unwritten rules of Brazil's racial hierarchy, historically underpinned by the insidious ideology of 'whitening', were central to the emerging star system's visual aesthetics, and it was no coincidence that an article in *Cinearte* in 1929 stated:

> Making quality films in Brazil must involve purifying our reality, by selecting aspects that deserve to be shown on screen: progress, works of modern engineering, our beautiful white people, our natural wonders. No documentaries, since you cannot totally control what is shown and undesirable elements can infiltrate them; we need a studio-made cinema, like the North American model, with well-decorated interiors featuring agreeable people.[11]

Cinelândia *magazine*

In Brazil in the 1950s, *Cinelândia* magazine was the main vehicle for creating 'star texts', taking over the baton from *Cinearte*. Inspiration was provided by US magazines like *Photoplay* or the *Moving Picture World*, and *Cinelândia* borrowed their techniques for constructing star discourse, such as reviews of Brazilian and Hollywood films, film stills and publicity shots of stars supposedly in their real home environment, and gossip columns direct from Hollywood, such as that of the infamous Hedda Hopper (which was printed in Portuguese in the Brazilian magazine). *Cinelândia* actively sought the co-operation of the Brazilian studios in its creation of a star system, as its editorial declared in the debut number of May 1952: 'We hope that national studios will organise themselves to facilitate our task, having photos taken of stars and their homes, facilitating reports, supplying, in short, previously unpublished and interesting material.' Nevertheless, in the editorial of the magazine's second number, the lack of publicity material, especially photos of 'stars', and of Brazilian films was bemoaned.

Miss Cinelândia

Like the North American magazines, *Cinelândia* targeted female readers, as the predominance of adverts for beauty products attests. It often also contained articles on the beauty tips of Hollywood stars. The magazine also promoted its own beauty contest, designed to 'discover' and launch the careers of future screen stars, copying the competitions organised by the major Hollywood studios and promoted in the press, a strategy adopted by many national film industries. As early as 1928 a 'Contest for Female and Male Photogenic Beauty' was held in Brazil, which tantalised would-be stars with the first prize of a contract with Fox studios in Hollywood.[12] The 'Miss Cinelândia' contest offered readers of the magazine the chance to win a contract with the Atlântida studio to appear in at least one feature film. Some winners were also treated to a trip to California and a screen test at a Hollywood studio, such as Wilma Sozzi, Miss Cinelândia 1955, who is pictured in the magazine chatting intimately with Tony Curtis, and visiting both Universal Studios and Warner Brothers.[13] Entry coupons were printed in the magazine, and the possibility of becoming a film star through this competition was emphasised by countless articles about or interviews with 'stars' who had been 'discovered' in this way. The judges were clearly looking for a pale-skinned brand of Hollywood beauty, as is evidenced by the entry form, which required entrants to state their *tez* or complexion, as well as sending in two photographs of themselves. The possible categories of *tez* are suggested by an advertisement for Coty beauty advice that appeared in the magazine, asking readers if their complexion was *clara* (pale), *rosada* (pink) or *morena* (dark). An interview with Miss Cinelândia 1954, Avany Maura, tellingly describes her as having 'a *slightly* dark complexion'.[14]

Carmen Miranda (1909–55)

Samba star

Before her departure for the United States in 1939, and her subsequent landslide success on Broadway and in Hollywood, Carmen Miranda was a star of the Brazilian recording industry, radio and talking cinema. She had by then made almost 300 records in Brazil, and was recognised in the local press as the biggest female singing star. As early as 1933 she was among the most popular interpreters of samba to emerge from the song festivals or concerts that popularised the genre among the middle class, and in recognition of her status she was invited to perform on Rio's radio stations. In 1933 she won a national competition to act as the 'Ambassador of Samba' and perform on stage and radio in Argentina. The following year she was voted 'Queen of Rio Broadcasting' by readers of the newspaper *A Hora*.[15] Even before her own appearance on screen, Miranda's recordings were played to entertain cinema audiences before the curtain went up, alongside those of the leading male crooner of the era, Francisco Alves.

Screen stardom

Miranda's star billing within the recording industry in Brazil in the 1930s virtually guaranteed her a place in early Brazilian sound films. She first appeared on screen singing a selection of her hit songs in the 1933 production *A voz do carnaval* (The Voice of Carnival), and went on to star in the musicals *Alô, alô, Brasil!* (Hello,

Hello, Brazil!, 1935) and *Alô, alô, Carnaval!* (Hello, Hello, Carnival!, 1936), which premiered in the run-up to carnival, as well as the musical comedy *Estudantes* (Students, 1935). Her last appearance in a Brazilian film came in 1939 in the film *Banana da terra* (see Figure 10.1).[16]

Much has been written on the artifice of Miranda's representation of a generic Brazilian/Latino identity in Hollywood movies such as *Down Argentine Way* (1940) and *The Gang's All Here* (1943).[17] Her star text in Brazil before her departure to the USA has, however, been largely overlooked. In the late 1920s she had already begun to tap into Brazil's emerging star system. She sent a photograph of herself wearing an elegant hat and wavy, shoulder-length hair to *Cinearte* magazine, which was published alongside that of another hopeful on 18 December 1929 with the caption 'Readers of *Cinearte* who wish to be involved in Brazilian cinema'.[18] Just six years later, shortly after the premiere of *Alô, alô, Brasil!* in 1935, the magazine consecrated her star status: 'Carmen Miranda is, today, the most popular figure in Brazilian cinema, judging by the impressive correspondence that she receives.'[19] Copious numbers of readers' letters were published that requested the publication of photos of or interviews with Miranda, and there were constant rumours of future film projects in Brazil, Argentina and Europe.

Performing Brazilian identity: the baiana

In the 1930s Miranda was already articulating a complex negotiation of Brazilian urban identity. She became the darling of President Vargas's nationalistic regime, particularly after the creation of the authoritarian New State in 1937, whose propaganda machine sought to transform her into its unofficial 'cultural ambassador' in North America and beyond. She represented the muse of the 'Good Neighbour Policy' not only for the US administration but equally for Brazil.[20] In *Alô, alô, Carnaval!* she and her sister Aurora perform a memorable rendition of the song 'Cantoras do rádio' (Radio singers), wearing striking silver lamé trouser suits, bow ties and top hats. Like their outfits, the lyrics of the carnival *marcha* (march) they perform celebrate modernity: 'We are the radio singers / Our songs cross blue space / and unite in a big embrace / hearts from north to south.' As McCann observes,

> the Miranda sisters do not dance the *marcha* the way a Brazilian carnival dancer might, with syncopated elbow and hip movements, but instead high-step on the beat, in vaudevillian fashion. The overall effect is decidedly cosmopolitan, a page out of a contemporary Hollywood musical.[21]

In contrast, in 1939 Carmen Miranda appeared on screen for the first time in what would become her trademark, the caricatured, folkloric *baiana* costume, in the musical film *Banana da terra*, released in February, the same month in which she recorded the smash hit song from the film, 'O que é que a baiana tem?' (What

Figure 10.1 Carmen Miranda wearing a *baiana* costume in a scene from *Banana da terra* (Banana of the Land, 1939), produced by the Sonofilmes studio (courtesy of BBC Wales; reproduced with kind permission from Maria Byington, and with the technical assistance of Rosângela Sodré, CTAv, and Mauro Domingues, Labdigital, Arquivo Nacional)

has the *baiana* got?). In an iconic sequence on a primitive set of a stylised colonial-style street under a full moon, coconut palm and street lamp, she sings this song by Dorival Caymmi. Taking her cue from the song's lyrics, Miranda (who had previously trained as an apprentice milliner) went with Caymmi to the dressmakers to choose the fabric for her outfit and the two then set off in search of *balangandãs* (the metal, ornamental amulets worn by real-life *baianas*). Her costume incorporated all the other key aspects of this traditional Afro-Brazilian dress, in line with the song's self-referential lyrics. But the addition of fruit to the turban was Miranda's inspired initiative, transforming the baskets of fruit that the female street vendors of Salvador da Bahia carried on their heads into what would become the first of many edible turbans. In 1939 real-life *baianas* could be found not only selling food on the streets of Rio and Salvador, but also leading the rituals of the Afro-Brazilian religion, *candomblé*, or in the ranks of Rio's so-called samba schools, the neighbourhood carnival groups, paying homage to the Bahian women, such as Tia Ciata, responsible for bringing samba from the North-East to the capital and subsequently the rest of the nation in the first decades of the twentieth century.[22] The *baiana* persona was already popular in the revues of the low-brow *teatro de revista* or music hall in the 1920s. The costume was thus intimately associated with Brazil's poor, marginalised black population, and Miranda's adoption of it was a pioneering move, prompting its popularity as a carnival costume among white Brazilians, not least men. Indeed, she once referred in interview to being warned off adopting this racialised persona: '"You can't put theez dress . . . because theez dress only Negroes put." Bah! I put gold an' silk an' velvet, an' I seeng song in movie.'[23]

The Afro-Brazilian elements of Miranda's screen costumes, gestures and dance moves have been analysed in detail by José Ligiero Coelho.[24] The dance she performed while singing the duet 'Pirolito' in *Banana da terra* has been kept for posterity only in the form of a series of five snapshots, which reveal that she

> did not assume the character of a black girl as a parody or caricature, but rather as another aspect of her own expression. Her behavior is very far from the glamour girl she showed off in the beginning of her career.[25]

When performing 'What has the *baiana* got?' in the film she wore large hoop earrings, a typical adornment for women of African descent in Brazil, and used her arms and hands to emphasise the meaning of the lyrics, pointing to the items referred to in the following verse as if she were a street vendor:

> What has the *baiana* got?
> She's got a silk turban
> A golden necklace
> A *pano da costa* [shawl]
> An embroidered blouse
> A gold bracelet
> A starched skirt
> Decorated sandals

Some of the poses and movements she adopted are of her own invention, but others can be traced to the Bantu tradition taken to Brazil by African slaves, creating a stylised samba inspired by Afro-Brazilian performers in Rio's samba parades or informal black gatherings or parties she attended with her Afro-Brazilian composer friends.[26] 'Miranda', Coelho writes, 'embodied the gestures of the Afro-Brazilian population, which she knew very well because of her background in Lapa and her numerous *sambista* collaborators.'[27]

Miranda catapulted the ethnically loaded persona of the *baiana* to the elite Urca casino, where Afro-Brazilians were allowed on stage but not in the audience. In doing so she was confirming her identification with an underdog, Afro-Brazilian culture that was nevertheless being moulded into an expression of national identity by the Vargas regime. (It was this performance of 'What has the *baiana* got?' which attracted the attention of US show business impresario Lee Shubert.) Nevertheless, for the upmarket context of the Urca casino, a more sophisticated version of the costume was required. She wore a white dress, with a wide black band across it, embellished with an image of Sugar Loaf Mountain, designed by the artist Gilberto Trompowski, accessorised with necklaces and a turban decorated with tiny baskets of fruit.[28] The stylised look was born, and it soon caught on. Shortly after Miranda signed a contract with Shubert to star on Broadway, Josephine Baker arrived in Rio and performed her own version of 'What has the *baiana* got?' at the Urca casino.[29]

Personifying 'Brazil' at home and abroad

Miranda was 'epidermically white',[30] having been born in Portugal to Portuguese parents just a few short years before the family's arrival as immigrants in Rio de Janeiro. She nevertheless embraced Afro-Rio from the start, frequenting the samba circles of the then capital's poorer quarters and shantytowns, rubbing shoulders with the emerging genre's Afro-Brazilian creators. In her repertoire she favoured compositions written by black or mixed-race artists such as Assis Valente, Pixinguinha and Dorival Caymmi, recording countless sambas whose lyrics asserted the music's ethnic background.[31] She maintained this preference even into the late 1930s and 1940s, when the propagandists of the *Estado Novo* and the growing respectability of samba both among white radio listeners and record buyers and among white popular composers ensured that the genre conveyed an increasingly 'national' rather than racially marked identity.

On 4 January 1939 she performed Ari Barroso and Luís Iglesias's composition 'Boneca de Piche' (Tar Doll) in the official 'Popular Music Day' celebrations at the New State's 'Feira de Amostras' fair, a song that she had recorded on disc the previous year. She sang: ' Jet black, the colour of berries / I'm a tar doll', and, in a photograph taken during this performance, she can be seen on stage with the singer and radio presenter Almirante, her face clearly darkened with exaggerated make-up, as was the tradition when performing this particular samba.[32] Indeed, Miranda often appeared in blackface when performing songs featuring Afro-Brazilian characters. In *Banana da terra* she was originally due to perform 'Boneca de Piche' in duet with Almirante, but the song was replaced with 'Pirolito' owing to a dispute with Ari Barroso over copyright payments. In the film, she and Almirante perform the new song, which contains no references to black culture, wearing the same costumes and blackened faces that had been planned for the performance of 'Tar Doll'.[33]

Miranda's personification of Brazil as 'fertile land of plenty/banana republic' in Hollywood was seen by many Brazilians as patronising and mildly offensive. More recently critics have identified a knowing parodic element in her stage persona, betraying a creative use of some of the empty clichés of Hollywood's *Latinidad*. Her increasingly farcical costumes, heavily accented English and frequent malapropisms can be interpreted as 'a nod to the requirements of a conception of foreignness and "otherness" necessary to maintain the validity of the text in question as well as her persona as a gesture of good neighborliness'.[34] A further clue as to Miranda's agency within what appears to be an imposed Latino stereotype lies in her first screen appearance as a *baiana* back in Brazil in 1939. *Banana da terra* was set in the fictitious Pacific island of Bananolândia that is faced with a surplus of bananas, a thinly veiled caricature of North America's hackneyed vision of Brazil/Latin America. In this context, Miranda's incongruous appearance as a white woman in stylised Afro-Brazilian dress could be seen as part and parcel of the film's self-deprecating humour and tongue-in-cheek critique of Hollywood stereotyping and sanitising of the true ethnic make-up of South America.

Her Hollywood *baianas* made a huge impact back in Brazil and appeared to play a role in shaping Brazilian national identity, regardless of the glitz they acquired in California. The creations she wore in *That Night in Rio* (1941), designed by Travis Banton, were so widely commented on in the Brazilian press that the organisers of the Rio carnival parade requested replicas from the Twentieth Century Fox wardrobe department, to serve as inspiration for carnival revellers back in Brazil. Her stylised version of the costume became the template for Brazil's national costume in international beauty pageants, the outfit worn by the white Brazilian hatcheck girls at the restaurant in the Brazilian pavilion at the 1939 World's Fair in New York, and even the clothes worn by souvenir dolls. Thanks to her performance of 'What has the *baiana* got?' in *Banana da terra*, the largely unknown regional term *balangandã* entered the everyday vocabulary of Brazilians all over the nation. In August 1939 a stage production entitled *Joujoux e balangandãs* (Trinkets and amulets) was performed at Rio's Municipal Theatre, to raise funds for the charitable works of Brazil's First Lady, Darcy Vargas, a sure sign that the ethnically loaded term had now gained national respectability. The show culminated with the performance of the song 'Nós temos balangandãs' (We have amulets) by a group of white women in caricatured *baiana* costumes. Just a few weeks later the Brazilian press was advertising a forthcoming show to be held at the Urca casino called *Urca's Balangandãs* and billed as 'the voice and the music of Brazil for tourists'.[35] This 'exotic' term had captured the Zeitgeist and had become a metonym for Carmen's *baiana* persona, and in turn Brazilian national identity. Her wider legacy within Brazilian cinema was most closely felt in the scores of white look-alikes who appeared in the musical and dance sequences of the 1950s *chanchadas*, and particularly the penchant shown on screen by Eliana Macedo for the Hollywoodesque *baiana* look.

Eliana Macedo (1925–90)

Eliana Macedo, in her heyday known throughout Brazil simply as Eliana, starred in over twenty films and was Brazil's screen sweetheart. On her death in 1990, Luiz Carlos Merten wrote in the newspaper *Estado de São Paulo*: 'For a long time – throughout the 1950s – she was the biggest and perhaps the only female star in Brazilian cinema.'[36] Eliana was the quintessential *mocinha* or girl-next-door of the Atlântida musical comedies or *chanchadas* of the late 1940s and 1950s, the pretty, clean-cut heroine of the narrative, who also appeared in the song and dance numbers.

A worthy star

Eliana's star status, evidenced by her top billing in movie credits, is confirmed by her frequent presence in *Cinelândia* magazine, in which she was among a small minority of Brazilian stars who appeared on the front cover. From an analysis of Eliana's star text as constructed in this magazine, it appears to constitute what Dyer would term a 'perfect fit' with the roles she played in the *chanchadas*.[37] In fact, the magazine even goes so far as to blur the boundaries between Eliana and the roles she plays on screen. The following description of the plot of the *chanchada Vamos com calma* (Let's Go Quietly, 1956) is a clear illustration of this:

> Luís Carlos [Cyl Farney] doesn't have time to suffer as a result of this setback in his love life since Sandra (Eliana, who just gets prettier and prettier!) is on hand to console him. And who wouldn't be consoled in a split second learning to love a girl like Eliana, sorry, Sandra?[38]

Dyer argues that there are four rules to becoming a star:

1 You have to be an ordinary person, like the rest of us.
2 Fate/luck has to shine on you – the idea that 'it could happen to anyone'.
3 You have to have something special, a talent or gift that makes you different.
4 To reach stardom requires hard work and professionalism.

In a given star text, one or more of these 'rules' may be emphasised more than others, but in the case of Eliana all four are dutifully abided by. Descriptions of her young life in *Cinelândia* magazine stress that she was like any other girl of her time – 'the girl next door'. She travelled from the countryside to the then capital of Brazil, Rio de Janeiro, to visit her uncle (who just so happened to be a film director). Many people made this same migratory journey in real life in the 1940s and 1950s, as did the characters of the *chanchadas*. But fate took a hand in her life – she 'just so happened' to visit her uncle, the director Watson Macedo, in the Atlântida studio in Rio. She maintains that she did not ever dream of becoming a star, and that it happened almost against her will. Her sweet nature, innocence, playfulness and prettiness are emphasised in the magazine's reports and interviews. The combination of all these desirable qualities sets her apart from ordinary girls and makes her a deserving star. She is portrayed as totally lacking in vanity, and a clean-living, exemplary housewife, who does not like expensive clothes (preferring to make her own, and allowing her mother to make her costumes for her film roles). An article published in *Cinelândia* in July 1954 claimed that she only wore glamorous outfits on screen, preferring a more modest wardrobe more suited to her discreet life in Niterói, the city across the bay from Rio de Janeiro, which is inevitably overshadowed by its iconic neighbour.

Cinelândia magazine and the star system in Brazil were clearly moulded on Hollywood's versions, but there were some important differences that reflected the norms of a patriarchal, Catholic society in Brazil in the 1950s. Thus Brazilian female stars like Eliana are always depicted as being closely linked to their families and homes, nurturing girls who turned their back on luxuries and nightlife (unlike their Hollywood counterparts). In this respect Brazilian filmmakers continued to employ a tactic developed in the silent era, by which they succeeded in catering to female spectators by creating stars who 'curiously adapted patriarchal ideology, and mediated between the public persona of the new woman and the traditional domestic female sphere'.[39] The dominant impression that Brazilian readers gained of Eliana was just how much she was like them – an ordinary young woman who simply found herself in a very extraordinary position and posed no threat to the country's age-old social and gender hierarchies. Her love of sports forms part of her youthful vitality, but is equally a way of controlling her potentially threatening screen sexuality. In interviews she stresses how hard she had to work to perfect her skills as an actress. Her efforts to control her weight and preserve an adolescent body are equally part of the hard work and discipline required in order to become and remain a star.

The Brazilian 'Debbie Reynolds'

Cinelândia continually emphasised that Eliana was the match for any Hollywood star, and her star text was clearly modelled on those of her North American rivals. She is referred to, for example, as the Brazilian 'pin-up' or the Brazilian 'Miss Sweater' (the English terms are used). The magazine also assures its readers that she is an equal match for Betty Grable or Jane Russell.[40] Her similarity to US star Debbie Reynolds, in particular, as commented on by João Luiz Vieira and Robert Stam,[41] can clearly be seen in two of the front covers of *Cinelândia* magazine (see Figures 10.2 and 10.3).[42] Both were their respective nations' sweethearts, epitomising youth, vitality, prettiness, sweetness and whiteness. In film stills and publicity shots both Eliana and Debbie are dressed to appear younger than their years, often with their hair in ponytails. Their promotion in *Cinelândia* also stressed their childlike/adolescent qualities, even when both were married women in their mid- to late 20s. An article on Eliana entitled 'Assim é Eliana' (This is what Eliana is like) supposedly catches her unawares, thus revealing the 'truth' behind her star text.[43] It focuses on her recent weight loss that makes her look and act even more like a teenager. She is described as 'the blond, radiant, youthful star of Brazilian cinema', and is photographed playing with a teddy bear and cuddly toy dog, part of her collection of soft toys. Unlike Debbie Reynolds's celebrity union with Eddie Fischer (the same issue of the magazine dedicates two pages to their wedding), Eliana's marriage to radio star Renato Murce was downplayed (although a rare, and admittedly small, photo of them together appears here). Murce was much older, previously married and thus not seen as a fitting enhancement of her youthful image. Instead, she was often pictured in film stills, reproduced by *Cinelândia*, with the heart-throb of the *chanchada*, Cyl Farney, equally chosen for his Hollywood-style good looks. A publicity still of them smiling and gazing into each

Figure 10.2 Eliana Macedo on the cover of *Cinelândia* magazine (courtesy of the Biblioteca Nacional, Rio de Janeiro)

Figure 10.3 Debbie Reynolds on the cover of *Cinelândia* magazine (courtesy of the Biblioteca Nacional, Rio de Janeiro)

other's eyes bears the caption: 'Cyl Farney and Eliana are together again. Brazil's most adored romantic couple co-star in *Vamos com calma*.'[44]

Eliana, the baiana

In apparent contradiction of her epidermis and innocent, homely roles in the narrative, Eliana often appears in the song and dance sequences of the *chanchadas* wearing the sexy stylised *baiana* costume revealing her bare midriff. Her 'whitening' of this ethnically marked persona should also be considered within the context of her often ludicrous 'racial' casting, such as in *Samba em Brasília* (Samba in Brasilia), where she plays a humble shantytown inhabitant well versed in *macumba*, who claims to be a priestess of this Afro-Brazilian religion. Black culture, in the form of samba, was central to the soundtrack of these films, yet its creators were consistently sidelined on screen (the notable case of leading actor Grande Otelo being the exception that proved the rule). People of colour typically appear as musicians or dancers in the background, there to support the white stars and 'to visually "set off" the beauty and elegance of the white elite', as Stam has argued.[45] Eliana's *baianas* are the ultimate example of the stylisation and ethnic cleansing of symbols of black Brazil. Paradoxically, her whiter-than-white face is the acceptable face of Afro-Brazilian culture in these films.

In her first film, *E o mundo se diverte* (And the World has Fun, 1948), Eliana sings the well-known samba 'No tabuleiro da baiana' (On the *baiana*'s tray), a performance that is strikingly reminiscent of Aurora Miranda's rendition of another of Ari Barroso's sambas, 'Os quindins de Yayá' (Missy's coconut cakes), in Walt Disney's partially animated feature film *The Three Caballeros* (1945). Eliana's celluloid *baianas* clearly owe a debt of gratitude to such Hollywood images, not least those of Aurora's famous sister, Carmen. Whereas Carmen Miranda adopted the *baiana* as her alter ego in Brazil in order to give credibility to her performances of sambas with Afro-Brazilian themes, Eliana's rehashing of the persona in the late 1940s and 1950s formed part of her compliance with Hollywood ideals of beauty and sanitised Latino identity.

Oscarito (1906–70)

The white-skinned Oscarito's star text, endorsed by *Cinelândia* magazine, which hailed him as 'without doubt one of the biggest Brazilian stars',[46] hinged on his representations of the 'small man' in a constant, albeit comic, battle with the powers that be and the perils of urban life. Critics have likened this Brazilian icon, virtually unknown outside Brazil, to the Mexican star Cantinflas, Harpo Marx, Stan Laurel, Harold Lloyd, Buster Keaton and Charlie Chaplin, for both his comic genius and the roles he played.[47] He frequently portrayed a displaced rural–urban migrant, or an equally unassuming character, who from being down on his luck finds his fortunes temporarily overturned in a carnivalesque inversion of societal hierarchies that was the trademark of a *chanchada* plot. His screen persona encapsulates the very Brazilian concept of *jeitinho* or using one's wits to evade the law or get around an obstacle in life. He is an archetypal *malandro*, another pole of popular identity in Brazil, who rejects 'respectability' and hard toil in favour of a lazy existence on the margins of society. After a minor role as an exploited *otário* or sucker (the antithesis of the *malandro* hustler in Brazilian popular culture) in *Alô, alô, Carnaval!* (1936), in which he is tricked into handing over his money in a casino to a pair of con men (who declare 'Three cheers for the gullible stranger!'), Oscarito soon became synonymous with the downtrodden but ultimately triumphant anti-hero, a champion of popular identity who by the end of the *chanchada* always scores a small victory over authority or the social elite, usually by a quirk of fate or slightly underhand ruse.

Oscarito's parents were itinerant circus performers, who emigrated to Brazil a few years after their son had been born during a stay in Malaga, Spain. Oscarito claimed that his family had links with the circus dating back some 400 years, and when he was young he appeared in a circus act with his mother and sister, performing acrobatics, and with the black clown Benjamin de Oliveira, where he equally became skilled at physical comedy. In 1931 he took on the guise of a clown named Excêntrico (Eccentric) at the Democrat Circus in Rio de Janeiro. In 1932 Oscarito Brenier, as he was then known, made his first appearance in the *teatro de revista*, Brazil's brand of music hall or vaudeville, in the characteristically irreverent show *Calma, Gegê* (Calm down, Gegê – a common nickname for President Getúlio Vargas). It was on stage that his comic skills were honed and popular audiences began to identify with him and his Everyman persona. He enjoyed a successful career in popular theatre, travelling to Portugal in 1933 with Jardel Jércolis's company. He then made a smooth transition to cinema screens, making his film debut in *A voz do carnaval* (The Voice of Carnival, 1933) and earning his first leading role in *Banana da terra* (1939). He appeared in nine productions from the Cinédia and Sonofilmes studios, before signing the longest exclusive contract with the Atlântida studio in 1944, for which he worked until 1962, appearing in thirty-three films, invariably in a starring role, becoming the company's unofficial trademark and, according to Luiz Severiano Ribeiro, its 'gold mine'.[48]

The Brazilian underdog

On screen Oscarito became the stupid, socially marginalised Brazilian par excellence, designed to be laughed at but also empathised with. He was neither the first nor the last Brazilian actor to become synonymous with the *matuto* or *caipira*, the yokel or hick, bewildered upon his arrival in the big city. Audience members could laugh at and yet identify with the characters that Oscarito played, such as the impoverished rural migrant in *O homem do sputnik* (Sputnik Man, 1959) who does not understand how to behave in a city-centre bank in Rio, the henpecked Felismino in *Esse milhão é meu* (That Million Is Mine, 1958) who cowers in the face of his formidable wife, played by his real-life wife, Margaret Louro (in a further comic twist), or the yellow-bellied sheriff in the *High Noon* spoof *Matar ou correr* who bursts into tears as the villains approach. In *Treze cadeiras* (Thirteen Chairs, 1957) he again plays the role of an alienated yokel in the city, who openly admits 'Eu não conheço ninguém aqui' (I don't know anybody here). As Jerry Palmer has argued, for humour to be successful there must be a close correlation between the culture out of which it is produced and that of the receiver – a common 'frame of mind', a shared stock of information and an agreement on the emotional significance of the events portrayed in the joke/humour. Shared pleasure depends on some kind of common agenda.[49] There is little doubt that Oscarito struck a comic chord with mass audiences all over Brazil.

Slapstick, cross-dressing and parody

Oscarito's physical clowning on screen clearly owed a debt of gratitude to his circus background and formed an important part of his comic appeal. He embodied the tradition of the clumsy, socially inept man of the people, who almost gets knocked down by a bus in the chaotic streets of Rio de Janeiro in *Esse milhão é meu*. In this film his character, Felismino, appears in a ludicrous mock-flamenco dance sequence during which he drunkenly falls twice into the lap of an unattractive, portly and stony-faced female member of the audience. Male sexual desire is ridiculed in this film when Felismino makes a fool of himself with the showgirl Arlete by falling for her deception, and visually by way of his fumbling advances, which contrast sharply with her poise and almost choreographed seduction routine. As Alan Dale writes, 'the slapstick hero's skill at deploying his paradoxically acrobatic clumsiness is central to his status as an Everyman . . . It's one of our comic rituals because it's common – it happens to everyone.'[50] Oscarito's memorable appearances in drag equally gave ample evidence of his slapstick skills. In *Este mundo é um pandeiro* (This World Is a Tambourine, 1946) he performed a legendary parody of Rita Hayworth in the movie *Gilda*, for which he studied the relevant section of the Hollywood film assiduously. His very visual comedy appealed to children and adults, and his brand of humour afforded the poor, uneducated masses, many displaced migrants, a sense of belonging by being 'in on the joke' rather than it being at their expense, creating an intimacy through mutual comprehension.

Oscarito came to be known for his parodic skits of authority figures. In *Nem Sansão, nem Dalila* (Neither Samson nor Delilah, 1954) he parodies President Getúlio Vargas, mimicking his intonation and gestures, and refers to himself as *um homem de ação* (a man of action), just a short hop from one of Vargas's self-styled nicknames, *o homem de ação* (the man of action). In *Aviso aos navegantes* (Calling All Sailors, 1950) he plays a poor stowaway on a ship who manages to pass himself off as the vessel's doctor by spouting pseudo-medical nonsense in order to gain a closer examination of a female patient's cleavage and take a comic swipe at authority figures. Turning the tables on the elite and laughing at their expense provided welcome relief for marginalised audiences and ensured Oscarito's appeal as 'the man in the street'.

Star status

Oscarito's star status is confirmed by his presence in extra-filmic 'texts', such as film magazines. A short piece about his daughter's wedding that was published in *Cinelândia* in February 1956 (first fortnight), is accompanied by a photograph of him pulling a typically goofy face whilst unravelling a reel of his supposedly latest film, *Vamos com calma*. Other issues feature stills from this same film which emphasise his visual comedy, such as one of him in a skeleton costume[51] and another of him in an incongruous Scottish kilt next to an elegant Eliana in a ball gown and tiara.[52] 'Our very much loved and very funny Oscarito'[53] is an ordinary family man whose comic appeal, nevertheless, transcends social boundaries. *Cinelândia* (April 1956, first fortnight) dedicated several pages to a major feature on this Brazilian star, entitled 'A Happy Family'. Alongside photographs of him supposedly 'at home', inspecting the contents of a pan on the stove in his kitchen or jokingly performing in an 'improvised jazz band' with his family, we learn that:

> There is no one like Oscarito for getting the biggest laughs from the masses, and even from people less accustomed to this popular brand of humour . . . There is nobody so content with his life, at least when he is at home, surrounded by the love of his family, as we found him, on Saturday afternoon when we did this report . . . A happy family, indeed, that knows how to divide its time well, working a lot, it's true, but also enjoying a simple, honest life, as God would wish.

Oscarito's star text hinged on his physical propensity for comedy; he admitted in interview that he became aware early in his career that his looks were not conducive to serious, dramatic roles, and thus emulated his Uncle Alfonso's facial expressions and clowning, honed in the circus ring.[54] The film press reinforced this screen image by repeatedly referring to his childlike antics and publishing film stills which self-consciously drew his persona in marked contrast to that of the handsome leading men with whom he co-starred. In a still from *De vento em popa* (Wind in the Sails, 1957), for example, published in *Cinelândia*,[55] he appears pulling a characteristic grimace alongside the broad-shouldered, Hollywoodesque good looks of Cyl Farney, described as follows by the magazine: 'Tall, dark and friendly, he has a very similar physical presence and demeanour to Hollywood's youngest stars'.[56] In comic counterpoint to such screen glamour, Oscarito represented an essential Brazilian comedic response to the trials of life, an anti-hero with whom those on the bottom rungs of the social hierarchy could identify.

Grande Otelo (1915–93)

The diminutive Grande Otelo is, with the exception of Pelé, perhaps the most instantly recognisable black face in Brazil. He was a most accomplished actor in both comic and dramatic roles, who was described by Orson Welles as 'the greatest

Figure 10.4 Oscarito (centre) and Grande Otelo (left), in a scene from *E o mundo se diverte* (And the World Has Fun, 1948) (courtesy of the Cinemateca of the Museum of Modern Art, Rio de Janeiro; reproduced with kind permission from Atlântida)

comic actor of the 20th century' and by the Brazilian novelist Jorge Amado as 'the epitome of Brazil', and who appeared in over 100 Brazilian feature films.[57] He rose to prominence in the *chanchadas*, which tended to feature Afro-Brazilian performers only as bit-part actors or extras. Grande Otelo was the notable exception that proved the rule, starring as part of a double act, firstly with Oscarito and later with Ankito, both of whom were white. This section will examine Grande Otelo's 'star text' prior to 1960, focusing on its socio-racial implications.

Show business beginnings

Roberto Moura begins his biography of Grande Otelo by calling him 'A cara do Rio!' (the face of Rio!), forever associated in the popular memory of his generation with the *chanchadas* set in Brazil's then capital.[58] Born Sebastião Bernardes de Souza Prata in the provincial town of Uberlândia, in the state of Minas Gerais, to poor Afro-Brazilian parents, Grande Otelo became synonymous on screen with the black and mixed-race *carioca* (Rio) underclass. Educated in the best school in Uberlândia thanks to his unofficial 'adoption' by a well-off white family, a not uncommon practice in Brazil, the young Sebastião soon stood out, not only for his skin colour but equally for his exceptional intelligence, vivacity and natural comic skills. He found work as a singer in a local hotel when still a young boy, and soon showed a keen interest in the world of entertainment, especially the visiting circus troupes and the cinema. He was taken on as a *peludo* or helper by these itinerant circuses from São Paulo during their spells in the town, and when just 8 years of age he made his first appearance in the big top, dressed in drag as the wife of a clown. The story goes that he put on a long dress with pillows tied to his buttocks to create the impression of an amply proportioned matron. In the middle of a scene he tripped and his fake bottom fell to the floor, to great hilarity. He had discovered his slapstick comic skills.[59] He spent his earnings on trips to the cinema, but his natural charm soon gained him free access to the Brazilian and Hollywood movies. He took a particular interest in the first black faces he saw on screen, initially white actors in blackface but later Afro-Americans in patronising, stereotypical roles. He identified especially with Hollywood's comic character Topsy, a young black girl played by Mona Ray, and the African-American child star Allen Clayton Hoskins, who played Farina in the 'Our Gang' series of comic shorts between 1922 and 1931. Grande Otelo's big break came in 1924 when he was spotted performing in his home town with the Serrano circus by the classical singer Abigail Gonçalves, who took him to São Paulo and began teaching him the rudiments of acting.

The teatro de revista

Grande Otelo's first theatrical role established him as the perennial butt of jokes premised on his racial identity; he played 'the son of a German' who is, unsurprisingly, questioned about his skin colour.[60] He was then taken on by Genésio Arruda's theatre group in the city of Campinas,[61] in the interior of São Paulo state, where he probably came into direct contact with the first all-black Brazilian theatre group, the *Companhia Negra de Revistas*, formed by the Afro-Brazilian performer from Salvador, Bahia, João Cândido Ferreira, better known as De Chocolat, who had travelled to Paris and been inspired by Josephine Baker's *Revue Nègre*. When the Brazilian group staged their first show, aptly entitled *Tudo preto* (All black) on 31 June 1926, the press deemed it ridiculous, scandalous and even grotesque. Dubbed by journalists the 'eccentric jet black troupe',[62] they nevertheless took Rio by storm. The group later split into two, forming the *Companhia Negra de Revistas* and the *Ba-ta-clan Preta*, but both continued to put on shows which dealt, in a non-aggressive, understated way, with the theme of blacks in Brazilian society. Their shows had racially marked titles, such as *Café Torrado* (Roasted coffee), *Preto e Branco* (Black and white), *Carvão Nacional* (Brazilian coal) and *Na Penumbra* (At dusk). Sebastião introduced himself to the group when they performed at the Apolo theatre in Campinas, no longer under the command of De Chocolat, but still very much influenced by him. He was soon incorporated into its shows, under the name of 'Pequeno Othelo' (Little Othello), and shortly after arrived on the Rio stage for the first time.

After a spell out of the limelight, following the break-up of the *Companhia Negra de Revistas* and the *Ba-ta-clan Preta*, Grande Otelo began singing for a São Paulo radio station, from which he joined Zaíra Cavalcanti's travelling theatre group working around São Paulo state, and later made the acquaintance of show business impresario Jardel Jércolis, who took him back to Rio, where he became a leading light in the former's acting company, travelling with them to Argentina, Uruguay, Portugal and Spain.[63] He threw himself headlong into the city's bohemian night life and Afro-Brazilian culture, gaining a valuable insight into the cultural reference points and humour of the local population. Indeed, he went on to become an accomplished samba composer himself; around thirty of his sambas were recorded on disc and many found their way into film soundtracks. He appeared for the first time on stage under the name of 'The Great Othelo' at the João Caetano theatre in the production *Goal*, in recognition of his acting skills and in a joke at the expense of his physical stature and racial features.

Afro-Brazilian iconicity

In spite of the 'whitening' ideology of Brazil's Euro-elite, Afro-Brazilians had already represented popular identity to great success in popular entertainment, and in many ways Grande Otelo followed in the footsteps of the black clown Benjamin de Oliveira, the main attraction of the Spinelli circus at the turn of the century, and Eduardo das Neves, singing sensation in the *teatro de revista*, both of whom became 'respectable' emblems of the nation. On screen Grande Otelo became the acceptable face of black Brazil, but was racially stereotyped and infantilised in order to remove any threat to established socio-racial hierarchies. He made his cinematic debut in *Noites cariocas* (Rio Nights, 1935), and there followed a string of minor roles, as racially typecast errand boys, in films such as *João Ninguém* (Johnny Nobody, 1937) and *Futebol em família* (Family Football, 1939). In spite of his cinematic marginalisation he showed early evidence of his acting range; in *João Ninguém* he develops from a goofy young boy into a figure of pathos who is knocked down by a car at the climax of the film. 'He made the most of the opportunity', Moura writes, in 'a small role that underlined his already provisionally established notoriety'.[64] Moura adds that the mannerisms and facial expressions that Otelo incorporated into these roles, to such great effect, were *carioca* parodies of the parodies of American blacks performed by the Hollywood character Stepin Fetchit, played by the first black adult actor to be contracted by one of the major Hollywood studios, Lincoln Theodore Monroe Andrew Perry.[65] The characteristic physical clowning and exaggerated face-pulling of Grande Otelo, whom McCann calls 'bug-eyed'[66] and Vieira vividly describes as having 'rolling eyes, a wide white smile, thick lips that were always threatening to kiss you',[67] can also be seen in a more negative light. He could be interpreted as playing into the hands of racist caricature and stereotype, rather than sending it up, in the manner of the Jim Crow character of North American and subsequently British minstrelsy tradition, who performed a perceived 'nigger eccentricity' in his odd movements and dances.[68]

Like Oscarito, Otelo 'tended to incarnate a popularesque type in the grand comic tradition, characterized by broad gestures, exaggerated facial expressions, and acrobatic corporality'.[69]

Perhaps Grande Otelo could only be afforded star status when Afro-Brazilian culture had finally achieved a sanitised respectability, the latter possibly only achievable in the context of an international vogue for the African exotic. He thus only consolidated his star persona after appearing alongside Josephine Baker and, in turn, Carmen Miranda in shows for upper-crust audiences at the Urca casino (where blacks were not permitted in the audience, but where Otelo worked under contract for seven years) at the end of the 1930s. From then on he was given bigger parts in a series of musical comedies, such as *Pega ladrão* (Catch the Thief, 1940) and *Laranja da China* (Orange from China, 1940), in which he played a lowly pickpocket named Boneco de Piche (Tar Doll). His character's name in this film was an obvious comic reference to his skin colour, but it also played on the title of a popular song, 'Boneca de Piche', recorded by Carmen Miranda in 1938. Otelo's star status was confirmed by his collaboration with Orson Welles on the ill-fated film project *It's All True*. The US administration's 'cultural ambassador' to Latin America, charged with making a film to improve US–Brazilian relations in the context of the 'Good Neighbour Policy', chose Otelo as the protagonist of one of the film's three sections, entitled 'The History of Samba'. As Moura perceptively writes, 'It was in these years that Otelo constructed *carioca* identity, which was fundamental for his show business career.'[70] It was in the twenty-two productions that he appeared in for the Atlântida studio that his identification with the Rio underclass would be consolidated.

The Atlântida years

Atlântida's first feature-length production was a fictionalised semi-biography of Grande Otelo entitled *Moleque Tião* (Little Kid Tião, 1943). Combining location shooting with a socio-racial theme, this pioneering melodrama, which put Rio's poorer classes centre stage, proved to be a success both at the box office throughout Brazil's major cities and with the critics. Grande Otelo, the film's star, was thus established as a national icon. In Atlântida's *Tristezas não pagam dívidas* (Sadness Won't Pay Your Debts, 1944), Grande Otelo reverted to his theatrical comic persona, as a master of ceremonies cum narrator, who dances and clowns around for the amusement of the audience. Brazil's most famous 'black and white' double act, Oscarito and Grande Otelo (a pairing that played with oxymoronic physical contrasts as with many famous comic duos[71]), first appeared on screen together in the studio's musical comedy *Não adianta chorar* (It's No Good Crying, 1945). Between 1945 and 1955 Grande Otelo worked exclusively for Atlântida in partnership with Oscarito.[72]

In spite of his starring role in Atlântida's first production, *Moleque Tião*, and this film's courageous engagement with the issue of race in Brazil, Grande Otelo was destined to play second fiddle to Oscarito throughout their partnership on screen.

Whenever they appeared in the same film, it was always Oscarito who received the top billing. Only after the break-up of their partnership, when Grande Otelo starred in films such as *Malandros em quarta dimensão* (*Malandros* in the Fourth Dimension, 1954) alongside the lesser-known comics Colé and Jayme Costa, did the Afro-Brazilian actor appear at the top of the bill. Although this very topic was the central theme of Atlântida's 1953 production *A dupla do barulho* (The Terrible Twosome), this black actor, who had given considerable evidence of his professional talents, was overwhelmingly forced into a straitjacket of secondary roles as Oscarito's comic, rather childlike sidekick, the constant target of throwaway racial slurs and cheap physical jokes. In *E o mundo se diverte* (And the World Has Fun, 1948), for example, he answers the phone and describes himself to the woman on the other end of the line as follows: 'tall, neither fat nor thin, narrow nose, thin lips'. When asked if he is *moreno* (dark), he replies that he is more on the fair side. As Stam argues, 'the "gag" is premised on the self-rejection engendered by the "ideology of whitening"'.[73] In a later scene, a camera explodes in his face and that of his white co-star, Oscarito. The latter is covered with black soot, whereas Grande Otelo is dusted with white powder, in a typically carnivalesque overturning of ethnic hierarchies. Society's ethnic prejudices are seemingly endorsed in this film, when a middle-class white character condescendingly says to the lowly stagehand, played by Grande Otelo: 'Não sei como uma cabeça tão preta pode ter um pensamento tão claro' (I don't know how such a black head can have such clear [also literally 'pale'] thoughts). His characters seem happy to go along with the status quo, accepting their lot with the stereotypical good humour of the passive Afro-Brazilian.

Racism and stardom

As recently as 1990 a journalist from the respected newspaper *O Globo* posed the following question to Grande Otelo: 'What is it like being black, ugly and short in show business in Brazil?'[74] His characters were invariably likeable *malandros* or urban survivors, such as the illegal street vendor he plays in *De pernas pro ar* (Topsy-Turvy, 1957),[75] but who physically embodied the bottom of the heap in contemporary society, allowing disenfranchised, poor spectators to feel better about themselves by laughing at the ultimate other, the physically ill-favoured, very dark-skinned Afro-Brazilian. There is ample evidence of racism within Rio's show business circles in the 1930–60 period; the artistic director of the shows performed in the Golden Room of the ultra-chic Copacabana Palace hotel, for example, prohibited blacks from appearing, with the notable exception of Grande Otelo. He thus became the token black face, par excellence, chosen to represent Afro-Brazilians at official functions attended by President Vargas alongside mixed-race artists like the samba singer Orlando Silva, as 'evidence' of the mythical racial democracy that was taking shape within nationalist rhetoric. Otelo's face stands out clearly from the crowd in official photos of such events. His star text in the press is also tacitly racist; hinging on the stereotype of the *malandro* libertine, it drew heavily on his chequered personal life, love of women and alcohol, unreliability and violent events in his life, such as the murder of his child by his wife and her subsequent suicide. His lack of respectability, synonymous with his racial identity, explains his marked absence, save for a few brief lines and a handful of small black and white photos, from the pages of the magazine *Cinelândia*, where much lesser-known white Brazilian stars are afforded double-page spreads.

Grande Otelo personified the *zé-povinho* or Everyman figure of urban Brazil, as did Oscarito. Between them they covered a broad racial spectrum of the urban masses. Their embodiment of the pervasive ethos of *malandragem* on screen, an unofficial tenet of Brazilian popular identity, coupled with their physical appearances, 'permitted them to each become the synecdoche of large swathes of an ethnically diverse population'.[76] But Otelo's very marked racial features, which the roles he played required him to play up to, meant that he represented the very lowest rung of the social ladder, the 'Maldito negro!' ('Damned black!'), as he is referred to in the *chanchada O caçula do barulho* (The Topsy-Turvy Kid, 1949), in which he plays a suitably meek and poorly treated cleaner.

> The privileging of the figure of Grande Otelo as the key black actor, and his pairing with white co-stars, had the effect of isolating him from his black brothers and sisters. As a lone representative of black Brazil, he was made to bear a heavy 'burden of representation'.[77]

Conclusion

Very different film stars can be claimed to embody an essential 'national' identity at a given time. As we have seen in this chapter, stars of predominantly white European physiognomy (Miranda, Eliana and Oscarito) came to embody 'Brazilianness' in the popular comedies of this era, with the token nature of the presence of Grande Otelo, the very dark-skinned Afro-Brazilian, on screen being underlined by his striking absence from film magazines. In the 1940s and 1950s neither the United States nor Brazil was ready for images of the black masses to appear centre stage on cinema screens, as reflected in the censuring of Orson Welles's project *It's All True*, with its documentary footage of Afro-Brazilian shantytown inhabitants performing samba. If this were true in Hollywood it was no less the case in Brazil itself, where both Carmen Miranda and Eliana performed an ethnically cleansed version of Afro-Brazilian identity.

In these films, Grande Otelo was the ultimate *uber*black, a virtual caricature, 'blacker'/more racially marked than the audience members, a large percentage of whom were undoubtedly of partial African descent. As Carl N. Degler has shown, a rigid racial ideology like that which developed in North America was unworkable in Brazil as a consequence of the historical and demographic evolution of the colony and then the independent nation. Degler coined the phrase 'mulatto escape-hatch', the theory that lighter-skinned mulattos in Brazil could ascend the social and economic hierarchy and distance themselves from Afro-Brazilians of darker complexions and more limited horizons, in marked contrast to the biracial identificatory system of the USA.[78] Grande Otelo is referred to on screen as 'negro', a term 'reserved for reference to very dark skinned individuals who seem, at least by physical appearance, to be entirely of African ancestry'.[79] *Chanchada* audience members were largely those of mixed racial origin, but in relation to Grande Otelo those of African descent could place themselves in different, lighter-skinned categories of Brazil's extensive taxonomy of ethnicity. Regardless of their physical similarities to Grande Otelo, such spectators could perceive themselves as higher in the social pecking order than the poor, underdog characters that he played on screen, an added aspect of the 'feel-good factor' provided by this escapist cinematic fare.

Carmen Miranda, Eliana and Grande Otelo perform 'blackness' from very different ethnic starting points, but ultimately underlying these representations is a disavowal of real Afro-Brazilians, and an implicit engagement with the pervasive ideology of whitening. Even in the 1950s there is a populist dimension to representations of black identity that dates back to the First Republic, if not earlier. It could be argued that by the 1950s these images of black identity had become acceptable to popular filmmakers and audiences in Brazil as a consequence of Hollywood's fascination with the *baiana* and international representations of Afro-identity. Brazilian audiences were equally fascinated with the stars of Hollywood, with whom their own leading men and leading ladies, not least Cyl Farney and Eliana, were favourably compared and consciously aligned in the film press. These domestic screen gods and goddesses of Caucasian good looks functioned most effectively in opposition to the comic foil of Oscarito. White-skinned yet as downtrodden as the marginalised poor in the audience, Oscarito embodied an intrinsic 'Brazilianness' in the *chanchada*, a genre whose claims to 'national' essentialism rely on its humour. The *chanchada* delighted in juxtaposing the downmarket, unglamorous realities of life in Brazil with the exotic images of Hollywood for humorous effect,[80] a comic technique that was equally central to the casting of Oscarito alongside a broad-shouldered leading man worthy of a Hollywood contract.

11

ICONS OF POPULAR CULTURE POST-1960

This chapter deals with the contribution to Brazilian cinema of three successful filmmakers/stars: Renato Aragão (known to his legions of fans as Didi), Amácio Mazzaropi (immortalised on screen as Jeca, the country bumpkin) and José Mojica Marins, otherwise known as the incomparable and now internationally renowned horror performer Zé do Caixão (Coffin Joe). These three stars have been chosen because of their considerable popular appeal, their unique performative styles, their intense involvement in filmmaking (from writing scripts to directing, production and distribution), which sets them apart from other screen stars, and thus for their impact on Brazilian cinema.

Renato Aragão

Renato Aragão was born in the North-Eastern state of Ceará in 1935, where he was brought up with his twelve siblings. As well as being one of Brazil's most successful film producers and screen actors (he is said to be the only Brazilian producer never to have lost money on a film, and he has starred in forty-four films to date, all of which were box-office hits), Aragão was one of the nation's first TV stars. In 1960 he was offered a part on a television comedy programme in Ceará called *Vídeo alegre*, on which he used for the first time his stage name Didi (Didi Mocó Sonrisal Colesterol Novalgino Mufumbo, in its fuller version). He moved to the then very successful TV Tupi in Rio de Janeiro in the early 1960s, and in 1963 he made a TV series with his future long-term acting partner Manfriedi Santana (Dedé) entitled *Adoráveis Trapalhões* for TV Excelsior, about a gang of dopey, clumsy, scruffy ne'er-do-wells (all of these are implied in their name in Portuguese) and the amusing scrapes they invariably get themselves into. Thus began one of the most successful and longest-running TV shows in Brazil's history, a show that since 1977 has been produced and screened by the all-powerful TV Globo, and which spawned the most successful film series of the same name.

Thus, Aragão is one of the most, if not the most, cherished TV stars in Brazil, currently enjoying his fifth decade at the top of the TV ratings. In order to understand the reasons for the success of a performer like Renato Aragão, it must be borne in mind that in Brazil stars and programme formats enjoy much greater longevity than in many other TV cultures.[1] Furthermore, national television series, especially those shown on TV Globo, are often more popular than foreign series. As a result, the television audience's relationship with the national product is very different from the cinema audience's relationship to national films, for example. By way of illustration, 27 million people regularly tuned into the Trapalhões TV series at the height of its popularity.[2]

Didi on screen

Aragão's screen persona Didi is very reminiscent of the stock *chanchada* hero. Like the *chanchada* stars before him, Aragão is not famed for his matinée idol looks or elegant speech. To compensate, his performances as Didi are often very physical (acrobatics, stunts and pratfalls, often shot in fast-forward). While, like many a comedian, Didi plays the underdog, the marginalised and the subaltern on screen, he does not have to rely purely on luck for a carnivalesque reversal of his fortunes to take place. Didi is a problem solver, but, more than this, he has the physical strength to defeat his enemies. He is a kind of Popeye figure, then, without the spinach. Aragão, in fact, bears an uncanny resemblance to the Popeye cartoon character, both physically and in terms of his speech. His physical prowess has always played an important role in the development of his star text, and was perhaps used to confirm his superiority to the rest of the stars who made up the Trapalhões team. Two of the team died young: one from an Aids-related illness and one from alcohol poisoning. The other surviving member of the Trapalhões, Dedé Santana, has fought very public battles with obesity and depression. By contrast a sexagenarian Aragão, positively oozing good health, became a father for the fourth time, scaled the 127-foot Christ the Redeemer statue in Rio de Janeiro live on television for charity, ran with the Olympic torch and wrote a best-selling self-help book.

Like Popeye, Didi is always the moral leader of his gang, his success as a comedian on screen relying on the 'hysterical cowardice and the selfishly motivated heroism' of his sidekicks.[3] While the humour in both his big screen and his television performances in the 1960s and 1970s, at the height of his stardom, was decidedly infantile, aimed as it was at a young audience, the plotlines of sketches and films tended to lack a linear narrative structure, and their resulting surreal and anarchic quality appealed to an older generation of viewers. These qualities continue to provide a source of nostalgia for Brazilian adults who watched Aragão as children.

Renato Aragão's widespread fame in Brazil, then, is ultimately predicated on his special relationship with children, which, like Xuxa's star text,[4] serves to draw attention away from the wealthy business empire he has built up. Aragão has been UNICEF special envoy for Brazil since 1991, he regularly plays a key role in TV Globo's children's charity telethon *Criança esperança*, and the birth of his fourth child when he was 64 was one of the media events of the year in 1999. Promoted as children's cinema (the TV series was closer to the standard definition of light entertainment), the Trapalhões films tapped into an important market in Brazil, allowing children to go and watch familiar faces and their antics, which had been previously rehearsed on television, without the interference of dubbing or subtitles.

Didi may be the leader of his gang and the main star in his films, but he rarely plays the romantic lead. His 2003 film, *Didi, o cupido Trapalhão* (Didi, the Trapalhão Cupid) literalises the role he takes on in his films: that of facilitator, bringing together the (much younger) love interests in his films. In *O casamento dos Trapalhões* (The Marriage of the Trapalhões, 1988), based loosely on *Seven Brides for Seven Brothers* (1954), the 53-year-old Didi and his gang find themselves brides, but so too does a group of younger stars, who form the focus of the film's happy ending. Thus, unlike Mazzaropi and Coffin Joe, Aragão has never shied way from sharing screen space with other (younger) stars.

Didi and the Trapalhões

The Trapalhões were essentially a quartet of comedians who dominated the national box-office listings in Brazil throughout the 1970s and 1980s. No fewer than fourteen of the twenty-five highest-grossing films released between 1970 and 1984 were from the Trapalhões series, the most successful of which, *Os Trapalhões nas minas do rei Salomão* (The Trapalhões in King Solomon's Mines, 1977), was seen by almost 7 million people by 1984. Manfriedi Santana, the other founding member, had a background in the circus and Brazilian vaudeville in Rio de Janeiro. Together they made seven films, before being joined in 1976 by another *carioca*, Antônio Carlos Bernardes Gomes (Mussum), who had made a name for himself first in a travelling musical troupe/circus and later on television as a good-humoured *sambista*. Mauro Gonçalves (Zacarias), a radio star from Minas Gerais, completed the quartet in 1978. The four made a remarkable twenty-one films together, all of which were box-office hits, until the death of Zacarias in 1990.

In terms of popular appeal the Trapalhões series of films work in similar ways to the *chanchada* films of the 1950s: very strong evidence of the traditions of the circus and popular theatre (in terms of humour, sentimentality and the structure of the films) and references in film titles and plots to recent cinema and television successes. They are filled with nods to expressions of popular culture in vogue at the time, such as TV talent competitions (*Na onda do iê-iê-iê* (On the Wave of Rock 'n' Roll, 1965), the Brazilian version of country and western music (*O casamento dos Trapalhões*) and Beto Carrero's famous rodeo theme park in the South of Brazil (*Os Trapalhões no reino da fantasia* (The Trapalhões in the Land of Make Believe, 1985). In the films the Trapalhões play characters who start off as lowly and marginalised, who are then called upon to aid the forces of good, represented by young lovers, in overcoming evil in the form of a male figure of authority. A series of adventures and misfortunes befall them on the way, involving chase sequences which take up the bulk of the films' running time, but justice prevails in the end and they are rewarded for their efforts. When political issues are tackled in these films (and Aragão dealt increasingly with contemporary social themes in his films after 1982), discussion is limited to clear-cut, easy issues, such as the need for water in the North-East, or that vote buying and the illicit sale of children for adoption abroad are wrong.[5]

With the might of TV Globo behind Aragão and the Trapalhões gang from 1977, it is hard to imagine their celluloid outings failing. For a start, saturation advertising of the biannual release of their films was guaranteed. To give an idea of the extent of their exposure, by July 1983 Renato Aragão had starred in no fewer than 530 hours of weekly programmes on TV.[6] The average number of spectators for a Trapalhões film in the 1970s and 1980s was around 4 million. Aragão recently argued that, even though spectator numbers for his films are consistently high, they would be higher still if the rules of distribution were fairer, and if US and multinational distribution companies did not throw their weight around to get their own films widely exhibited. He cites the example of his 2006 'solo' film *Didi, o caçador de tesouros* (Didi, the Treasure Hunter): despite placing 150 copies of the film in circulation, and despite healthy box-office returns, the film was pushed out of the cinemas after only one week by rival Hollywood blockbusters.[7]

Further testament to the power of Aragão, and to the usefulness of his relationship with Globo, can be found in the ease with which Brazil's top celebrities were brought in to star alongside the Trapalhões in their films. In the 1980s the Trapalhões could frequently rely on a supporting cast taken from the most successful TV programmes, such as Globo star Xuxa (for example, *O Trapalhão na arca de Noé* (The Trapalhão on Noah's Ark, 1983), *Os Trapalhões e o mágico de Oroz* (The Trapalhões and the Wizard of Oroz, 1984) and *A Princesa Xuxa e os Trapalhões* (Princess Xuxa and the Trapalhões, 1989)) and rival channel SBT's Gugu Liberato, already in the 1980s being groomed to become the nation's most popular TV variety show presenter, along with the successful boy bands that he managed at the time (*Os fantasmas Trapalhões* (The Ghostly Trapalhões, 1987), *O casamento dos Trapalhões* and so on). In one film, *O cangaceiro Trapalhão* (The Bandit Trapalhão, 1983), Aragão was able to convince two of TV Globo's soap authors to adapt their own successful miniseries for the troupe for the big screen.

Not only was Didi the leader of the Trapalhões gang, but Renato Aragão was the main driving force and decision maker behind the highly lucrative outfit. Aragão's production company, Renato Aragão Produções Artísticas, was responsible for producing the Trapalhões films from the mid-1970s onwards. He has also written most of the material that he has performed throughout his career. Unlike many film producers, Aragão has always recognised the importance of looking beyond box-office receipts in terms of potential filmmaking profits: at the height of their fame the Trapalhões produced comic books, toys and even a children's clothing line. Many of the products endorsed by the Trapalhões were advertised in their films, and Aragão made clever use of product placement, a practice which had always been both common and perfectly acceptable on Brazilian television. Take, for example, the consistent plugging of Itapimirim coach travel in Trapalhões films. Beto Carrero, one-time rodeo star and now the owner of a popular theme park called Beto Carrero World, enjoyed a special relationship with the Trapalhões, in terms of both personal appearances in their films and profitable plugs for his theme park: *O noviço rebelde* (The Rebel Novice, 1997) contains the most blatant advertising of the park. As if in recognition of the marketing boost offered to the theme park by the Trapalhões, it now houses a cinema named after Aragão (the Cine Renato Aragão).[8]

Didi post-Trapalhões

With the deaths of Zacarias in 1990 and Mussum in 1994, the writing was on the wall for the Trapalhões. Aragão and Dedé Santana made three more commercially successful movies together in the 1990s, their fan base maintained thanks to TV Globo broadcasting repeats of their TV shows, before Aragão, building on the success of his solo Globo TV show *A turma do Didi* (Didi's Gang), began going it alone in the twenty-first century with *Um anjo Trapalhão* (An Angel Trapalhão, 2000). Didi has appeared (to 2006) in four films without Dedé.[9] With the end of the Trapalhões, Dedé Santana struggled to find a niche on television, and ended up making evangelical programmes. In the face of accusations of abandoning Santana, who has never shied away from sharing with the press the bitterness he felt as a result of the collapse of the Trapalhões troupe, Aragão has always avoided the claim/counterclaim style of publicity that feeds the machine of the 'entertainment' press in Brazil, limiting his observations instead to the fact that the decision not to continue making TV programmes with the remaining Trapalhões was taken by TV Globo, which preferred to screen repeats of old Trapalhões series.[10] Aragão did invite Santana to star in three Trapalhões films after the demise of the TV show, but was seemingly forced to go it alone after Santana began to accuse Aragão directly of playing a role in his own televisual downfall.

Although Didi and Dedé were reunited in 2004 for a one-off performance as part of TV Globo's *Criança esperança* telethon, Aragão's relationship (personal and professional) with Santana continues to be a touchy subject. Aragão alleges that he was poised to invite him to take part in one of his films, but Santana then went head to head on rival TV channel SBT with *Dedé e o comando maluco* (Dedé and the Crazy Command), a comedy programme in which Santana resurrects his familiar stage persona. The show is produced by none other than Beto Carrero and filmed in Beto Carrero World. Like Aragão, Santana also regularly takes part in his channel's charity telethon and, with the weight of Beto Carrero Produções behind him, his comedy show is enjoying unexpected publicity and success. With the occasional participation in the show of, for example, Mussum's grandson, Santana is clearly staking his claim as a rightful inheritor of the Trapalhões name.

While Aragão's skilful handling of the 'break-up' with his long-term comedy partner ensured that his status of national treasure remained intact, an incident occurred which would force a growing section of the viewing public to question the validity of his screen persona in contemporary society. With the gradual establishment of an alternative comedy scene in Brazil, with its (albeit limited) readjustments in terms of who and what can be considered comedic fair game, it was, perhaps, only a matter of time before Aragão's form of humour came under attack. In July 2004 Aragão was accused by gay rights groups in Brazil (led by the very influential Grupo Gay da Bahia) of causing offence by making fun of gay people on his children's TV programme (*A turma do Didi*), while being a UNICEF goodwill ambassador.

In the Trapalhões films and TV series references to homosexuality were usually limited to the use of slangy and often neologistic euphemisms such as 'rapaz alegre' (the literal translation of the term 'gay'), and 'ele é chegado' or 'ele camufla', suggesting a closet kind of homosexuality. It is interesting that such references were not aimed at Zacarias, the character played by the gay Mauro Gonçalves. Zacarias's persona was asexually camp and was understood to be weak in a tender and affectionate way. Furthermore, references in the Trapalhões films to the nether regions, for example, are silly rather than sexualised, but the odd joke that would be deemed inappropriate for children in Britain and the United States does slip through.

The sketches singled out by gay rights organisations involved a more direct form of homophobia. In one, Didi both humiliated a male ballet teacher and referred to one male character uneuphemistically as 'boiola' (poof). In another sketch one character appeared in a stag costume, at which point, after declaring that the *veado* (stag in Portuguese, but also the most commonly used slang word for gay in Brazil) was a very dangerous animal, Didi proceeded to beat the character up.

Perhaps as a result of being wholly unused to the level of criticism, which made headline news, aimed at him by the gay community, Aragão's initial reaction was to be unmoved and unrepentant. He argued that he was just a clown and that much greater insults were levelled against the gay community on television elsewhere. Aragão failed to see the irony in declaring that he had been cracking the same jokes for over forty years and that his intention was not to offend anyone. Any attempt to make him change the content of his programmes would represent a challenge to his freedom of speech. The extent to which he had mishandled the controversy was evident in the fact that within a matter of days a now repentant Aragão was obliged to apologise on live television for any offence that he might have caused, with the guarantee that he would cease to crack homophobic jokes.

Didi, o cupido Trapalhão was both the last film to use the Trapalhão moniker and the first of a series of three (so far) of films including the word Didi in its title. Despite Aragão's denials, it was also the only film to try (unsuccessfully, as the attempt was never repeated on the big screen) to rebuild the Trapalhões team. In the film Marcelo Augusto plays the pseudo-macho role played in the past by Dedé Santana, while Jacaré replaces Mussum as the black musician with the big smile, and Tadeu Melo plays a weak and infantilised comedian reminiscent of Zacarias.

Perhaps as a result of this failure to rekindle the box-office success of the Trapalhões quartet, since 2004 the all-important words Trapalhão and Trapalhões have been dropped from Aragão's films, to be replaced with Didi. As Aragão grows older, the comedy in his films has become less physical, and Didi now shares more screen space than ever with other stars of the moment. There is also a greater emphasis in his films on childhood and family values. For example, in *Didi, o caçador de tesouros* the timeless plot revolving around a search for hidden treasure has been carefully chosen to appeal to children. Didi plays the butler (older friend, confidant, protector) in the house of 10-year-old Pedro, with whom he shares the screen. This emphasis on children is reflected in the production as well as the plot: the film was produced by Aragão's son Paulo, and stars both his young daughter Livian and Mussunzinho, the young son of Mussum. In Aragão's next film, *O cavalheiro Didi e a princesa Lili* (Gentleman Didi and Princess Lili, 2006), Livian got equal billing with her father.

Having seemingly learned from his run-in with the Grupo Gay da Bahia, the *deboche* or cheeky and at times schoolboy humour, which in the 1970s endeared Aragão to a generation of Brazilians but which in the twenty-first century inevitably brought to light the inherent prejudice in much mainstream comedy in the country, has been replaced by an almost tangible sentimentality. As a result, Aragão continues to be the focus of intellectual scorn, only now his critics are mourning the loss of the spirit of the Trapalhões.

Amácio Mazzaropi

The single most successful star of the big screen in Brazil in the 1960s was *paulista* comedian Amácio Mazzaropi, who appeared in thirty-two films between 1951 and his death in 1981. Mazzaropi was born in the city of São Paulo in 1912 to lower-middle-class parents (his father was a taxi driver and later ran a grocery store) and he literally ran away to join the circus when he was 15, becoming an assistant to a famous fakir. After working the interior of the state of São Paulo for years with his own travelling theatre-circus,[11] the Troupe Companhia Amácio Mazzaropi, made up of assorted members of his family, he signed a contract with Rádio Tupi in 1946 for eight years, starring in the popular *Rancho alegre* programme. He made his TV debut in 1950 on Channel 3, securing his own show (a live version of *Rancho alegre*) on São Paulo's TV Tupi, the most watched show on TV at the time in São Paulo. Despite being remembered as a film performer, his credits include being the first comedian ever to appear on Brazilian television.

The story goes that shortly after his TV debut he was approached by legendary *chanchada* producer Abílio Pereira de Almeida and encouraged to make movies. He made his first film, *Sai da frente* (Get Out of My Way, 1951) for the Vera Cruz studios at the age of 39. The film, in which he plays the lead role as a *paulista* taxi driver, was a box-office hit. He starred in two more *chanchadas* for Vera Cruz: *Nadando em dinheiro* (Swimming in Money, 1952) and *Candinho* (Little Candide, 1953), before being enticed away to Rio, where he made four more *chanchadas*. It was while working with Aníbal Massaini, owner of the successful Cinedistri film production company, on *Chico Fumaça* (1958) and seeing how much money Massaini could make on the back of his stars' hard work and success, that Mazzaropi decided to take a chance: he paid Massaini to be released from his contract with Cinedistri and set up on his own.

From the ruins of the bankrupt Vera Cruz, Mazzaropi built PAM Filmes (Produções Amácio Mazzaropi): at first renting studio space from Vera Cruz and borrowing equipment, then later buying up the equipment when it was auctioned off. With PAM Filmes Mazzaropi became responsible for the production and distribution of his films and the use of his image.[12] He even built his own film studios in the grounds of his farm in Taubaté in the state of São Paulo in the early 1970s. He produced (and starred in) twenty-four films, all of which were commercially successful.

Mazzaropi's screen persona

The social type that was forever associated with Mazzaropi's stage and screen performances is the *caipira*. The traditional definition of *caipira* is country bumpkin or hick from any rural area in Brazil, although now its use tends to be limited to describing folk from the interior of the states of São Paulo, Minas Gerais, Mato Grosso do Sul and Goiás. In fact it is most associated with the interior of the state of São Paulo, where the differences between the state capital (one of the world's largest cities and one of the richest and most sophisticated in Latin America) and the rural hinterland are most striking.

The inspirations behind Mazzaropi's screen persona are manifold: the rural lifestyle of both his Italian immigrant grandfather, whom he would visit as a child, and upstate São Paulo, where he spent part of his childhood; the performances of Genésio and Sebastião Arruda, two well-known comedic actors who also interpreted country bumpkins; and the character Jeca Tatu, created by the great writer and intellectual from Taubaté, Monteiro Lobato (1882–1948).

Lobato first referred to the character Jeca Tatu in an article entitled 'Urupês' in 1918, in which he described a backward-looking, lazy and sickly *caipira* from the interior of Sao Paulo, by way of a critique of the lack of progress in the Brazilian countryside. On realising his potentially negative contribution to race and class relations in Brazil, Lobato rethought the character in 1924, transforming him into Jeca Tatuzinho, now with the power to change his own destiny. Jeca Tatuzinho appeared in the *Almanaque Fontoura*, a freely distributed magazine purporting to teach Brazil's backward, unhealthy rural masses about the importance of sanitation, nutrition and so on, but which ultimately served to advertise a tonic (Tônica Fontoura). According to the Monteiro Lobato official website, the Jeca Tatuzinho edition of the *Almanaque Fontoura* has sold over 100 million copies and is thus regarded as Brazil's most successful marketing campaign.[13]

Although Mazzaropi only plays a character called Jeca in nine of the thirty-two films in which he starred, the association between his screen persona and Monteiro Lobato's Jeca Tatu is clear is see. Take, for example, Mazzaropi's gait, his clumsy, animal-like walk, and his tatty garb, with the waistband of his trousers practically up round his armpits, which was strikingly similar to the images of Jeca Tatu that appeared in the *Almanaque Fontoura*. Furthermore, in 1960 Mazzaropi produced and starred in a film entitled *Jeca Tatu*, acknowledging Lobato as the source of the story in the film's credits.[14]

The uneducated countryman who grapples with life in urban spaces, reflects on the speed of modernisation and change, and reveals that not everything is better in the city is, of course, a staple in much popular comedy. Jacques Tati in France and Cantinflas in Mexico, for example, played very similar roles in their respective cinemas. However, as we have established, the roots of Mazzaropi's comedic performance do not lie in the cinema, but in Brazilian popular culture, and specifically the popular theatre, where the *caipira* clown and plays revolving around the city/countryside dichotomy had been popular throughout the twentieth century. The roots of Mazzaropi's performance can, of course, also be traced to the Zanni of the Italian *commedia dell'arte*, an important pre-modern influence on much popular cinema throughout the world. The Italian comedy tradition was particularly strong in São Paulo, and Mazzaropi for one was associated with the so-called Italian-Brazilian theatre of melodrama, the *filodrammatici*.

During his early days on radio Mazzaropi was said to have been encouraged to change his name. The one concession he made was to omit his first name, thereby reducing the number of syllables from an unfeasible eight to a reasonable four and at the same time staking his claim for superstardom (most superstars in Brazil – Pelé, Xuxa and Didi, as well as the great comedy performers, such as Oscarito, Ankito and Costinha – have one stage name only). The fact remained, however, that Mazzaropi's name sounded (and was) very Italian. But it worked as the name of a *caipira* because Mazzaropi's performance would also have spoken to Southern Brazil's very large immigrant populations, of which the Italian was by far the largest, as they too would have been affected in cultural and economic terms by processes of industrialisation, the growth of cities, the power of international capital, and the clash between the archaic and the modern.

Although Geni Prado, who had starred alongside Mazzaropi on *Rancho alegre*, appears in most of his films as his long-suffering *caipira* wife, the only real star of Mazzaropi's films is Mazzaropi himself. Unlike Renato Aragão, Mazzaropi did not rely on appearances in his films by other popular stars to entice audiences to the cinema. Mazzaropi's image was maintained in the public imaginary, not by complementary roles on television, but by the widest and longest possible distribution and exhibition of his films, together with occasional personal appearances in the kind of small-scale theatre and circus operations that he had been involved in before finding fame on the radio. His fear of 'wearing out his image' through overexposure on TV and his approach to ensuring the longevity of his stardom was, then, very different from the saturation techniques employed on behalf of the Atlântida stars of the 1940s and 1950s, for example, or later performers such as Renato Aragão and Xuxa.

More a performer of popular melodrama than a comedian per se, Mazzaropi would reiterate that his role, as he saw it, was to make people laugh and cry. His performances, then, did not rely solely on humour in terms of entertaining the audience. The sudden switching that we see in Mazzaropi's performances from humour to tragedy/pathos, and the sentimentality that the uninitiated spectator may find cloying were codes that were familiar to his audience, given their origins in popular theatre and their ubiquity in TV soap operas.

Mazzaropi was proud to describe himself as never changing. The level of stardom that he had reached, particularly in São Paulo, was such that all audiences really needed was to see his familiar image on screen: plot and dialogue were of little importance. In Mazzaropi's later films, for example, there is surprisingly little dialogue, and remarkably little effort is made to play the *caipira* for laughs. Mazzaropi tapped into a real need for community entertainment, in that Mazzaropi the 'star' brought people together in cinema halls, where they would meet, chat and only occasionally look up (usually when Mazzaropi appeared on screen) and pay attention. Mazzaropi was arguably the last of this kind of film star, and it is the loss of the sense of collective experience that his cinema represented that has produced the current nostalgia for Mazzaropi and other *chanchada* stars.

The figure of Jeca or the *caipira* continues to provide a source of amusement in Brazil: after the death of Mazzaropi a number of performers vied to take his place on the big screen, with varying degrees of success.[15] A number of other filmic incursions into the world of the *caipira*, particularly those linked to Brazil's much-maligned *música sertaneja* or country music tradition, have enjoyed success at the box office, although this success can at least partly be explained by the fact that the principal home of *caipira* culture, São Paulo, also supplies the bulk of Brazil's film audience.[16]

Filmmaking hillbilly-style

Mazzaropi had a special, personal relationship with his public: having worked the interior for many years before becoming a successful film star via radio and television meant that he had a good idea of what his audience wanted and how to make them laugh. The style and content of his films were strongly influenced by popular theatre and the circus. All of Mazzaropi's films have a large number of features in common, the most striking of which is the *dramalhão* or element of sentimental drama. The plots revolve around a battle between good and evil (good commonly being represented by a young couple in love and evil by the local landowner). Mazzaropi's characters almost lose their faith halfway through the movies but are implicitly reconciled with God at the end as good is victorious over evil. As someone is invariably killed off midway, his films tend to include a funeral sequence as well as a wedding at the end, again firmly rooting these films in popular cultural traditions.

While Mazzaropi's character and performance may reassuringly remain the same, the plots of his films reflect on the constant change to which the inhabitants of rural Brazil were subjected. These included the accommodation of new immigrant groups, as witnessed in films such as *Meu Japão brasileiro* (My Brazilian Japan, 1964) and *O lamparina* (The Little Oil Lamp, 1964), generational differences that reveal a clash, experienced by much of Brazil's migrant population, between the traditional, conservative values of the interior and the modernity of town and city life (*O puritano da rua Augusta* (The Puritan of Rua Augusta, 1965) and *Portugal, minha saudade* (Longing for Portugal, 1973)), and the increasing popularity of alternative religious practices (the syncretic *macumba*, and spiritism, for example, in *O Jeca macumbeiro* (Jeca Does Voodoo, 1974), *Jeca e seu filho preto* (Jeca and His Black Son, 1978) and *Jeca e a égua milagrosa* (Jeca and the Miraculous Mare, 1980). The deliberately timeless quality to Mazzaropi's performance is counterbalanced by a number of techniques employed to situate the spectator in the present day. First of all, there are musical references to instantly recognisable soundtracks to Hollywood movies and hit television shows. Secondly, there are references at the level of plot to contemporary culture, from allusions to cinema and televisual genres, to sport.

In one sense, Mazzaropi was a kind of model strategist for the Brazilian film industry. Unlike the seeming majority of Brazilian filmmakers he made a point of never going over time or budget on his films. Mazzaropi was an astute businessman whose experience setting up and running his own theatre troupe meant that he understood the discipline required to make a profit from filmmaking. Despite criticism of the quality of his films,[17] he did make the more expensive investments where he felt they needed to be made, for example in colour film stock and equipment, to enable him to record sound directly, and in the construction of a hotel in the grounds of his studios, to accommodate his cast and crew. He kept things simple in other regards (take, for example, the predominance of uncomplicated and therefore quick-to-film medium-length shots, and the absence of 'stars', with their attendant lawyers and contracts with Globo). For the plots and dialogue of his films, which Mazzaropi wrote himself, he sought inspiration from popular theatre[18] and from the characters he met on his travels through the interior. He made his feature films longer in order not to have to profit-share with an accompanying short film,[19] and he spent time producing trailers for his films, in all of which the one word 'Mazzaropi' remains emblazoned in capital letters for the maximum amount of time. Mazzaropi aimed to premiere his films on the same date (25 January, the anniversary of São Paulo) and in the same place (the Art Palácio cinema in the centre of the city) every year,[20] arguably tapping into the sense of continuity and familiarity that we see with spectatorship practices relating to television in Brazil, and serving to highlight the extent to which Mazzaropi was a producer and star of 'event cinema'.

Mazzaropi was able to observe closely the lessons to be learned from the failure of the Vera Cruz company and, in particular, the two key mistakes to be avoided: needless spending on production and direct competition with foreign films, both of which, ironically, were also identified as challenges by the *cinema novo* group. Mazzaropi dealt with the issue of competition by taking charge of distribution himself. By setting up his own production company, Mazzaropi assumed control of all aspects of the filmmaking process: direction (or at least the selection of directors), scriptwriting, contracting actors, fiscal control and, perhaps most importantly, distribution. Mazzaropi invested in a number of distribution offices in large state capitals. It is also worth noting that in the eight films in which he had starred before setting up on his own he had played characters based on the *caipira* figure of his comedic interventions on radio and television, so in a sense the 'product' of his new business venture, his screen persona, was already fixed in the public imaginary, and thus demand was there.

Mazzaropi was the bane of many a left-wing film critic during the 1970s in particular, because of his undeniable conservatism. He was a well-known friend and supporter of many figures linked to the dictatorship (Presidents Médici and Figueiredo, to name just two), and his films were understood as reinforcing both conservative moral values and the political and social status quo. Mazzaropi defended himself against accusations of being overly familiar with Brazil's authoritarian rulers by arguing that, as with many a wily businessman, his only desire was for peace, and any government that could deliver peace would have his support. He did, however, use his contacts in Brasília to ensure that his films were never held up by the bureaucracy associated with an over-zealous censor.[21]

Mazzaropi both shunned contact with other filmmakers[22] and assumed a decidedly 'anti-intellectual' position which went against the grain, given that filmmakers in the 1960s and 1970s played a crucial role in national cultural and political debates. Mazzaropi as a result was highly suspicious of journalists and film critics, and seemed to take a particular delight in undermining *cinema novo*'s contribution to national cinema, in a kind of tit-for-tat for the perceived abuse he and his audience received at the hands of critics. He said in interview: 'Critics don't understand that I make films industrially. Cinema is an industry like any other.'[23] Mazzaropi declared in interviews that he was just an ordinary guy who believed in national cinema, and that it was his mission to set up *the* Brazilian film industry, suggesting, then, that one did not already exist. For Mazzaropi, a film industry clearly meant the self-sustainable production of commercially successful films. He voiced pride at never having to rely on State sponsorship to produce films.[24] It was perhaps inevitable, then, that Mazzaropi, producing highly popular commercially oriented (and, for some, ideologically suspect) films in the 1960s and 1970s, became enemy number one of critics, filmmakers and cinephiles who supported *cinema novo*. Mazzaropi declared, at a time when *cinema novo* films were being acclaimed by critics (but ignored by audiences) and garnering awards abroad, that 'Brazil is my public.'[25] Mazzaropi reproached critics for preferring 'a cinema full of symbols, confused, complicated, pretentious, but with no spectators'.[26]

Eva Bueno has argued that the *caipira* was neither exotic enough, nor ethnic enough, nor tragic enough to merit the attention of the *cinema novo*,[27] and in this sense Mazzaropi's appropriation of the Jeca character and *caipira* culture served as a kind of trump card in the battle to win his rightful place in the Brazilian national cinema canon:

> by acknowledging the existence of these films, as well as by watching them, the subaltern, displaced, disenfranchised *caipira*, crowded in *cortiços* – poor neighbourhoods – and slums around the industrial cities,

> effectively commits an act of insubordination against the official culture of the country, which ignores Jeca and what he represents.[28]
>
> . . .
>
> [Mazzaropi's work] makes visible and audible a Brazil which has been historically effaced and silenced.[29]

From the 1960s onwards there have arguably been two distinct varieties of national cinema being produced in Brazil – the fiercely commercial, or industrial, type that sought to entertain the audience and sell the maximum number of tickets possible, and an intellectual/political cinema. The divide was arguably never as deep between the two as it was during Mazzaropi's reign as king of the box office. By way of illustration, Mazzaropi's *Meu Japão brasileiro*, a box-office hit made in colour and telling the sentimental tale of hard-working Japanese immigrants overcoming prejudice and finding a place in the melting pot that is Brazil, was produced in the same year (1964) as Glauber Rocha's seminal *Deus e o diabo na terra do sol* (*Black God, White Devil*), with its bleak portrayal of misery in the backlands and contrasting message of rejection of the status quo and revolutionary call to arms.

Eva Bueno posits that there was a level of subversion present in Mazzaropi's films in the exaltation of the lazy, sickly, backward Jeca character, who refused to be 'civilised'.[30] What Bueno fails to recognise is that, while Jeca might be lazy, sickly and so on, the other rural types portrayed in Mazzaropi's films are not. Young farmhands are invariably honest and strong. In Mazzaropi's films the lazy, backward Jeca is a figure of amusement, as opposed to someone that the audience is encouraged to aspire to be like. Jeca serves as a reassuring representation of his audience's past: he is static while they keep moving, changing and growing.

Furthermore, while it is true to say that the bad guys of Mazzaropi's films are nearly always powerful landowners, they are bad as individuals – they nearly always have a good son who helps save the day. They therefore do not represent their class or political party, weakening the case for the existence of a narrative of resistance in the films. Another obstacle to reading Mazzaropi's critique of landowners in his films as a form of subversion is that, as Jeffrey Lesser reminds us, the military regime (1964–84) also took a dim view of landowners, seeing their oligarchic position as 'a challenge to the military's urban-industrial intentions'.[31] Resistance can perhaps at best be found in the audience's very evident approval of Mazzaropi's backward and slightly corrupt screen persona, who normally plays some kind of thorn in the side of the establishment.

It is worth bearing in mind also that a large part of Mazzaropi's audience would have been completely unaware of (urban) critics' views on his films, and their knowledge of *cinema novo* may well have been negligible, given the distribution limitations associated with 'erudite' cinema. Thus, the notion of resistance has to be treated carefully: to what extent could we argue that Mazzaropi's audience was resisting hegemonic culture if they did not know what it was? Mazzaropi's work was unlike that of his contemporary Augusto Boal and his 'Theatre of the Oppressed', for example, which actively borrowed from popular theatre traditions in order to raise the political consciousness of subaltern groups in Brazil; there is no suggestion of socio-political intent on the part of the filmmaker associated with Mazzaropi's work. Mazzaropi himself was the first to deny any ideological content in his films, and it is easy to see how this would have frustrated supporters of *cinema novo* in the 1960s and 1970s, for example. Mazzaropi said: 'I dream of full theatres . . . but more importantly, the public enjoying themselves. I love to see the public enjoy themselves.'[32] Of course, as Barsalini points out, just because Mazzaropi's screen persona appeared never to change, and just because his films had happy endings, it does not follow that viewers were not reading Jeca and his challenges to authority in interesting and diverse ways.[33]

Despite arguing the case for treating cinema like any other business, Mazzaropi was clearly troubled by accusations of being in it solely for the money. He protested:

> No one to this day in Brazil has invested as much as me in cinema. I have a plot of 220,000 square metres, where I have built twenty-six apartments with carpet and music to receive artists, a restaurant, studio, and the kind of equipment that few people have access to. So I have invested in national cinema. So it's not just a question of Mazzaropi wanting to make millions. I've got millions – money the public gave me. I don't like it when they say I only make films for the money. It's really not the case.[34]

Mazzaropi even argued, in an evident nod to *cinema novo*'s espousal of cultural nationalism, that by filling Brazilian cinema halls with national films he was preventing money from being sent abroad.[35]

One of the difficulties in holding up Mazzaropi as a proponent of national cinema is the fact that his filmmaking was to a very large extent a personal project. Accusations of megalomania could easily be aimed at him, given the degree to which he controlled PAM Filmes and his failure to groom anyone to take over from him. Mazzaropi would famously joke about how PAM Filmes would go to rack and ruin after his demise.[36] Despite his adopted son's ambition to continue filmmaking in Mazzaropi's studios, PAM Filmes, as Mazzaropi himself had predicted, was shut down and all the equipment auctioned off. Such was his concern with the state of abandon of Mazzaropi's film archive after his death that a private citizen, Norival Milan Jacob, filed a legal suit in 1984 asking the city of São Paulo to intervene.[37]

Mojica Marins: Coffin Joe and Brazilian horror

The final filmmaker to be considered in this chapter is Brazil's only true horror maestro, José Mojica Marins, otherwise known as Zé do Caixão or, in English translation, Coffin Joe.[38] Marins directed and starred in a total of twenty-six films between 1958 and 1986 and, after a number of years in the wilderness, his star is once more in the ascendant, thanks in large part to his success in the US video and DVD market. His long-awaited twenty-sixth film is currently in post-production.

Marins was born in 1936 and brought up in a working-class, Spanish immigrant community in the city of São Paulo. Like many of the exponents of popular cinema in Brazil, his background was rooted in popular culture: both his grandfathers had been Spanish bullfighters, and his own father had been brought up in bullrings and circuses in Brazil. He spent a good part of his childhood living in a flat above a popular cinema where his father worked as a manager. Both the dramatic, dangerous and ostentatious side of bullfighting, and his close link with 1940s cinema would influence his films throughout his career. He started filming when he was a teenager, making little more than home movies with friends and no budget.

Marins's credentials as Brazil's only real exponent of the horror genre, the fact that as a filmmaker he did not rely on State funding, and his move in the 1980s into the 'no-go' area of hard-core porn have all made it difficult to place him within the national cinema canon, with its emphasis on movements, local genres and State financing. The difficulty of placing him within a filmmaking tradition has also led to facile conclusions being drawn about his screen persona being inspired by the Western vampire tradition.[39] But like Aragão and Mazzaropi, Marins's work can be usefully viewed in the context of Brazilian popular culture. In Marins's case, inspiration is clearly drawn as much from Brazil's syncretic religions as from the Euro-American horror film tradition.

Marins's alter ego: Zé do Caixão

Marins first metamorphosed into Zé do Caixão in 1963. He apparently dreamed one night of a horrific gravedigger dressed in a black cape, with long fingernails and wearing a top hat. He woke up the next morning, desperate to recreate the excitement, fear and dramatic tension of his dream. He decided to make his first horror film and, after abandoning his search to find a suitable leading man, Marins's alter ego, Zé do Caixão, was born. Marins came up with Zé do Caixão's visual style when he borrowed a cape from a porter at his studio: the porter dabbled in the Brazilian Dark Arts and used the cape in his worship of Exú.[40] Exús are worshipped primarily in *Quimbanda*, which viewed in a simplified form is the Black Magic side (darkness, evil and association with cemeteries) to *Umbanda*, a syncretic religion celebrated mostly in urban areas of the South of Brazil.[41] In the *Gira dos Exús* ritual, which lies at the heart of *Quimbanda*, celebrants at midnight incorporate deities, dance, drink, smoke, gyrate and use bad language, all of which is very reminiscent of the grotesque excess portrayed in certain scenes of Zé do Caixão films. Musical accompaniments to the worship of Exú include refrains such as 'It's midnight – come and take what is yours', reminding us of the titles of Zé do Caixão's earliest and most successful films: *À meia-noite levarei sua alma* (*At Midnight I'll Take Your Soul*, 1964) and *Esta noite encarnarei no teu cadáver* (*This Night I Will Possess Your Corpse*, 1967).

Figure 11.1 José Mojica Marins as Zé do Caixão (Coffin Joe), 1966 (courtesy of Iberia Filmes/The Kobal Collection)

Many sectors of Brazil's population, while declaring themselves Catholic (Brazil is officially the largest Catholic country in the world), dabble in other belief systems on offer, ranging from *espiritismo*, based on the reincarnation theories of Alan Kardec, to *candomblé*, a religion of African origin brought to Brazil by slaves, to *umbanda*. Thus, while the percentage of the population who define themselves as *umbandistas* may be relatively small, and while there may be plenty of scepticism around with regard to the capacity of such religions to heal and do good, a large number of Brazilians are wary of the negative, destructive, vengeful powers associated with such religious practices. This is an important context to bear in mind when considering the impact of Zé do Caixão's trademark cursing on screen, a context which is ultimately lost on foreign audiences and, if anything, is a source of kitsch humour: Brazilian audiences may well have been terrified to see an Exú lookalike stare straight to camera and condemn the audience to eternal damnation.[42]

Combined with Marins's fondness for appearing in public dressed as Zé do Caixão, his unfeasibly long fingernails, his penchant for wearing black and his facial hair offer a visual link between the filmmaker and his Zé do Caixão persona which adds to the confusion between the two. As a result of the success of his films in the 1960s, Marins (or rather Zé do Caixão) made a number of TV programmes: the kind of gruesome audience participation shows in the style of 'I'll do anything to appear on television' that UK broadcasters, for example, only dared to air in the 1980s. Zé do Caixão is one of the most visually striking and therefore memorable creations of contemporary Brazilian popular culture, and therefore, despite years in celebrity wasteland,[43] Marins's alter ego has never lost his status as icon. This status was confirmed when he appeared at the head of a samba school in the Rio carnival in 1997 and when he inspired a fashion collection by respected Brazilian stylist Alexandre Herchcovitch in 2002.

Coffin Joe entered a second phase of popularity in 1993 when Mike Vraney of Something Weird, a US distributor of exploitation videos, discovered his films and marketed them for an English-speaking audience. Admiration for his work from US directors and writers such as Tim Burton, Joe Dante and Stephen King provoked in the 1990s an overdue reappraisal of his work by the press and public back home.[44] One of the results of Zé do Caixão's incursion into the US video market is an unusual collaboration with Necrophagia, an extreme death/black/horror/gore metal band from the USA. As well as starring in a music video shot in Brazil, which incorporates footage of Marins's real-life eye operation, Zé do Caixão appears on the cover of the band's album *The Divine Art of Torture*, which includes a track called 'Zé do Caixão'. The title track is entirely made up of a dialogue performed by Marins. Despite the interest in Zé do Caixão outside of Brazil, and despite the fact that his income is based almost exclusively on the sale of his DVDs in the USA and Europe, Marins makes few trips abroad, and to date has refused to film outside his native land, thus ensuring that his status as national icon remains intact.

Coffin Joe films

Zé do Caixão's first outing was in *À meia-noite levarei sua alma*, which is set in an unnamed town in the interior of the state of São Paulo. The local gravedigger, Zé do Caixão, is obsessed with finding a woman who will give him the perfect son. First, he kills his barren wife, Lenita, by tying her up and letting loose on her body a poisonous spider. Then he turns his attention to his best friend's fiancée, Terezinha. He drowns his best friend in a bathtub, and rapes Terezinha with a cry of: 'You're going to give me the child I've always wanted!' Terezinha hangs herself as a result of the rape, and a gypsy rightly predicts that on All Souls' Day, at midnight, the spirits of all the people Zé has killed will return to seek their revenge.

The film made a lasting impression on the public at the time because of one particularly blasphemous scene in which Coffin Joe tucks into a leg of lamb on Good Friday while laughing at an Easter procession passing by his house. Here was a director making, for the first time, a Brazilian horror film, with Brazilian concerns (the blasphemy scene would hardly have shocked Anglo-Saxon audiences as much) and a very Brazilian backdrop.[45]

Although the character Coffin Joe lived and worked in the small towns of the interior where Marins's films were set, he was not a man of the people like *chanchada* heroes tended to be, or Mazzaropi was in his films, for example. For a start, Joe had a distinctive, suave voice, with perfect diction, which contrasted on screen with the *caipira* accents of the townsfolk and helped to set him apart from the masses, whom he regularly ridiculed and victimised.[46] Those same masses who flocked to the cinema to see his films saw themselves being mocked on screen, but accepted this, as their mocker was immediately identified in the opening scenes of the films as evil, and therefore in the wrong.[47]

Coffin Joe's second cinematic outing, *Esta noite encarnarei no teu cadáver*, picks up where the story line of his previous film left off. Having survived an attack by the spirits of those he had murdered in *À meia-noite levarei sua alma*, Joe continues both his search for the perfect woman to bear him a child and his murderous ways. At the end of this film, he is drowned in a lake where he has dumped the bodies of his childbearing rejects. The character Coffin Joe appeared in only four more fiction films between 1968 and 1983: *O estranho mundo de Zé do Caixão* (*The Strange World of Coffin Joe*, 1968); *Ritual dos sádicos* (renamed *O despertar da besta*) (*Awakening of the Beast*, produced in 1969 but seized by the censor and not released until 1983); *O exorcismo negro* (*Black Exorcism of Coffin Joe*, 1974); and *Delírios de um anormal* (*Hallucinations of a Deranged Mind*, 1978).

Although Marins, during interviews, tends to come across as taking himself and his oeuvre very seriously, his capacity to send himself up is clear from Zé do Caixão's final celluloid outing. In *Delírios de um anormal*, Hamilton, a psychiatrist, suffers from paranoid hallucinations, fantasising that the horror film character Coffin Joe is trying to steal his wife, Tânia, in order (once again) to create the perfect child. Meanwhile Tânia, in an effort to aid her delusional husband, seeks the help of Hamilton's colleagues, who in turn seek the help of Mojica Marins himself. In the film, the director lives in a huge mansion and is attended to by blonde, uniformed maids: a far cry from the virtual penury that the real-life director was reportedly living in during the late 1970s and 1980s.

Meanwhile Mojica Marins continued, as he had always done, to make other, usually violent and sexually daring, feature films. In the 1970s and 1980s he followed the path of many an independent filmmaker in São Paulo: in order to make ends meet he produced both soft and hard-core porn films. The script for Zé do Caixão's latest feature film, *Encarnação do demônio* (Devil Incarnate), has reportedly been ready since 1967. After years of being unable to secure financial support, Marins recently received 500,000 reais (around £125,000) from the Brazilian Culture Ministry to finally get the film made. In the film, Zé do Caixão appears as a kind of storyteller, linking three discrete horror stories together, including one about a fashion show, which has ensured him some pre-launch publicity.

Filmmaking Marins-style

As Marins never learned to look after his money, and was constantly broke, even at the very height of his career his films are characterised by their very low budgets. In fact, it is a miracle that the films were ever made in the first place. Marins was arguably Brazil's finest exponent of 'popular' cinema, in that he did not rely on State funding for his films, nor did he have a wealthy family to fall back on financially when things went wrong. Instead, he made money and used free labour from his acting school and he often sold cheap pre-production shares in his movies in and around his neighbourhood, although admittedly few people ever saw a return on their investment.

Marins's filmmaking is equally characterised by constant battles with the censor. Marins had hoped to release *Esta noite encarnarei no teu cadáver* as soon as it was ready in 1966, in order to make the most of the positive publicity and box-office success of *À meia-noite levarei sua alma*. The censors, however, had other ideas and, as was the case with all of Marins's feature films, lengthy negotiations had to take place between the producer and the censors, resulting in the film being severely cut, and even rewritten in parts by the censors themselves (and therefore re-edited later). With the 1968 'coup within the coup', Mojica Marins's problems with the authorities only worsened, so much so that he is said to be Brazil's most censored director. For example, he was threatened with imprisonment in 1969 if he attempted to release *O despertar da besta*.[48]

Positive reviews of Marins's work tend to overlook the fact that the aesthetic choices that link his films to Brazil's avant-garde *cinema novo* and *cinema marginal* of the 1960s, such as the (politically motivated) revelation of technical shortcomings and the ironic use of excess, were not always made deliberately. As Fernandes admits, Marins had a number of filmmaking shortcomings, including the use of tacky scenery, poor photography and inauthentic dialogues.[49] Actors declaim (rather than deliver) pompous-sounding lines, and plots frequently involve cannibalism, mutilation, blaspheming and sadism. The result for many spectators, and in particular for an international audience made up of horror aficionados, and a contemporary national audience, is an involuntary humour.

To describe Marins's work as 'scandal cinema' – made up of strong images, of carnal and spiritual torment, that constantly evoke suffering, everyday violence, underdevelopment, the conditions of existence of the Third World – is to imply both a socio-political awareness and a conscious effort on the part of the filmmaker to produce such evocations: there is no evidence, even anecdotal, to suggest the existence of either. Nevertheless, Marins was clearly conscious that he was producing exploitation films and, as Dolores Tierney reminds us, 'exploitation cinema offers its own form of resistance to the bourgeois excesses of the avant-garde'.[50]

What is clear is that Zé do Caixão captured the imagination of a large number of cinema-goers, both at home and abroad, and that both Marins's filmmaking style and his tenacity in getting films made and screened inspired a number of key players in the Brazilian film industry. Glauber Rocha for one was said to be fascinated by Marins's early films, because of their deceptive simplicity, their shirking of the rules of filming and, perhaps more importantly, Marins's creative use of a shoestring budget which offered a new take on Rocha's 'aesthetics of hunger'.[51]

12

BOMBSHELLS: PIN-UP ACTRESSES POST-1960

This section will analyse the star texts of a group of 'sex symbol' actresses, concentrating on Sônia Braga, Vera Fischer and Xuxa Meneguel (known solely as Xuxa), who have dominated cinemas and glossy magazines in Brazil from the 1960s onwards. While there are, of course, award-winning 'character' actresses who have graced the Brazilian screen, such as Fernanda Montenegro and her daughter, Fernanda Torres, they are very much the exception to the rule that dictates that exceptional beauty and sexual attraction are pre-requisites for a career as an actor. The actresses discussed in this chapter were chosen for the fact that their star texts hinge on their representation of colour ('Nordic', as Brazilians like to describe those of Northern rather than the more common Southern European colouring and physique, as in the case of Vera Fischer and Xuxa, and *moreno/mulato*, as represented by Sônia Braga), rather than the body of work they have produced or their commercial success.[1] That said, Sônia Braga, Vera Fischer and Xuxa are easily the biggest stars of their generation in Brazil, and other iconic blonde stars such as Odete Lara, Norma Benguel and Darlene Glória have starred in a large number of critically acclaimed films.

In our discussion of Brazil's screen actresses and their star texts, it is important to bear in mind a number of issues which make Brazilian 'stardom' unique. For a start, it is worth considering the relationship that a number of mainstream screen actresses have with the soft-core porn industry. From around 1975 onwards, until the time of the *retomada* in the mid-1990s, Brazilian cinema was marked by a very high incidence of nudity, partly as a result of greater freedom from censorship and partly as a reaction to competition from the commercially very popular Italian soft-core porn films and the home-grown *pornochanchada* films.[2] It was, and continues to be, perfectly acceptable for actresses to promote upcoming roles in films, relaunch flagging careers and announce dramatic changes in style with highly suggestive and revealing photo shoots for soft-core porn magazines such as *Playboy* and *Revista Status*.[3] Both the now defunct *Revista Status* and the less 'highbrow' and more popular Brazilian *Playboy* were seen as essential vehicles for the marketing of female stars. It seems that, since the magazines' inception in the mid-1970s, actresses have had little to gain from taking the moral high ground and refusing to pose nude for such mainstream soft-core magazines to further their screen careers.

The dissemination of such images is arguably more widespread in Brazil than, say, in Britain. These magazines are not restricted to the 'top shelves': newsagents are scattered all over towns and cities in Brazil in the form of *bancas* or kiosks where the latest magazines are pinned up on display for passers-by to see. There is also a sizeable second-hand market for such magazines, which are displayed and sold by street traders in public squares.

Sônia Braga: Brazil's favourite *morena*

Sônia Braga was born in 1950 in the south of Brazil to a part-black father and part-Indian mother. Outside of Brazil she is perhaps best known for her role in Hector Babenco's Oscar-winning *Kiss of the Spiderwoman* (1985), as well as her numerous roles as the 'sultry *latina*' in Hollywood movies such as *The Rookie* (1990) and *From Dusk till Dawn III* (2000), and she is also known for the leading men with whom she has been linked over the years, including Robert Redford and Clint Eastwood. She was most recently seen in Britain in the popular US television series *Sex and the City*, in which she played, once again, the 'sultry *latina*' lesbian lover of the sexually rampant Samantha.

Braga was catapulted to stardom in Brazil in 1975 by her appearance in the title role in TV Globo's adaptation of *Gabriela*, a novel by the nation's most successful and prolific writer, Jorge Amado.[4] She would go on to play Gabriela in a film version in 1983, as well as two more of Jorge Amado's heroines on the big screen, including arguably Brazilian cinema's biggest ever role for a female lead, Dona Flor.[5] In 2001 on Jorge Amado's death, Braga acknowledged the debt she owed to the writer, declaring that his name alone represented her whole career. Earlier she had declared: 'he loves our people so much and he helped the Brazilian woman to understand that our beauty is how we are, brunette with brown eyes, it doesn't matter, we don't need to have blond hair or blue eyes!'[6]

When examining the star text and racialised sexuality of someone like Sônia Braga, we must be careful not to fall into the trap of understanding racial difference as it is understood in Britain or the United States, for example, as outlined below. That said, it is impossible to deny the 'structuring absence' of blacks and mixed-race people in Brazilian visual media, particularly when we contrast these with other popular cultural forms such as popular music, and particularly when we consider the extent to which many of the surviving and transformed legacies of African culture, such as samba and capoeira, have become part of the national culture, rather than an Afro-Brazilian ethnic culture.[7] Michael Hanchard points out that the Africanisation of the female bodily aesthetic as a national standard of beauty is a distinctive feature of Brazil, where scant attention is paid to breast size and emphasis instead is placed on large hips, buttocks and thighs and a narrow waist.[8] While this bodily aesthetic has slowly changed since the 1970s (consider, for example, the recent trend in breast enlargements as opposed to previously common reductions, possibly as a result of the success of Brazil's curvaceous 'Nordic' supermodel Gisele Bundchen), it is interesting to observe how few black or mixed-race pin-up girls there have been in Brazil, a country with such a large mixed-race population,[9] beyond the world of hard-core porn.

Racial definitions in Brazil are flexible and negotiated, and there is a strong tendency to identify as white people near the white/brown colour boundary.[10] Emphasis is placed on how people perceive themselves, just as much as on how people are perceived by others. Therefore, racial background, unlike, say, in the United States, does not always determine one's race and/or colour. Brazil's (white) ex-President Fernando Henrique Cardoso illustrated the difference between the nation's understanding of race and that of the home of the 'one-drop rule', by declaring, in a classic example of Brazilian political incorrectness when discussing race, that like most Brazilians he too had 'one foot in the kitchen', in a reference to the country's domestic slave-holding past.

Angela Gilliam points out that people who struggle to pass for white in the United States may not pass for black in Brazil, citing as one example the actress Lena Horne.[11] In this context, Sônia Braga's whiteness, in Brazil at any rate, is not open for discussion.[12] The racial definition most frequently applied to Braga is not *mulata* but *morena*. For many (including those who work in her publicity machine), Braga is *the* archetypal *morena*, a term meaning a dark-skinned or dark-haired 'white' woman, but which is often confusingly also used as a euphemism for *mulata* (mixed-race). *Mulata* in turn was until recently frequently used to mean black. Both *morena* and *mulata* have sexual as well as racial connotations.

In a book first published in 1942 on race in Bahia, Brazil's most Afro-Brazilian state in demographic terms, Donald Pierson described the *morena* in a way which still holds currency today:

> The 'ideal type' of Bahian femininity. She is in many cases an individual of remarkable beauty. Typically, she has dark-brown eyes and dark hair, quite wavy, perhaps even curly, and Caucasian features; her colour is *café com leite* (literally, 'coffee with milk'; i.e., like that of one 'heavily tanned') and she has a healthy appearance. The term *morena* is seldom mentioned to a Bahian male without there appearing an instant change in his expression. His face 'lights up', and a smile breaks on his lips. He pronounces *morena* with a tone indicative of admiration, affection, desire . . . The *morena* may, or may not, have African blood. But at least in Bahia this category includes many individuals of partial African descent.[13]

With her black, 'wiry' hair, wide hips and dark skin, Sônia Braga stands out, even among the new generation of stars, as physically one of the most Africanised of Brazil's successful white actresses. In an interview given in the USA, Braga described herself in the following terms: 'I am a typical Brazilian. I have a typical Brazilian bottom, typical Brazilian colouring, even a bit Africanish, and a typical Brazilian style.'[14]

Given the general absence of people of colour on television and cinema screens in Brazil, it is our contention that the *morena* frequently fills the role assumed by the *mulata* in other art forms. Braga's 'whiteness' did not prevent her from playing the lead in films with titles such as *A moreninha* (1970) (which roughly translates as Little Dark Girl) and *Mestiça, a escrava indomável* (1973) (about an indomitable mixed-race slave girl) earlier in her career. The screen *morena*, of which she is the most celebrated example, is very sensual and dark-skinned, with long wavy hair and European features.

Jorge Amado, the self-styled 'man of the people', was one of Brazil's most popular writers and one of its most successful exports. His novels of the 1960s and 1970s, for which he is best known, were commonly set in Bahia, and had 'exotic', sexy, mixed-race females as their protagonists (the character Dona Flor, for example, is a mixture of the three races believed to make up the typical Brazilian: white, Indian and black). It is worth noting that the work of Gilberto Freyre (1900–87), the sociologist most associated with the myth of Brazil's racial democracy, provided the inspiration for Amado's heroines and his interpretation of Brazilian culture. Freyre's description of the creation of Brazil's racial democracy in turn is strikingly similar to his own description of Sônia Braga, whom he considered to be the typical Brazilian woman. He described her as *the* Brazilian muse, and maintained that her mixture of blood gave her her beauty.[15]

Although not her most successful film, *Gabriela* (Bruno Barreto, 1983) was Sônia Braga's most significant big screen outing in terms of portraying the irresistible *morena*. Her tenth feature film, it gave her the opportunity to re-create on the big screen a role that had catapulted her to stardom on TV in 1975: the heroine of the adaptation of Jorge Amado's *Gabriela, cravo e canela* (Gabriela, clove and cinnamon). Here, Sônia moves away from the 'whiter', middle-class roles she had played in her three previous box-office hits: *Dona Flor e seus dois maridos* (*Dona Flor and Her Two Husbands*, 1976); *A dama do lotação* (*Lady on the Bus*, 1978); and *Eu te amo* (*I Love You*, 1981). With the exception of *Mestiça, a escrava indomável*, Sônia looks at her most 'untamed' in this film (especially her hair) and she appears on screen to be more dark-skinned than in the three previous films. Gabriela is one of Jorge Amado's archetypal mixed-race females from the North-East: *cor de canela* (cinnamon-coloured), devastatingly sexy without even trying, a free spirit and dirt-poor. In the film Gabriela bewitches an older man, bar owner Nacib (played by an incongruous Marcelo Mastroianni, with whom Braga had an affair during filming), and moves in with him. Thus begins a complicated love story played out against a backdrop of political intrigue.

Bruno Barreto, in his adaptation, treads familiar ground in the methods he uses to contrast the stuffy, conservative and predominantly white world of middle-class, small-town Bahia with the world of possibilities represented by Gabriela. She is tamed when she marries Nacib. Just as Dona Flor had seemed trapped and stifled by her second marriage, compared to the naked love scenes in which she appears with her first husband (in which the lighting of the shots reveals her to be much darker than when clothed), Gabriela is restricted by the new society she joins. This restriction is emphasised by her discomfort when wearing shoes (a trope used in numerous other films, including Nelson Pereira dos Santos's seminal *cinema novo*

Figure 12.1 Sônia Braga in Bruno Barreto's *Gabriela* (1983) (courtesy of Sultana/The Kobal Collection)

film *Vidas secas* (*Barren Lives*, 1963)). There are frequent shots of Gabriela looking uncomfortable in shoes, of her bare feet, and of shoes being removed and put on. In a typical scene, she goes to a conference, falls asleep, goes home and then slips out later and goes to the circus (barefoot of course), where the camera homes in on Gabriela's feet as she delightedly stamps them in time to the lively music.

The crucial undressing scene, which can be found in all of Sônia's films made in Brazil,[16] sees Gabriela carefully remove her smart white clothes, stockings and underwear and shake her hair loose. Totally naked, she then puts on a short, colourful dress, runs her fingers through her long wavy hair (see Figure 12.1) and is 'dressed' to go out on her terms. This has become the trademark outfit for the screen *morena* of the kind played by Braga[17] and described in novels by Jorge Amado. Imitations can be found, for example, in the wardrobe of Eurídice (Patrícia França) in Carlos Diegues's *Orfeu* (*Orpheus*, 1999) and Juma (Cristiana Oliveira) in the hit TV soap *Pantanal* (Manchete, 1990), whereby make-up, shoes, underwear and hairdressing are at best dispensable and at worst the tools of the prostitute.

Sônia Braga has often commented that her appearance on the acting scene in the 1970s marked a new, 'aesthetically nationalist' period in that people saw for the first time that they, with their dark hair and brown eyes, could be beautiful too.[18] With this she endeared herself to millions of Brazilian women. Just as Jorge Amado promoted himself as a 'man of the people', so too could Sônia Braga's star persona be read as populist. During the 1970s in Brazil, notions of racial harmony and national unity were being promoted more than ever by the military dictatorship. In a climate of cultural nationalism, the promotion of the racial democracy myth and the popularity of cultural representations of sexual transgression such as those seen in the *pornochanchada*, the dark-skinned Brazilian woman came to symbolise Brazilian culture in the 1970s. It is surely no coincidence that another big commercial hit of the mid-1970s that had a female lead, Carlos Diegues's *Xica da Silva* (1976), starred the black actress Zezé Mota playing a sexually rampant slave. Evidence of how attractive a notion the assertion of the dark-skinned character of Brazil can be, and how it is often unavoidably linked to the myth of racial democracy, can be found in respected cultural anthropologist Roberto DaMatta's dismissal in 1999 of the need for the introduction of positive discrimination in the country because, he argued, in Brazil practically everyone is a mulatto.[19]

In films such as *Dona Flor e seus dois maridos*, *A dama do lotação* and *Gabriela*, Sônia Braga became associated with the transgressive and liberated mood of the period of *abertura*, and this must be one of the reasons why she became such a popular movie star. Also, given the commercial success of the writers upon whose work the three films were based, Jorge Amado and Nelson Rodrigues, Braga's association with Brazilian popular culture and identity were firmly established during this period. Throughout the *abertura* period, in interviews at home and abroad, Braga actively sought to link herself with the boom in popular Brazilian culture, the Brazilian masses, good times, freedom (and not necessarily in political terms) and hope for the future. At times it becomes difficult to distinguish between Braga the woman, the roles she has played and the nation itself. In a lengthy interview to Brazilian *Playboy* magazine in 1982, she evidently considered herself to be the flag bearer for popular Brazilian cinema.[20] The journalist who interviewed her, Hamilton Almeida Filho, said of her: 'She reminds me of Brazil smiling, I don't know why.' Braga declared in the same article that she represented an unconscious desire for liberty, that she had been an ugly child, which had helped her be beautiful in adulthood, and that she had lived in poverty for a while. She then proclaimed: 'that's the story of Brazil'.

Sônia Braga, in terms of her racial background and how she portrayed herself and was portrayed in the media at the height of her career in Brazilian cinema in the late 1970s and early 1980s, fitted comfortably into notions of syncretism, hybridity and middle paths that were so popular in political and cultural terms at the time. She was often described in terms of contrasts: beauty and the beast, reality and fiction, a mixture of innocence and carnality. She was also seen by everyone at the time as being very Brazilian, as if there was something almost patriotic in her colouring and personality. She appeared at a time when there was a need to produce 'an authentic national culture for the people, a category both vague and all-embracing',[21] and the *morena*, as we have seen, is a widely encompassing term. She was also anti-establishment, in that she appealed to people partly because of her libertarian and transgressive qualities, on and off screen.

It is interesting that in the post-*abertura* period (after Braga starred in *Gabriela*) the offer of film work in Brazil dried up and media attention seemed to turn almost immediately to Xuxa Meneguel, the blonde, blue-eyed children's TV host and film actress and, later, media mogul. Xuxa has practically built a career on a carefully constructed image of whiteness. Sônia Braga, on the other hand, in her spontaneity, vitality, energy, exaggerated sensuality, alternative lifestyle, willingness to get naked on screen, 'natural' beauty and 'Africanised' body, came as close to representing the *mulata* on screen as Brazil's briefly nationalist but ultimately racist visual media of the 1970s and early 1980s would permit.

So if Sônia Braga in her major movies and the ones that cast her star text in stone played characters that can be described as hybrids (socially, racially, sexually and so on), and if she has come, rather like the *mulata* and *mestiça* in both specifically Brazilian and generally Latin American foundational fictions of the nineteenth century onwards, to be held as a symbol of nationhood, where does that leave actresses at the other end of the white colour bar, actresses such as Vera Fischer, who similarly made an impact on the Brazilian screen principally in the 1970s, who also has close associations with TV Globo and soap operas and who also, now in her 50s, continues to be very famous and seek work on the screen?

As loiras: Brazil's screen blondes

While reference will be made in this section to five iconic blonde actresses – Odete Lara, Norma Benguel, Darlene Glória, Vera Fischer and Xuxa Meneguel – we will concentrate on the star texts of Fischer and Xuxa, given their greater professional longevity, their impact at the box office and their greater reliance on their blonde hair and colouring in terms of career and self-promotion. Both Odete Lara (born 1929) and Darlene Glória (born 1943), having been well-known screen actresses in the 1960s and 1970s respectively, abandoned their film careers at the height of their popularity and have rarely appeared in public since.[22] Norma Benguel (born 1935), forever remembered as the blonde bombshell in films such as *O homem do sputnik* (Sputnik Man, 1959), in which she imitated Brigitte Bardot, and *Os cafajestes* (*The Unscrupulous Ones*, 1962) has reinvented herself as a (brunette) film director and producer.

Vera Fischer was born in 1951 in Blumenau in the Southern state of Santa Catarina and is of German descent.[23] She broke into television and movies on the back of her victory at the 1969 Miss Brasil beauty contest. She made her screen name starring in *pornochandadas*, the most memorable of which was Aníbal Massaini Neto's *A superfêmea* (Superwoman, 1973). In the film, Fischer plays a naive, distant and devastatingly attractive beauty queen who is used by a marketing Svengali to promote a product deemed impossible to sell because of its associations with impotence: the male contraceptive pill. A date with 'superwoman' is offered as first prize in the competition: the suggestion being that the lucky winner will be able to try out the new product with his prize, in whose company impotence would simply be impossible.

Vera Fischer to an extent became this much desired and sought-after 'superwoman' in the 1970s and early 1980s. She starred in a number of box-office hits after leaving behind the *pornochanchada* in the mid-1970s, including Braz Chediak's 1981 adaptation of popular Brazilian author Nelson Rodrigues's *Bonitinha mas ordinária* (Pretty but Wicked) and Arnaldo Jabor's *Eu te amo* (also 1981), and she was one of Brazil's most popular cover girls at the time. Having seemingly overcome a series of grave personal difficulties, she is now a regular once again on TV Globo primetime soap operas and, well into her 50s, she continues to make the headlines for her looks.[24]

In 1989 Fischer starred in a film entitled *Doida demais* (Just Too Crazy), and by doing so she handed gossip columnists a ready-made headline for reports on her stormy private life. Married twice (to actors Perry Salles and Felipe Camargo), her family life reads like a Globo soap opera. Both marriages were wracked by violence. Rather than being seen as a victim of domestic abuse, Vera is portrayed as giving as good as she gets and, more often than not, as provoking violence through her drug and alcohol abuse, which also caused her to be sacked from (but always later re-employed by a surprisingly forgiving) TV Globo. Felipe Camargo was hospitalised as a result of being attacked with a pair of scissors (one of Fischer's maids suffered a similar fate), eliciting from the press the cruel headline 'Vera Scissor-hands'. Vera's inability to keep control of her senses and stay sober saw her hit rock-bottom in the early 1990s when she notoriously lost custody of her young son.

Fischer is very much an extreme case in terms of star text, but there are a number of features of both her film career and perceptions of her private life that resonate with the star texts of other blonde actresses. For a start, blonde actresses not only tend to come from backgrounds that are associated, in Brazil at least, with the world of prostitution, but they play characters from similar backgrounds on screen. Norma Benguel was a showgirl, and in *Os cafajestes* she is required to perform naked in front of the two male leads and, in what is a consciously voyeuristic sequence, the film audience too. Darlene Glória was a cabaret singer, a role director Arnaldo Jabor later re-created for her in the film *Toda nudez será castigada* (*All Nudity Shall Be Punished*, 1972). And Vera Fischer was a beauty queen, a role she plays in *A superfêmea*. In 2000 in *Xuxa popstar*, Xuxa, after years away from the catwalks, played a supermodel.

Furthermore, these blondes have played prostitutes in their most memorable film roles (a total of twelve roles among them). In contrast, Sônia Braga has yet to play a prostitute on the Brazilian screen.

Blondes appear to be stereotypically linked to prostitution in Brazil and other places in Latin America in a way that they are not, for example, in the UK or the United States, and in this sense many of the tropes of feminine whiteness suggested by Richard Dyer, for example, cannot be so readily applied to the Brazilian cultural context.[25] This partly stems from the large population of poor 'Germanics' in the South of Brazil. While the international sex tourism industry in Brazil reflects a fascination on the part of foreign visitors with the 'exotic' *mulata* and black woman, many young Southern women of Northern European ancestry and colouring migrate to urban areas where they are prized for their exoticism by Brazilians. There is a sizeable market for such 'exotic' women in cities such as Rio and São Paulo, and many fall into prostitution as a result.

As well as a close association with prostitution, blonde leading ladies, seemingly without exception, have turbulent and deeply troubled private lives. Like Vera Fischer, Darlene Glória and Norma Benguel nearly destroyed themselves through alcohol and drug abuse. Odete Lara's tragic personal circumstances (her Italian immigrant parents committed suicide) became the subject of a film, *Lara*, in 2002. Norma Benguel, in the mould of the archetypal blonde, is thought of as a loose cannon. She may have been imprisoned briefly at the height of the military dictatorship in the 1960s for her outspoken views on censorship, but she seems to have garnered few supporters in artistic circles as a result. She came under considerable criticism, for example, in the 1990s when, as a fledgling film director, she approached then President Itamar Franco unilaterally to demand greater support for the Brazilian film industry, in the light of Fernando Collor's dismantling of state support mechanisms. The assumption was that Benguel was looking out for her own interests, rather than representing the aspirations of the industry.[26] When they are businesswomen, blondes like Benguel and Xuxa are perceived as ruthless and individualistic.

Blondes like Vera Fischer are perceived as being ultimately 'unhinged'. Both Odete Lara and Darlene Glória quit their film careers and sought refuge in new-age religions, while Vera Fischer went on a well-publicised 'soul-cleansing' trip to India at the height of her personal troubles. Xuxa, never one to miss a marketing opportunity, has declared her faith in the power of fairies and elves (and made two commercially successful films on the topic).

Given that Vera Fischer and Sônia Braga are contemporaries, it is useful to compare their star texts in terms of their representation of the Brazilian *loira* and *morena* respectively. For a start, there are clear differences in how both are photographed for features in magazines. In terms of lighting, Sônia Braga is frequently shot (particularly, it should be said, when releasing a film or TV series in which she plays a mixed-race character) as being literally 'cinnamon-coloured' (the *cor de canela* associated with mixed-race women discussed earlier). The colour of Vera Fischer's (and other blonde stars') skin is less significant, as it is the blonde hair, blue or green eyes, European features and 'doll-like' complexion, revealed in facial close-ups, that are seen as markers of whiteness and beauty.[27] That said, pale white skin has until very recently been rarely seen in glamour photography in Brazil. White stars are often, in fact, lit so that their skin looks very tanned.

The differences in the setting of glamour shots of Braga and Fischer are clear to see and arguably conform to stereotypes of race in Brazil. Braga, like the roles she has always played, is wild and untameable, with her *cabelo ruim* ('bad', as in unruly, hair) very much a marker of a racial other in Brazil: the common usage of the phrase makes it clear that 'Africanised' features are seen to deviate from an accepted standard of beauty. In a typical magazine feature she is photographed in a forest, surrounded by the natural world, and is not obviously 'made up'.[28] In contrast Fischer, in a feature for the same magazine, is wearing heavy make-up: glossy lips, heavy blusher and carefully coiffured hair.[29] In fact, she is photographed here (and elsewhere) very much in the style of the high-class prostitute, for example shot naked underneath luxurious furs, wearing expensive jewels, on the telephone, in a bubble bath, in what is understood to be a hotel room. The frequency of the voyeuristic overhead shots of Fischer staring straight into the camera contrasts with the level, sideways-on shots of Braga, suggesting a different relationship between the reader and the star.

Sônia Braga is generally photographed as having an all-over tan, whereas most models make a point of leaving the clear sunbathing bikini lines that are typical of pornographic iconography.[30] There are two exceptions in Braga's iconography: first, the poster still for Arnaldo Jabor's *Eu te amo*, in which Braga is shot pulling down one side of the top of her dress to reveal a bikini-marked breast; secondly, in the feature on her in *Status*, published on the eve of the release of *Gabriela*, her bikini marks are very clearly defined. *Gabriela* is arguably Braga's 'darkest' role. Newspaper articles reporting on the filming of *Gabriela* made mention of the fact that Braga was obliged by director Bruno Barreto to spend four hours per day sunbathing, to maintain her tan, thus emphasising that her natural colouring is not in fact all that dark. Both movies were made partly with the US market in mind and as a way of building on the name Braga was gradually making for herself abroad as a sex bomb. So while Gabriela the *morena* does not reveal bikini marks on screen, Sônia Braga the (white) soft-core porn star debuting in the US film market does, confirming her 'white' acceptability in the USA.

As we have seen already, the 'natural' quality of Sônia Braga that is emphasised in her film roles and photo shoots is also reflected in interviews. For example, in 1976 in an interview for *Fatos e Fotos* gossip magazine, Braga described how her ambition was to have a little farm, where she would pick fruit, make her own clothes or not wear any at all. In reality, Braga has gone on to become one of the most powerful Latino celebrities in Hollywood, but her simple ambitions do seem to stand in stark contrast to, for example, Vera Fischer's publicised desires to leave behind the world of the *pornochanchada* and to be taken seriously as an actress, or the European theatrical pretensions of Odete Lara and Norma Benguel, or the media empire created by a very astute Xuxa. Screen blondes are, then, set apart from the majority of the population, as indeed they are numerically: they are distant and difficult to fathom, qualities which make them irresistible, but as their star texts reveal they can ultimately be bought for the right price.

A significant shift in the portrayal of blondes in the media and their impact on popular culture took place in the 1980s in Brazil with the arrival on the scene of model-turned-actress and TV presenter Xuxa Meneguel. Xuxa was born in 1963 in Santa Rosa, a small town in Rio Grande do Sul, Brazil's southernmost state, the grandchild of Austrian, Polish, Italian and German immigrants.[31] Her family moved to the suburbs of Rio de Janeiro when she was 7 years old (her father was an officer in the Brazilian army) and she was 'discovered' and became a model in 1978. Around this time she embarked on a very widely publicised relationship with Brazilian football star Pelé, said to be the most famous black man on earth, certainly the most recognised Brazilian in the world at the time, and twenty-three years her senior. Amélia Simpson has argued that Xuxa's relationship with Pelé at the beginning of her TV and film career enabled her to play up her whiteness without accusations of being racially insensitive.[32] Her behaviour may have elicited comment from time to time from Brazilian feminists, concerned with her promotion of gender stereotypes and beauty myths in general, but little comment has been made on her explicit promotion of the ideal of whiteness.

Xuxa is, to an extent, incomparable with other actresses, not just because of her success first and foremost as a TV presenter and her singing career in the children's market, but because of her wealth and business empire. In the 1990s Xuxa regularly appeared in the Forbes Entertainment Rich List (in thirty-seventh place in 1992, with a fortune of $100,000,000).

Randal Johnson and Robert Stam may argue that 'Xuxa's films are commercial successes that are likely to be soon forgotten'[33] and that they thus do not form part of Brazil's cinematic canon, but it is impossible to deny the impact of Xuxa's stardom, both on Brazilian society in general and on commercial Brazilian cinema specifically. While Xuxa is undoubtedly better known for her television work and the intense merchandising opportunities that such work brings (she is also one of Brazil's most successful recording artists), her film career is far from insignificant. She has made fifteen films to date, nearly all of which, since 1980, have had the name 'Xuxa' in the title. So even though she plays characters with names other than her own, by having her own name in the title of her films the understanding is that she is playing herself. In other words, in her films she becomes a princess, a queen, a supermodel, a successful dancer and a goddess, all of which, in Brazil, are tropes of feminine whiteness. She began her children's movie career starring in three films alongside the Trapalhões, a comedy quartet who had also built a considerable following on television. She broke out on her own in 1988 in *Super Xuxa contra o baixo astral* (*Super Xuxa against Satan*), only to rejoin the Trapalhões (but now with top billing) in 1989 in *A Princesa Xuxa e os Trapalhões* (Princess Xuxa and the Trapalhões), one of the quartet's most popular movies. The formula was repeated the following year in *Xuxa e os Trapalhões em o mistério de Robin Hood* (Xuxa and the Trapalhões in the Mystery of Robin Hood, 1990), on which Xuxa's production company Xuxa Produções acted as associate producer.

In 1990 Xuxa teamed up with another hugely popular children's TV performer, Sérgio Mallandro, in a joint venture entitled *Lua de cristal* (Crystal Moon). With just under 5 million spectators, it was the biggest film of the 1990s, and it guaranteed Xuxa a second box-office hit at a time when the Brazilian film industry had all but ground to a halt. The years 1990 and 2000 were important landmarks in her movie career in that she made semi-autobiographical films – in *Lua de cristal* she plays Maria da Graça (her real name), a young girl who moves from the sticks to the big city, comes across all sorts of dishonest people and dangerous situations, and finds her way with the help of luck and, the film suggests, good friendships. In 2000's *Xuxa popstar* she plays a famous international model who returns to Brazil to find love.

Xuxa spent most of the 1990s making very lucrative straight-to-video films and CDs for children as well as TV programmes. She returned to cinemas in 1999 with *Xuxa requebra* (Xuxa Gets Down), in which she picked up on the fashion for dancing competitions in the style of *A Loira do Tchan* and faced head on and incorporated the (fake) blonde competition from Carla Perez.[34] Xuxa also picked up on a popular fascination with *duendes* (elves) and their magical powers in *Xuxa e os duendes* (Xuxa and the Elves, 2001) and the sequel, *Xuxa e os duendes II: no caminho das fadas* (Xuxa and the Elves II: The Fairies' Path, 2002). She released another couple of films in quick succession in 2003 and 2004, *Xuxa abracadabra* and *Xuxa e o tesouro da cidade perdida* (Xuxa and the Treasure of the Lost City), in which she manages to product-place even more Xuxa merchandising than in previous movie outings.

The great skeleton in Xuxa's cupboard is her role in Walter Hugo Khouri's *Amor, estranho amor* (*Love, Strange Love*, 1982). Khouri, considered (perhaps generously) to be the Bergman of Brazil, made a series of complex and highly sexually charged films in the 1960s, 1970s and 1980s which invariably starred blondes in the key roles (Xuxa, Vera Fischer, Odete Lara and Norma Benguel all starred in his films). In *Amor, estranho amor* Xuxa plays Tamara, a young prostitute who is brought from the South of Brazil to a high-class brothel in order to seduce a powerful politician. While at the house, she seduces the young son of prostitute Anna, played by Vera Fischer.

Xuxa, like many other blonde actresses, continues to this day to be dogged by rumours of affairs with men in high places, affairs that she has always denied. Part of Xuxa's star text is an 'alternative' discovery myth which confuses the plotline of *Amor, estranho amor* with real life, suggesting that Xuxa was brought by her military father to Rio de Janeiro to be sold to politicians. But such urban myths and the sexual content of the film did not in themselves preclude a career working with children, for within a year of the release of *Amor, estranho amor* Xuxa had secured her first TV presenting job with the now extinct TV Manchete, to be snapped up shortly afterwards by the all-pervasive TV Globo. *Amor, estranho amor* did Xuxa's career no harm in Brazil (if anything, it can be said to have offered another context with regard to the consumption of Xuxa's image on TV – for example, the 'shorts and thigh-length white boots look' that she sported and that was imitated by young girls throughout Brazil in the 1980s).[35] It would be difficult in the UK or USA, for example, for an actress who had made an 'art-house porn' film in which she performed a sexual act with a pre-pubescent boy, to rise to become one of the most successful children's television presenters. But as Amélia Simpson observes, the fact that Xuxa played a prostitute in the film made the initiation ceremony acceptable in Brazil,[36] given the relatively accepted tradition of young men experimenting sexually with maids and other 'subaltern' females. Where it posed potential problems was in Xuxa's move into the Argentine market and the Latino market in the USA.[37]

Remarkably enough, at around the same time as Xuxa's on-screen sexual relationship with a young boy failed to raise more than the odd eyebrow, Vera Fischer was also crossing the slippery boundaries of representations of art, sexual liberation and child abuse, when she appeared in a dedicated special edition of soft-porn magazine *Suplemento* (now a much-sought-after collector's item). As well as ultra-soft-focus shots of Fischer relaxing (naked) at home and in her garden, and joined by her (naked) husband, actor Perry Salles, their infant daughter, Rafaela, also appears (naked) in the magazine, in shots which range in 'innocence' from a re-creation of the 'Madonna and Child' to the three of them at play on a double bed. In 1998 Xuxa gave birth to a daughter, Sasha, who, like Rafaela, receives considerable media exposure and regularly appears on TV and in photo shoots with her mother.

According to Amélia Simpson, Xuxa 'established a public image as a compliant, sexually provocative woman with a childlike, innocent quality. That image tells females how to be, and males what to expect.'[38] Xuxa established herself first and foremost as a desirable sexual being, by posing nude for magazines and starring in a Walter Hugo Khouri film, and then retreated into the innocent (and financially lucrative) world of children's television, films and music, from which she could continue to flaunt her sexual attractiveness but in a way that posed no threat to the patriarchal order. While the *pornochanchada* of the 1970s, regardless of its inherent chauvinism, helped to bring debates on sexual freedom to the fore in Brazil, and while Darlene Glória's character in *Toda nudez será castigada* and Vera Fischer in an interview for *Playboy* openly discuss the proto-feminist issues of female masturbation and sexual desire, Xuxa in the 1980s and 1990s, through her childlike and coy observations on sex[39] and through her screen persona as kiddies' favourite, provoked a return to the infantilisation of female sexuality. She represented 'a specific gender role that was under attack by women's movements in Brazil and abroad [and thus] performed the important function of reasserting the validity of the old-fashioned way'.[40]

But Xuxa also has a complicated family life: like Vera Fischer she has to try hard to create an image of a happy family which ultimately feels forced and artificial and fails to convince. In the wake of talk of lesbian relations with her manager, the vilified Marlene Mattos, Xuxa became pregnant. She split up from boyfriend and father of her child, actor and model Luciano Szafir, before Sasha was born, eliciting rumours that the model, who is five years her junior, had been hand-picked by Xuxa to produce a designer baby. When they were together, she sounded as uncommitted and dispassionate about him as she had done about Pelé twenty years earlier.

Concluding remarks

In Brazil white female film stars are generally portrayed as detached, distant, unhinged, with turbulent, complex and complicated private lives, and incapable of finding peace of mind. They frequently play prostitutes on screen. By contrast, darker actresses like Sônia Braga, rather than playing prostitutes, play women who are happy to give it away for free without a second thought. Sônia Braga built her fame on her perceived accessibility, her warmth, her passion and many other qualities that Brazilians pride themselves on that make them distinctive and special. Like the *superfêmea* played by Vera Fischer, who is substituted by an automaton at one point in the film and no one seems to notice, Xuxa's screen performance (and that of the blonde clones in the world of children's television she helped spawn, such as Angélica and Eliane), while visually striking, comes across as formulaic in the extreme and rather soulless.

Sônia Braga early on in her career declared that she was not interested in having children and did not ever have any. Her childless status (i.e. her pursuit of sexual pleasure over the need to procreate) has not been held against her and she did not seem to fall under pressure, unlike Xuxa, for example, to reproduce. Having had a child in controversial circumstances, Xuxa, like Fischer, is frequently depicted in the media as a 'failed' mother. Such an acceptance of Sônia Braga's childless status can be viewed as conforming to the notion of the sterility of the *mulata* left over from Enlightenment ideas of racial degeneration. But Sônia is hardly an archetypal *mulata* in the sense that she is not seen as 'tragic' – tragedy and self-destruction are very much the domain of the screen blondes.

NOTES

INTRODUCTION

1 Valentina Vitali and Paul Willeman, 'Introduction', in Valentina Vitali and Paul Willeman (eds), *Theorising National Cinema* (London: BFI Publishing, 2006), pp. 1–14 (p. 3).
2 Colonisation by the Portuguese, early independence (1822), the replacement of colonial rule with a Brazilian monarchy (1822–89), and the late arrival of the abolition of slavery (1888) attest to Brazil's lack of common history with its neighbours, resulting in the country's relative cultural isolation in Latin America, a situation that is gradually changing with, among other initiatives, the MERCOSUL, the customs union of the countries of South America's Southern Cone.
3 See Zuzana M. Pick, *The New Latin American Cinema: A Continental Project* (Austin: University of Texas Press, 1993).
4 For more information on these, see Chapter 4.
5 As discussed by Stephen Crofts in his seminal essay 'Concepts of National Cinema', in John Hill and Pamela Church Gibson (eds), *The Oxford Guide to Film Studies* (Oxford: Oxford University Press, 1998), pp. 385–94.
6 See, for example, Christopher J. Berry and Mary Ann Farquhar, *China on Screen: Cinema and Nation* (New York: Columbia University Press, 2006).
7 As do the films of another *cinema novo* veteran, Ruy Guerra. See, for example, the discussion of Guerra's 1983 film *Erendira*, a French/Mexican/West German co-production, included in Randal Johnson and Robert Stam (eds), *Brazilian Cinema* (New York: Columbia University Press, 1995), pp. 438–41.
8 It is highly suggestive in the sense that the film itself depicts the road journey through a number of South American countries made by a young Che Guevara, surely the most transnational of Latin American revolutionaries. It is worth adding that discussions of the transnational generally exclude work produced in Hollywood. Walter Salles's first film, *Exposure*, a USA/Brazil English language co-production made for an international market, has been ignored by critics, and *Dark Water* (2005) is dismissed as just a Hollywood genre film. One notable exception to this rule is the interesting examination of Hector Babenco's 1991 Hollywood film *At Play in the Fields of the Lord* included in *Brazilian Cinema*, although admittedly the *raison d'être* of the piece is to reveal how the film debunks the kind of myths usually espoused in Hollywood films about Brazil: Robert Stam, João Luiz Vieira and Ismail Xavier, 'The Shape of Brazilian Cinema in the Postmodern Age', in Johnson and Stam (eds), *Brazilian Cinema*, pp. 432–4.
9 There are a number of interesting studies on both the portrayal of indigenous populations and filmmaking within their communities (the so-called Fourth Cinema, for example) that suggest that they could arguably be more usefully analysed as part

of transnational study. See, for example, Scott Mackenzie, 'Mimetic Nationhood: Ethnography and the National', in Mette Hjort and Scott Mackenzie (eds), *Cinema and Nation* (London and New York: Routledge, 2000), pp. 241–59; Patricia Aufderheide, 'Grassroots Video in Latin America', in Chon A. Noriega (ed.), *Visible Nations: Latin American Cinema and Video* (Minneapolis and London: University of Minnesota Press, 2000), pp. 219–38.

10 See, for example, Lima Barreto's Cannes-winning film *O cangaceiro* (*The Bandit*, 1953), discussed in Chapter 6, the award-winning *cinema novo* films, discussed in Chapter 7, and *Central do Brasil (Central Station*, 1998) and *Cidade de Deus* (*City of God*, 2002), analysed in Chapter 9.

11 Stam, Vieira and Xavier, 'The Shape of Brazilian Cinema in the Postmodern Age', p. 394.

12 Ibid., p. 395.

13 Randal Johnson, *The Film Industry in Brazil: Culture and the State* (Pittsburgh, PA: University of Pittsburgh Press, 1987), p. 107.

14 It is interesting to note that critics and the public debated and to a great extent resolved the issue of cultural imperialism in the music industry back in the days of *Tropicália*, the highly influential late-1960s avant-garde movement that mixed traditional Afro-Brazilian and Portuguese rhythms with rock 'n' roll. The equivalent kind of debate was begun by the *cinema marginal* of the late 1960s, but marginal cinema was seen by too few people to make an impact.

15 Carlos Diegues, 'The Cinema that Brazil Deserves', in Lúcia Nagib (ed.), *The New Brazilian Cinema* (London and New York: I.B. Tauris, 2003), pp. 23–35 (p. 33).

16 José Álvaro Moisés, 'A New Policy for Brazilian Cinema', in Nagib (ed.), *The New Brazilian Cinema*, p. 5.

17 'Even with the best of intentions Hollywood had trouble treating Brazil the way it deserved to be treated.' Sérgio Augusto, 'Hollywood Looks at Brazil: From Carmen Miranda to *Moonraker*', in Johnson and Stam (eds), *Brazilian Cinema*, pp. 352–61 (p. 360). For further information on the relationship between Hollywood and Brazil at the time of the Good Neighbour Policy, see Lisa Shaw and Maite Conde, 'Brazil through Hollywood's Gaze: From the Silent Screen to the Good Neighbor Policy Era', in Lisa Shaw and Stephanie Dennison (eds), *Latin American Cinema: Essays on Modernity, Gender and National Identity* (Jefferson, NC: McFarland Press, 2005), pp. 180–209.

18 One of the dangers, of course, of attempting through filmmaking to 'correct' the foreigner's understanding of Brazil is that it can lead to self-censorship, and to a refusal to place on screen stories that could be said to reinforce a negative image of Brazil abroad. Anecdotal evidence suggests that there is a sizeable part of the cinema-going population that avoids national films (such as *Cidade de Deus*) that depict Brazil as a land of violence, and their concerns are more often than not echoed by critics when such depictions are presented in foreign films. This is clearly illustrated by the commotion that John Stockwell's *Turistas/Paradise Lost* (2006) has created in Brazil.

19 Andrew Higson, 'The Limiting Imagination of National Cinema', in Hjort and Mackenzie (eds), *Cinema and Nation*, pp. 63–74 (p. 71), quoting John Hill.

20 Randal Johnson and Robert Stam's *Brazilian Cinema*, the most important and useful guide to Brazilian cinema produced to date in English, focuses almost exclusively on 'worthy' films, and the most complete guide to Brazilian cinema published in Portuguese also strongly favours analysis of such films: Fernão Ramos (ed.), *História do cinema brasileiro* (São Paulo: Arte Editora, 1987).

21 As aptly summarised by Susan Hayward in 'Framing National Cinemas', in Hjort and Mackenzie (eds), *Cinema and Nation*, pp. 88–102 (p. 92).

22 Ibid., p. 93.

23 See, for example, Chapter 6 and the discussion of Vera Cruz film studios. The

nationalist project of Vera Cruz is implied even in the title of the studios: it is the original name given to Brazil by its first Portuguese 'discoverers'.

24 See, for example, Chapter 3 and the role of Embrafilme in the development of the Brazilian film industry.

25 The national squad is referred to as *a seleção brasileira* or simply *a seleção*.

26 For a useful summary of scholarship on the national cinema question to date, see Crofts, 'Concepts of National Cinema', and Paul Willeman, 'The National Revisited', in Vitali and Willeman (eds), *Theorising National Cinema*, pp. 29–43.

27 Erstwhile *cinema novo* filmmaker Arnaldo Jabor is an interesting example of this phenomenon: Jabor has reinvented himself as a (deliberately controversial) political and social commentator on TV Globo's evening news programme *Jornal nacional* and in the national press.

28 Jean-Claude Bernardet, *Historiografia clássica do cinema brasileiro: metodologia e pedagogia* (São Paulo: Annablume, 1995), p. 27.

29 Alex Viany's *Introdução ao cinema brasileiro*, first published in 1959 and republished by Embrafilme in 1987, included a national cinema filmography, the first of its kind. Viany published his first piece on Brazilian cinema in 1951, 'Breve introdução à história do cinema brasileiro' in *Revista Fundamentos*. Glauber Rocha published two key texts at both the beginning and the end of the *cinema novo* movement: *Revisão crítica do cinema brasileiro* in 1963 and *Revolução do cinema novo* in 1981. He also launched the highly influential manifesto 'Estética da fome' ('Aesthetics of Hunger') in 1965. See Chapter 7.

30 See the entry on Salles Gomes written by José Inácio de Melo Souza in Fernão Ramos and Luiz Felipe Miranda (eds), *Enciclopédia do cinema brasileiro* (São Paulo: SENAC, 2000), pp. 274–6.

31 Paulo Emílio Salles Gomes, *Jean Vigo* (London: Faber and Faber, 1998). His work on Vigo has been praised by, among others, André Bazin and Chris Marker.

32 Humberto Mauro is one of the 'pioneer' filmmakers discussed in Chapter 5.

33 First published in *Argumento* magazine in 1973. The essay appears in English translation in Johnson and Stam (eds), *Brazilian Cinema*, pp. 244–55.

34 Ibid., p. 245.

35 Ibid.

36 'No intelligent discussion of Brazil's cultural production can ignore the central fact of its economic dependency': Randal Johnson and Robert Stam, 'The Shape of Brazilian Film History', in Johnson and Stam (eds), *Brazilian Cinema*, pp. 17–51 (p. 17).

37 Despite the promotion by important Brazilian film critic and academic Lúcia Nagib, who occupies the Chair of World Cinema at the University of Leeds, of a polycentric approach to reading world cinema, Brazilian film culture, partly under the influence of Salles's essay, continues to be viewed by many as peripheral in its relation to Hollywood as centre.

38 Gomes, 'Cinema: A Trajectory within Underdevelopment', in Johnson and Stam (eds), *Brazilian Cinema*, p. 253.

39 Ibid., p. 255.

40 See entry on Bernardet written by Luiz Felipe Miranda in Ramos and Miranda (eds), *Enciclopédia do cinema brasileiro*, pp. 56–7. See also Fernão Ramos, 'Os novos rumos do cinema brasileiro', in Ramos (ed.), *História do cinema brasileiro*, p. 358.

41 For more on the Bela Época, see Chapter 1.

42 Jean-Claude Bernardet, *Historiografia clássica*, pp. 47–8. Bernardet argues on the same pages that, if a filmmaking Belle Époque did exist, it was restricted to the then capital, Rio de Janeiro.

43 Vitali and Willeman, 'Introduction', p. 1.

44 See the entry on *cineclubes* written by André Gatti in Fernão Ramos and Luiz Felipe Miranda (eds), *Enciclopédia do cinema brasileiro*, pp. 128–30.

45 Ibid., p. 130; see also Diegues, 'The Cinema that Brazil Deserves', p. 25, and Felipe Bragança, 'Um pouco do óbvio, um pouco do novo, um pouquinho de imaginação: produção e difusão do cinema no Brasil', available at www.contracampo.com.br/81/artdifusao.htm: Bragança describes the *Espaço/Estação* phenomenon as the 'aubergine and sundried tomato sandwich outlets of the Avenida Paulista and the Zona Sul carioca', alluding to a certain kind of (ultra-bourgeois) cinema-going experience, which is nominally alternative.

46 See entry on *cinematecas* written by Hernani Heffner in Ramos and Miranda (eds), *Enciclopédia do cinema brasileiro*, pp. 146–7.

47 An insurer's nightmare, Brazil's cinémathèques and film libraries (for example, the library at ECA in São Paulo University) all appear at one time or another to have been affected by fire or flood.

48 This feature of Brazilian film culture also serves to illustrate the difficulty experienced by those who work with Brazilian film. The precarious conditions in which films and filmic material are often stored in cinémathèques (and elsewhere), and in which their employees and researchers are obliged to work, often have to be seen to be believed.

49 African slavery in Brazil was abolished as late as 1888. The country has the largest population of African descendants outside of Africa, and second in the world only to Nigeria.

50 Brazil's 'Indians' were regarded as 'relatively incapable' and thus in need of protection from the State. It was only with the publication of the new constitution of 1988, in which all Brazilians were declared equal before the law, that they ceased to be regarded as *tutelados* or wards of court.

51 For examples of this 'structuring absence', see Chapters 1 and 10.

52 Stam, Vieira and Xavier, 'The Shape of Brazilian Cinema in the Postmodern Age', p. 396.

53 Bernardet, *Historiografia clássica*, p. 26.

54 Ibid., p. 27.

55 Much of our current research seeks to redress this balance: see, for example, Stephanie Dennison and Lisa Shaw, *Popular Cinema in Brazil* (Manchester: Manchester University Press, 2004).

56 Diegues, 'The Cinema that Brazil Deserves', p. 24.

57 Bernardet, *Historiografia clássica*, p. 68.

58 See Chapter 8.

59 Diegues, 'The Cinema that Brazil Deserves', p. 25. Notwithstanding the current high price of cinema tickets, the proliferation of shopping centres in working-class suburbs of large cities, equipped with multiplexes, means that a much wider demographic has access to cinema halls than Diegues admits.

60 Ibid.

61 Nuria Triana-Toribio, *Spanish National Cinema* (London and New York: Routledge, 2003), p. 8.

62 Mônica Rugai Bastos, *Tristezas não pagam dívidas: cinema e política nos anos da Atlântida* (São Paulo: Olho d'Água, 2001).

63 Ibid., pp. 85–6.

64 Ibid., p. 134.

65 These include *Pequeno dicionário amoroso* (*Little Book of Love*, Sandra Werneck, 1997), *Como ser solteiro* (*How to Be Single in Rio*, Rosane Svartman, 1998), *Bossa nova* (Bruno Barreto, 2000), *Copacabana* (Carla Camurati, 2001) and *Os normais* (*So Normal*, José Alvarenga Jr, 2003).

66 *Pequeno dicionário amoroso* ranked twenty-fourth in the top Brazilian films 1994–2003, while *Como ser solteiro* ranked forty-third, cited in Randal Johnson, 'TV Globo, the MPA, and Brazilian Cinema', in Shaw and Dennison (eds), *Latin American Cinema*, pp. 25–6.

67 Triana-Toribio, *Spanish National Cinema*, p. 8.
68 This term, coined by Chilean anthropologist Alejandro Lipschutz, is explained by Stam as 'a social pyramid where the light skinned dominate the top and where indigenous people, blacks, and mestiços constitute the base'. Robert Stam, *Tropical Multiculturalism: A Comparative History of Race in Brazilian Cinema and Culture* (Durham, NC, and London: Duke University Press, 1997), p. 47.
69 Ibid., p. 84.

1 THE FIRST REPUBLIC (1889–1930)

1 Just six months after Lumière unveiled his *cinématographe* in Paris in late 1895, his invention, known as the 'omnigraph' in Brazil, gave its first screening in Rio de Janeiro on 8 July 1896.
2 See Tom Gunning, 'The Cinema of Attractions: Early Film, Its Spectator, and the Avant-Garde', *Wide Angle* 8, nos 3–4, 1986, pp. 63–70, reprinted in Thomas Elsaesser and Alan Barker (eds), *Early Cinema: Space, Frame, Narrative* (London: British Film Institute, 1990), pp. 56–62.
3 Ana M. López, 'Early Cinema and Modernity in Latin America', *Cinema Journal* 40, 1, Fall 2000, pp. 48–78 (p. 52).
4 Ibid.
5 I am very grateful to Dr Maite Conde, Columbia University, for her generous assistance in researching this section.
6 Randal Johnson and Robert Stam, 'The Shape of Brazilian Film History', in Randal Johnson and Robert Stam (eds), *Brazilian Cinema* (New York: Columbia University Press, 1995), pp. 15–51 (p. 20). These boom years for Brazilian cinema were brought abruptly to a halt by the takeover of the Brazilian market by the European and chiefly the North American film industry, the latter having established itself as an international concern. 'No one, it seems, had thought of rendering the importation of foreign films difficult in order to protect the budding national industry.' Ibid., p. 22.
7 Lambertini was an immigrant, as were many of Brazil's first filmmakers and technicians, who hailed from Italy. Italo-Brazilian Affonso Segreto, for example, introduced the first filmmaking equipment into Brazil in 1898, and over the next few years he filmed various public ceremonies, official functions and festivals.
8 One of the most famous of these *ambulantes* was João Carriço, who travelled around the towns and villages of his native Minas Gerais with his portable 'machine for showing views' before becoming the owner of cinema theatres. Jurandyr Noronha, *No Tempo da Manivela* (Rio de Janeiro: Embrafilme/Ebal/Kinart, 1987), p. 3.
9 On taking office, President Peçanha had promised the Brazilian people 'peace and love'.
10 'Pátria' means fatherland in Portuguese; Ipiranga was the name of a stream on the outskirts of the city of São Paulo on the banks of which the regent Pedro (later the Emperor Pedro I) issued the so-called *Grito do Ipiranga*, the declaration of the independence of Brazil from Portugal on 7 September 1822 (the topic of the silent film *Grito do Ipiranga*, 1917, as documented by Alex Viany, *Introdução ao cinema brasileiro*, Rio de Janeiro: Revan, 1993, p. 35); and Guanabara is the name of the bay where the city of Rio de Janeiro is located and of the surrounding state until 1974, when it became part of the state of Rio de Janeiro.
11 Núria Triana-Toribio, *Spanish National Cinema* (London and New York: Routledge, 2003), p. 18.
12 These included *Inocência* (Innocence, Vittorio Capellaro and Santiago Giannatasio, 1915), based on the eponymous novel by the Viscount de Taunay, *O Guarani* (The Guarani Indian, Vittorio Capellaro, 1916) and *Iracema* (Vittorio Capellaro, 1920), both based on the novels of the same name by José de Alencar.

13 Maite Conde, 'Cinematic Encounters in Premodernist Brazilian Literature', Ph.D. dissertation, UCLA, 2004, p. 162.
14 *Partida para a Itália dos reservistas no 1 de julho* (Reservists' Departure for Italy on 1 July, Antônio Campos, 1915), for example.
15 Films such as *Pátria e bandeira* (Fatherland and Flag, Antônio Leal, 1918) and *Pátria brasileira* (Brazilian Fatherland, Guelfo Andaló, 1917).
16 Noronha, *No Tempo da Manivela*, pp. 36–49.
17 Ibid., p. 42.
18 Mônica Rugai Bastos, *Tristezas não pagam dívidas: cinema e política nos anos da Atlântida* (São Paulo: Olho d'Água, 2001), pp. 28–9.
19 Sheila Schvarzman, *Humberto Mauro e as imagens do Brasil* (São Paulo: Editora UNESP, 2003), pp. 54–5. See Chapter 5, pp. 49–50 for a transcription of these opening titles.
20 Bastos, *Tristezas não pagam dívidas*, p. 29.
21 Paulo Emílio Salles Gomes, *Cinema: trajetória no subdesenvolvimento* (São Paulo: Paz e Terra), 1996, p. 66.
22 Conde, 'Cinematic Encounters in Premodernist Brazilian Literature', p. 237.
23 Francisco Foot Hardman, *Nem patria, nem patrão! Vida operária e cultura anarquista no Brasil* (São Paulo: Brasiliense, 1983), pp. 65–6.
24 Johnson and Stam, 'The Shape of Brazilian Film History', p. 20.
25 Kristin Thompson, *Exporting Entertainment: America in the World Film Market 1907–1934* (London: BFI, 1985), p. 134.
26 See Chapter 5, pp. 44–5, and Chapter 10, pp. 118–19.
27 See Jurandyr Noronha (1988) 'Imigrantes no cinema brasileiro', *Cinemin* 40, January, pp. 28–30.
28 Ana M. López, '"A Train of Shadows": Early Cinema and Modernity in Latin America', in Vivian Schelling (ed.), *Through the Kaleidoscope: The Experience of Modernity in Latin America* (London: Verso, 2000), pp. 148–76 (p. 163).
29 Alice Gonzaga, *Palácios e poeiras: 100 anos de cinema no Rio de Janeiro* (Rio de Janeiro: Funarte, 1996), pp. 92–3.
30 João Luiz Vieira and Margareth C.S. Pereira, 'Cinemas cariocas: da Ouvidor à Cinelândia', *Filme Cultura* 47, 1986, pp. 25–34 (p. 25).
31 Johnson and Stam, 'The Shape of Brazilian Film History', p. 23. This parodic vein was to reach its zenith in the *chanchadas* of the 1950s, as discussed in Chapter 6.
32 Ibid., p. 24.
33 Quoted by Carlos Roberto de Sousa in the *Jornal do Brasil*, 14 May 1977, and reproduced in Johnson and Stam, 'The Shape of Brazilian Film History', p. 25. The career of Humberto Mauro is analysed in depth in Chapter 5, pp. 47–55.
34 See Chapter 6 for a detailed analysis of the *chanchada*.

2 THE VARGAS YEARS (1930–45 AND 1951–54)

1 The sound for this film was recorded on to discs using the so-called Vitaphone method.
2 *Cinearte*, 2 December 1931. This film was, however, produced and directed by an American, Wallace Downey, a record company executive who worked in Brazil. The sound was recorded on to the film stock in synchrony with the images, a first in Brazil.
3 Getúlio Vargas, 'O cinema nacional: elemento de aproximação dos habitantes do país', in *A nova política do Brasil*, vol. 3 (Rio de Janeiro: José Olympio, n. d.), pp. 187–9, quoted in Anita Simis, 'Movies and Moviemakers under Vargas', *Latin American Perspectives*, Issue 122, Vol. 29, No. 1, January 2002, pp. 106–14 (pp. 107–8).
4 Carlos Roberto de Souza (ed.), Introduction to *Catálogo: filmes produzidos pelo INCE* (Rio de Janeiro: Fundação do Cinema Brasileiro, 1990), p. iii.

5 Luiz Simões Lopes was a staunch supporter of Vargas in the run-up to the 1930 coup, and in March 1937 became a member of his cabinet. In 1938 he was appointed as president of the new *Departamento Administrativo do Serviço Público* (DASP – Administrative Department of the Public Service), and then president of the newly created *Fundação Getúlio Vargas* (Getúlio Vargas Foundation) in 1944.
6 Letter sent by Luiz Simões Lopes to Getúlio Vargas from London on 22 September 1934. Document archived at CPDOC (Centre for Research and Documentation), Fundação Getúlio Vargas, Rio de Janeiro.
7 Documents consulted in the Cinemateca Brasileira, São Paulo.
8 Sheila Schvarzman, *Humberto Mauro e as imagens do Brasil* (São Paulo: Editora UNESP, 2003), p. 129.
9 For more details of Mauro's filmmaking career and work for the Vargas regime's INCE (*Instituto Nacional de Cinema Educativo* – National Institute of Educational Cinema), see Chapter 5, pp. 47–55.
10 Mauro uses the word *triste* or sad here, but its literal translation into English conveys only the pathos of the scene, whereas the accusation made by the censors clearly also alluded to what they perceived as the aesthetically displeasing inclusion of too many non-whites.
11 Quoted in Alex Viany (ed.), *Humberto Mauro: sua vida/sua arte/sua trajetória no cinema* (Rio de Janeiro: Artenova/Embrafilme, 1978), p. 206. Mauro said that this incident led to speculation that he was a Communist. Ibid.
12 Souza (ed.), Introduction to *Catálogo: filmes produzidos pelo INCE*, p. iv.
13 Quoted in Simis, 'Movies and Moviemakers under Vargas', p. 109. For extensive details and statistical data concerning the activities of the INCE see Schvarzman, *Humberto Mauro e as imagens do Brasil*, pp. 199–231.
14 Document consulted at the Cinemateca Brasileira, São Paulo.
15 Schvarzman, *Humberto Mauro e as imagens do Brasil*, p. 220.
16 Souza (ed.), *Catálogo: filmes produzidos pelo INCE*, p. 113. See also Chapter 5, pp. 54–5.
17 Carlos Roberto de Souza, 'Cinema em tempos de Capanema', in Helena Bomeny (ed.), *Constelação Capanema: intelectuais e políticas* (Rio de Janeiro: Fundação Getúlio Vargas, 2001), pp. 153–82 (p. 168).
18 Silvana Goulart, *Sob a verdade oficial: ideologia, propaganda e censura no Estado Novo* (São Paulo: Marco Zero, 1990), p. 52.
19 Ibid.
20 Anita Simis, *Estado e cinema no Brasil* (São Paulo: Annablume, 1996), p. 64.
21 Ibid., p. 117.
22 See, for example, Bryan McCann, *Hello, Hello, Brazil: Popular Music in the Making of Modern Brazil* (Durham, NC and London: Duke University Press, 2004), pp. 26–34.
23 José Inácio Mello Souza, 'Ação e o imaginário de uma ditadura: controle, coerção e propaganda política nos meios de comunicação durante o Estado Novo', MA dissertation, School of Communication and Arts (ECA), University of São Paulo, 1990, p. 339. Mello Souza also shows how the DIP failed to impose its authority on Rádio Nacional, the regime's so-called 'official' radio station. Ibid., p. 174.
24 See Chapter 6.
25 Robert M. Levine and John J. Crocitti (eds), 'The Vargas Era', *The Brazil Reader: History, Culture, Politics* (London: Latin America Bureau, 1999), pp. 149–55 (p. 150).
26 Daryle Williams, *Culture Wars in Brazil: The First Vargas Regime, 1930–1945* (Durham, NC and London: Duke University Press, 2001), p. 12.
27 Randal Johnson, *The Film Industry in Brazil: Culture and the State* (Pittsburgh, PA: University of Pittsburgh Press, 1987), p. 58.
28 This cinematic tradition is examined in detail in Chapter 6.

29 Sérgio Augusto, 'Watson Macedo, o rei da chanchada detestava fazer rir', *Filme Cultura* 41–42, May 1983, p. 32.
30 On the retirement of Roquette-Pinto, Pedro Gouveia, a medical practitioner, and Paschoal Lemme, an educationalist, took over the headship of the INCE in March 1947.
31 Schvarzman, *Humberto Mauro e as imagens do Brasil*, p. 232.
32 Carlos Augusto Calil, 'Panorama histórico da produção de filmes no Brasil', *Estudos de Cinema* 3, 2000, pp. 13–34 (p. 25).

3 FILMMAKING AND THE DICTATORSHIP (1964–84)

1 Randal Johnson, *The Film Industry in Brazil: Culture and the State* (Austin: University of Texas Press, 1987), p. 87.
2 John King, *Magical Reels: A History of Cinema in Latin America* (London and New York: Verso, 2000), p. 112.
3 See Johnson, *The Film Industry in Brazil*, p. 95. In the twenty-first century, for a film to be considered Brazilian, it can either meet the criteria as established in 1961 or it can have a Brazilian director and Brazilian co-producer.
4 Ibid., p. 97.
5 Ibid., pp. 122–3.
6 Ibid., p. 105.
7 Quoted in ibid., p. 109.
8 Ibid., p. 110.
9 Ibid., p. 117.
10 Ibid.
11 The notion of promoting 'historical' cinema had been discussed by the Ministry of Education and Culture (MEC) in 1971–2 and was to come back into vogue at Embrafilme in 1975, precisely at a time when the success of and tacit support for the popular soft-core porn films known as *pornochanchadas* were beginning to irritate the government and left-wing cultural producers alike.
12 Johnson, *The Film Industry in Brazil*, p. 119.
13 Ibid., p. 116.
14 Ibid., p. 121.
15 Ibid., pp. 137–8.
16 Jorge A. Schnitman, *Film Industries in Latin America: Dependency and Development* (Norwood, NJ: Ablex, 1984), p. 69.
17 Johnson, *The Film Industry in Brazil*, p. 155.
18 Schnitman, *Film Industries in Latin America*, p. 68.
19 King, *Magical Reels*, pp. 115–16.
20 Johnson, *The Film Industry in Brazil*, p. 143.
21 José Mário Ortiz Ramos, *Cinema, Estado e lutas culturais: anos 50/60/70* (Rio de Janeiro: Paz e Terra, 1983), p. 136.
22 José Mário Ortiz Ramos, 'O cinema brasileiro contemporâneo', in Fernão Ramos (ed.), *História do cinema brasileiro* (São Paulo: Arte Editora, 1987), p. 410.
23 See Chapter 11.
24 See Chapter 8.
25 Johnson, *The Film Industry in Brazil*, p. 161.
26 Ibid., p. 61.
27 Ibid., pp. 213–14.
28 Ibid., p. 158.
29 Although democracy for Brazil was still a long way off in 1974, a moderate military president, General Ernesto Geisel, assumed power in that year, with the promise of

gradually relaxing military control over the country. His presidency ushered in a period of political opening up, a kind of Brazilian *glasnost*. After the international oil crisis of 1973, the bottom had rapidly fallen out of Brazil's so-called economic miracle, which had guaranteed much of the dictatorship's support through the dark days of the 1968–72 period. Geisel was thus a compromise candidate, a general who could ensure that the military both oversaw and controlled any future return to democracy.

30 Johnson, *The Film Industry in Brazil*, p. 171.

31 Embrafilme came in for considerable criticism when it produced, amid severe economic crisis in Brazil, Glauber Rocha's indulgent *A idade da terra* in 1980, until then the most expensive Brazilian film ever ($1 million), and a box-office flop.

32 Johnson, *The Film Industry in Brazil*, p. 177.

33 Ibid., p. 172.

34 Ibid., p. 190.

35 Gustavo Dahl, 'Embrafilme: Present Problems and Future Possibilities', in Randal Johnson and Robert Stam (eds), *Brazilian Cinema* (New York: Columbia University Press, 1995), p. 106.

4 CINEMA AND REDEMOCRATISATION (1984–2006)

1 See Chapter 8.

2 José Alvaro Moisés, 'A New Policy for Brazilian Cinema', in Lúcia Nagib (ed.), *The New Brazilian Cinema* (London and New York: I.B. Tauris, 2003), p. 5.

3 Lúcia Nagib, 'Introduction', in Nagib (ed.), *The New Brazilian Cinema*, p. xvii.

4 Randal Johnson, 'TV Globo, the MPA, and Brazilian Cinema', in Lisa Shaw and Stephanie Dennison (eds), *Latin American Cinema: Essays on Modernity, Gender and National Identity* (Jefferson, NC: McFarland Press, 2005), p. 18.

5 Pedro Butcher, *Cinema brasileiro hoje* (São Paulo: Publifolha, 2005), p. 21.

6 Ibid., p. 20. Riofilme was also able to lend a useful hand with post-production.

7 Moisés, 'A New Policy for Brazilian Cinema', p. 3.

8 Ibid., p. 4.

9 Ibid., pp. 12–13.

10 Ibid., pp. 14–15.

11 Butcher, *Cinema brasileiro hoje*, p. 72.

12 Ibid., p. 75.

13 Pedro Butcher reports that in both 2003 and 2004 over 90 per cent of tickets sold were for Globo-linked productions. *Cinema brasileiro hoje*, p. 76.

14 Cacilda M. Rêgo, 'Brazilian Cinema: Its Fall, Rise and Renewal (1990–2003)', *New Cinemas: Journal of Contemporary Film* 3, 2, 2005, pp. 92–3.

15 Carlos Diegues, 'The Cinema that Brazil Deserves' (Summary of the address given to the cinema sub-committee of the Brazilian Senate, 8 June 2000), in Nagib (ed.), *The New Brazilian Cinema*, p. 30.

16 The Brazil–Portugal Accord (2002), which promotes the exchange of technology between the two nations and whose results are yet to be seen, is also a potential source of funding for the Brazilian film industry in the twenty-first century.

17 Johnson, 'TV Globo, the MPA, and Brazilian Cinema', p. 28.

18 Moisés, 'A New Policy for Brazilian Cinema', p. 11.

19 José Alvaro Moisés reminds us that, globally, only 25 per cent of a given film's income comes from box-office receipts. 'A New Policy for Brazilian Cinema', p. 25.

20 Johnson, 'TV Globo, the MPA, and Brazilian Cinema', p. 28.

21 See the discussions on alternative distribution strategies on the Cinemando website: www.cinemando.com.br.200306/entrevistas/andiefischer_03.htm (accessed 8 August 2006).

22 Randal Johnson, 'From the Ashes? Brazilian Cinema in the 1990s', paper presented at the conference 'Latin American Cinema: Theory and Praxis', University of Leeds, June 1999.

5 THE PIONEERS

1 Humberto Mauro in interview with Barros Vidal in *Cinearte* magazine in 1929, quoted in Alex Viany, 'O cinema brasileiro de Humberto Mauro: um pioneiro', *Senhor*, March 1962, pp. 36–41 (p. 38).
2 Ana Pessoa, *Carmen Santos: o cinema dos anos 20* (Rio de Janeiro: Aeroplano, 2002).
3 Interview with Francisco Alves dos Santos entitled 'Gilda de Abreu: "Eu morri com Vicente Celestino"', in *Panorama*, 15 March 1978.
4 See Chapter 10, pp. 118–19.
5 See pp. 47–55.
6 Letter written by Adhemar Gonzaga to Humberto Mauro in August 1928, Arquivo Cinédia, quoted in Sheila Schvarzman, *Humberto Mauro e as imagens do Brasil* (São Paulo: Editora UNESP, 2003), p. 56.
7 Biographical information taken from Carlos Fonseca, 'Gonzaga, um pioneiro', *Filme Cultura* 8, March 1968, pp. 2–17.
8 See Chapter 10, pp. 118–19.
9 Ismail Xavier, 'O sonho da indústria: a criação de imagem em *Cinearte*', in *Sétima arte: um culto moderno* (São Paulo: Perspectiva – Secretaria da Cultura, Ciência e Tecnologia do Estado de São Paulo, 1978), p. 176.
10 Schvarzman, *Humberto Mauro e as imagens do Brasil*, p. 348.
11 João da Avenida (pseudonym of Olegário Mariano), *Correio da manhã*, 14 June 1929.
12 Fonseca, 'Gonzaga, um pioneiro', p. 6.
13 Ibid., p. 7.
14 See Chapter 6, p. 71.
15 See pp. 64–8.
16 As Gonzaga openly admitted: 'The film was very successful and helped Cinédia out, since it had been through a difficult period due to the war.' Quoted in Alice Gonzaga, *50 anos de Cinédia* (Rio de Janeiro: Editora Record, 1987), p. 102.
17 Luiz de Barros, *Minhas memórias de cineasta* (Rio de Janeiro: Artenova, 1978), p. 144.
18 See pp. 47–55.
19 Adhemar Gonzaga, quoted by Roberto M. Moura and Luiz Alberto Sanz, text for the *Mostra Humberto Mauro* exhibition, organised by Roberto Parreira and Carlos Augusto Calil, p. 11.
20 This interview features as an extra on the DVD *Humberto Mauro* (Rio de Janeiro: Funarte).
21 Humberto Mauro, 'O cinema brasileiro e as suas possibilidades', *Correio da manhã*, 29 June 1930.
22 Schvarzman, *Humberto Mauro e as imagens do Brasil*, p. 15.
23 See Chapter 7, p. 81.
24 This film marked the debut of future silent movie star Eva Nil, Pedro Comello's daughter, who enjoyed a brief but intense film career in Rio de Janeiro, before unexpectedly retiring from show business to return to Cataguases.
25 This detail is mentioned by Humberto Mauro in interview with Alex Viany and David Neves, included in the DVD *Humberto Mauro* (Rio de Janeiro: Funarte).
26 This biographical information is provided by Paulo Perdigão, 'Trajetória de Humberto Mauro', *Filme Cultura* 3, January–February, 1967, pp. 4–19.
27 This film and many others subsequently directed by Mauro are extant, unlike the vast majority of those produced by Adhemar Gonzaga's Cinédia studio or Carmen Santos's

Brasil Vita Filmes. The reason for this is that Mauro deposited the original prints and copies in the archives of the INCE, greatly facilitating the subsequent restoration and preservation projects carried out by Embrafilme and other bodies.

28 Perdigão, 'Trajetória de Humberto Mauro', p. 8.
29 This point is also made by Enrique de Resende, 'Humberto Mauro e o cinema nacional', *Pequena história sentimental de Cataguases* (Belo Horizonte: Editora Itatiaia, 1969), pp. 127–41 (p. 129).
30 Published in *Cinearte*, 1929, and quoted in Viany, 'O cinema brasileiro de Humberto Mauro', p. 39.
31 See pp. 58–9.
32 See Chapter 2.
33 See Chapter 1, p. 19.
34 The censorship body at this time was the Delegacia de Costumes e Jogos – Gabinete de Investigações, Censura Cinematográfica e Teatral (Inspectorate for Games and Traditions – Cabinet for Research and Film and Theatre Censorship). Gonzaga, *50 anos de Cinédia*, p. 37.
35 Carlos Ortiz's words are quoted in Viany, 'O cinema brasileiro de Humberto Mauro', p. 39.
36 Viany, 'O cinema brasileiro de Humberto Mauro', p. 39.
37 See, for example, 'Tudo que o País deve ao Mauro', *Folha de São Paulo* (no date, no page).
38 Glauber Rocha, 'Humberto Mauro e situação histórica', *Jornal do Brasil* (*Suplemento Dominical*), 7 October 1961. See pp. 83–6.
39 Glauber Rocha, *Revisão crítica do cinema brasileiro* (Rio de Janeiro: Civilização Brasileira, 1963), pp. 28–9.
40 Quoted in 'Tudo que o País deve ao Mauro'. The nickname Freud of Cascadura was given to Mauro by his friend and collaborator Henrique Pongetti.
41 Resende, 'Humberto Mauro e o cinema nacional', p. 134. Resende quotes Mauro as saying: 'only one of my films was a success at the box office. I'm referring to *Favela dos meus amores*. The others did not even cover their costs.' Ibid.
42 He also performed the duties of scriptwriter, cinematographer and editor on this production. Ibid.
43 Jorge Amado, 'Favela dos meus amores', *Boletim de Ariel*, s. d., pp. 10–11 (p. 10).
44 Carlos Roberto de Sousa, *Jornal do Brasil*, 14 May 1977. Quoted in Randal Johnson and Robert Stam (eds), *Brazilian Cinema* (New York: Columbia University Press, 1995), p. 26.
45 Henrique Pongetti's words are quoted in Viany, 'O cinema brasileiro de Humberto Mauro', p. 40.
46 See Chapter 6 for details of the *chanchada* tradition in Brazilian cinema.
47 Moura and Sanz, text for the *Mostra Humberto Mauro* exhibition, p. 16.
48 João Máximo, 'A música na lente de Humberto Mauro', *O Globo*, 31 July 1992 (*Segundo Caderno*), p. 3.
49 Moura and Sanz, text for the *Mostra Humberto Mauro* exhibition, p. 19.
50 Schvarzman, *Humberto Mauro e as imagens do Brasil*, p. 300.
51 This film was restored by the Fundação Nacional de Arte (Funarte) in Rio de Janeiro in the 1990s.
52 Schvarzman, *Humberto Mauro e as imagens do Brasil*, p. 155.
53 *O Globo*, 31 October 1937, quoted in Schvarzman, *Humberto Mauro e as imagens do Brasil*, p. 146.
54 Quoted in Schvarzman, *Humberto Mauro e as imagens do Brasil*, p. 149.
55 Ibid., p. 178.
56 Ibid., pp. 156–7.
57 Ibid., pp. 162–3.

58 See, for example, Richard A. Gordon, 'Recreating Caminha: The Earnest Adaptation of Brazil's Letter of Discovery in Humberto Mauro's *Descobrimento do Brasil* (1937)', *Modern Language Notes* 120, 2, March 2005, pp. 408–36.
59 Resende, 'Humberto Mauro e o cinema nacional', p. 135.
60 Hernani Heffner, 'Notas sobre *O descobrimento do Brasil* de Humberto Mauro', in *O descobrimento do Brasil: restauração* (Rio de Janeiro: Ministério da Cultura/Fundação Nacional de Arte/Funarte/Centro Técnico Audiovisual/CTAv, 1997), p. 19. See pp. 62–3 and 67–8.
61 Schvarzman, *Humberto Mauro e as imagens do Brasil*, p. 138.
62 Mauro was appointed as head of the INCE's Film Technology Service (*Serviço de Técnica Cinematográfica*).
63 *Um apólogo – Machado de Assis, 1839–1939* (1939), made to commemorate the one hundredth anniversary of the great nineteenth-century novelist's birth.
64 This film recounted the life of the great Brazilian writer and focused on the War of Canudos that he wrote about in his most famous work, *Os sertões* (Rebellion in the Backlands).
65 Quoted in Schvarzman, *Humberto Mauro e as imagens do Brasil*, p. 278.
66 For a detailed, nuanced analysis of the *Brasiliana* series see Randal Johnson, 'Documentary Discourses and National Identity: Humberto Mauro's *Brasiliana* Series and Linduarte Noronha's *Aruanda*', *Nuevo Texto Critico* XI, 21/22, 1998, pp. 193–206.
67 An *urutau* is a type of bird. This film had an alternative title, *Eterna história* (Eternal Story).
68 *Palcos e Telas*, year II, number 67, 3 July 1919. I am very grateful to Dr Maite Conde, Columbia University, for her insightful feedback on a first draft of this section.
69 Santos's words are quoted in Heloísa Buarque de Hollanda (ed.), *Quase Catálogo 3 Estrelas do Cinema Mudo, Brasil 1908–1930* (Rio de Janeiro: Escola de Comunicação UFRJ/Fundação Museu da Imagem e do Som, 1991), p. 55.
70 Pessoa, *Carmen Santos*, p. 65.
71 *Cinearte*, 21 March 1928.
72 Pedro Lima, 'O preço da fama', *Selecta*, year XII, number 39, 29 September 1926, quoted in Pessoa, *Carmen Santos*, p. 56.
73 Her choice of film roles further emphasised this facet of her 'personality'.
74 Pessoa, *Carmen Santos*, p. 38.
75 *Palcos e Telas*, 10 June 1920.
76 The novel sold 75,000 copies in the first five years after it was published, but was banned immediately following its first publication, copies being literally torn off shelves in bookshops only to reappear in 1924, just before Santos's project was commenced.
77 Pedro Lima, 'Ouvindo estrelas . . . Quem é Carmen Santos', *Selecta*, year X, number 21, 24 May 1924. Quoted in Pessoa, *Carmen Santos*, pp. 50–1.
78 Letter written on 19 January 1929, Humberto Mauro's correspondence with Adhemar Gonzaga, Arquivo Cinédia, quoted in Schvarzman, *Humberto Mauro e as imagens do Brasil*, p. 56, footnote 36.
79 *Folha da Noite Mineira*, no date, pp. 1, 5.
80 Letter from Carmen Santos to Humberto Mauro, 19 June 1929, archive of the Cinemateca Brasileira, São Paulo. Quoted in Schvarzman, *Humberto Mauro e as imagens do Brasil*, p. 85.
81 Ibid., p. 90.
82 *Cinearte-Album*, 1930, p. 15.
83 Ibid., p. 27.
84 Ibid., p. 18.
85 Letter from Carmen Santos to Humberto Mauro, 19 June 1929, archive of the Cinemateca Brasileira, São Paulo. Quoted in Pessoa, *Carmen Santos*, pp. 93–4.

86 Another, completed version of *Lábios sem beijos* starred Lelita Rosa, see pp. 50 and 68.
87 *Cinearte*, year IV, number 190, 16 October 1929. Quoted in Pessoa, *Carmen Santos*, p. 96.
88 Ibid., pp. 102–3.
89 Helena Salem, *90 anos de cinema: aventura brasileira* (São Paulo: Instituições Financeiras Sogeral/Nova Fronteira, 1988), p. 133.
90 Pessoa, *Carmen Santos*, pp. 116–17.
91 *A Scena Muda*, year XI, number 538, 15 July 1931. Quoted in Pessoa, *Carmen Santos*, p. 120.
92 Pessoa, *Carmen Santos*, p. 120.
93 Afonso de Carvalho, 'Carmen', *Cinearte* 312, 17 February 1932, p. 6. Quoted in Pessoa, *Carmen Santos*, p. 159.
94 Pessoa, *Carmen Santos*, p. 160.
95 *A Scena Muda*, year XI, number 554, 3 November 1931. Quoted in Pessoa, *Carmen Santos*, p. 128.
96 Barros Vidal, 'O cigarro na boca das mulheres . . . ', *A Scena Muda*, year XI, number 565, 19 January 1932. Quoted in Pessoa, *Carmen Santos*, p. 135.
97 Pessoa, *Carmen Santos*, p. 140.
98 'O filme de Carmen Santos', *Correio da Manhã*, 10 October 1933, p. 8.
99 *Cinearte*, 15 June 1933, p. 8.
100 Pessoa, *Carmen Santos*, pp. 142–4.
101 Speech published in *A Scena Muda*, year XI, number 571, 1 March 1932, p. 8. Quoted in Pessoa, *Carmen Santos*, pp. 152–6.
102 *Cinearte*, number 429, 15 December 1935, p. 28.
103 *A Scena Muda*, year XVI, number 814. No date.
104 Alice Gonzaga Assaf, 'Carmen Santos: Retrospecto' (no further publication details), p. 23. Santos's subsequent production was the romantic melodrama *Argila* (Clay, 1940), in which she plays the lead role of the predatory, wealthy blonde widow Luciana, who seduces one of her male employees in a controversial tale of inter-class desire and female sexual agency, see p. 52.
105 The acclaimed Edgar Brasil was employed as director of photography, and the historian Brasil Gerson was commissioned to write the script.
106 The first was Cléo de Verberena, who made *O mistério do dominó negro* (The Mystery of the Black Cape) in 1931.
107 See pp. 24–5.
108 Correspondence held in the archive of the Cinemateca Brasileira, São Paulo.
109 She states 'sou um cérebro', literally 'I am a brain', which translates figuratively as 'I am an intelligent person' or 'I have a brain'.
110 Correspondence held in the archive of the Cinemateca Brasileira, São Paulo.
111 Gonzaga Assaf, 'Carmen Santos', p. 26.
112 Regina Glória Nunes Andrade, 'Estrela luminosa', *ECO* (da Pós-Graduação em Comunicação e Cultura, Universidade Federal do Rio de Janeiro) 4, 1993, pp. 75–88 (p. 79).
113 *Cinearte* 449, 15 October 1936, p. 8, says that the film will be the 'first real Brazilian superproduction' and 'will exceed all expectations'. This term is also used by Orlando L. Fassoni, 'Morreu Gilda, pioneira do cinema', *Folha de São Paulo*, 5 June 1979, p. 29.
114 Ary Théo, *Cinearte* 454, 1 January 1937, p. 8.
115 *Cinearte* 449, 15 October 1936, pp. 12–13.
116 Ibid.
117 João Luiz Vieira, 'A chanchada e o cinema carioca (1930–1955)', in Fernão Ramos (ed.), *História do cinema brasileiro* (São Paulo: Art Editora, 1987), p. 157.

118 Ibid., p. 158. In a reflection of the enduring appeal of *O ébrio* throughout Brazil, it is the only film that is shown by the travelling projectionist in the backlands of Brazil's North-East in Carlos Diegues's *Bye Bye Brazil* (1979), set in the late 1970s.
119 See review by Fernando Albagli, 'Resgate do clássico da dor-de-cotovelo', *Programa* supplement, *Jornal do Brasil*, 7 to 13 August 1998, p. 12.
120 Luiz Zanin Oricchio, 'MIS exibe "O ébrio", clássico do melodrama', *O Estado de São Paulo* (*Caderno 2*), 18 July 1996, p. D2.
121 Quoted in Pedro Butcher, '"O ébrio" recuperado', *Jornal do Brasil* (*Caderno B*), 22 March 1997, p. 4.
122 Hernani Heffner, quoted in Butcher, '"O ébrio" recuperado'.
123 'Público exigia repetição de cena com Celestino', *O Estado de São Paulo* (*Caderno 2*), 15 July 1998, p. D3.
124 Information taken from a brochure produced by *Prefeitura/Rio Filme* to accompany the release of the restored print of *O ébrio*, consulted at the Cinemateca Brasileira, São Paulo.
125 'Dramalhão comovia público', *Folha de São Paulo* (*Ilustrada*), 27 June 1998, p. 5.
126 Roberta Jansen, '"O ébrio" ganha cópia nova e sem cortes', *O Estado de São Paulo* (*Caderno 2*), 28 June 1996, p. D4.
127 '"O ébrio": filme não é obra-prima, é fenômeno mercadológico', *Folha de São Paulo* (*Ilustrada*), 27 June 1998, p. 5.
128 'Remontagem "descobre" uma outra obra', *Folha de São Paulo* (*Ilustrada*), 27 June 1998, p. 5.
129 Helena Salem, '"O ébrio" volta às telas com seu grande apelo popular', *O Estado de São Paulo* (*Caderno 2*), 15 July 1998, p. D3.
130 Fassoni, 'Morreu Gilda, pioneira do cinema', p. 29.
131 Interview with Gilda de Abreu recorded at the Museu da Imagem e do Som, 2 October 1974.
132 'Trombose mata cantora e atriz Gilda de Abreu', *Estado de Minas* (Belo Horizonte), 5 June 1979.
133 Andrade, 'Estrela luminosa', p. 86.
134 Eduardo Giffoni Flórido, *As grandes personagens da história do cinema brasileiro, 1930–1959* (Rio de Janeiro: Fraiha, 1999), p. 76.
135 Schvarzman, *Humberto Mauro e as imagens do Brasil*, p. 72.

6 THE *CHANCHADA*, THE ONLY BRAZILIAN GENRE

1 Sérgio Augusto, *Este mundo é um pandeiro* (São Paulo: Companhia das Letras, 1993), p. 88.
2 See Chapter 5, pp. 46–7.
3 See Chapter 10, p. 120.
4 Mônica Rugai Bastos, *Tristezas não pagam dívidas: cinema e política nos anos da Atlântida* (São Paulo: Olho d'Água, 2001), p. 66.
5 Ibid., p. 44.
6 Luiz de Barros, *Minhas memórias de cineasta* (Rio de Janeiro: Artenova, 1978), p. 53.
7 Augusto, *Este mundo é um pandeiro*, p. 104.
8 See Chapter 10 for sections on both these stars, Eliana Macedo and Carmen Miranda.
9 Renato Ortiz, 'Preface', in Bastos, *Tristezas não pagam dívidas*, pp. 9–12 (p. 9).
10 Bastos, *Tristezas não pagam dívidas*, p. 40. In spite of the best efforts of private initiative, and the limited support offered by official legislation on quotas, at the peak of their production *chanchadas* represented only 6 per cent of the films exhibited in Brazil. Ibid., p. 58.
11 In a further comic inversion, in the final scene of the film the baby in the pram is revealed to have Oscarito's face.

12 This term refers to the counter-cultural lifestyle of the *malandro*, a street-wise hustler, often of mixed race, who evades the law and the world of work in favour of a life of petty crime, gambling, womanising and drinking. The real-life *malandros* of Rio's shantytowns and poorer districts in the first decades of the twentieth century, who after the abolition of slavery in 1888 found themselves discriminated against and rejected coercion into poorly paid physical labour, were given mythical status in the lyrics of samba in the 1920s and 1930s. The ethos of *malandragem* permeates Brazilian popular culture and is often referred to as an unofficial tenet of national identity.
13 See Chapter 10 for more details of Oscarito's film roles.
14 See Chapter 10 for more details of Grande Otelo's screen career.
15 Robert Stam, *Tropical Multiculturalism: A Comparative History of Race in Brazilian Cinema and Culture* (Durham, NC and London: Duke University Press, 1997), p. 135.
16 Breixo Viejo, '*O Cangaceiro*', in Alberto Elena and Marina Díaz López (eds), *The Cinema of Latin America* (London: Wallflower, 2003), pp. 63–9 (p. 65).
17 Ibid.
18 Carlos Augusto Calil, however, argues that Vera Cruz's commercial failure was partly the consequence of the maintenance of cinema ticket prices at an artificially low level by the populist Vargas government (1951–54), and the fact that North American film distributors were granted an additional subsidy to the order of 70 per cent of box-office receipts. As Calil states, this arrangement was only made public after Vera Cruz went into liquidation in 1954, and remained in force until 1957. Carlos Augusto Calil, 'Panorama histórico da produção de filmes no Brasil', *Estudos de Cinema* 3, 2000, pp. 13–34 (p. 25).
19 John King, *Magical Reels: A History of Cinema in Latin America* (London and New York: Verso, 1990), p. 57. The Atlântida studio hit back, however, with the 1952 production *Carnaval Atlântida* (Atlântida Carnival), which pokes fun at the unrealistic artistic pretensions of Vera Cruz, personified by a fictitious filmmaker who wants to produce a big-budget historical epic in Brazil, but is ultimately forced to accept that only a carnival musical is a viable option.
20 In *Sai da frente* two minor characters who form part of a circus troupe just happen to be called Samson and Dalila, in a throwaway comic swipe at Cecil B. de Mille's biblical epic *Samson and Delilah* (1949), and a man appears in a gorilla suit and carries off a beautiful damsel, in a clear parody of *King Kong* (1933), starring Fay Wray.
21 See Chapter 10, pp. 121–4 for more details of this costume.
22 See Chapter 10.
23 Mazzaropi plays the title role of Candinho, inspired by Voltaire's character Candide, a hillbilly who leaves the countryside behind in search of his mother in the city of São Paulo.
24 Stam, *Tropical Multiculturalism*, p. 156.
25 Atlântida's *chanchadas* were extremely popular among São Paulo audiences. Luiz Severiano Ribeiro did not own any cinemas in the city, but the Pedutti company distributed the films locally, to great success. Calil, 'Panorama histórico da produção de filmes no Brasil', p. 23.
26 Stam, *Tropical Multiculturalism*, p. 156.
27 See Chapter 1, p. 18.
28 João Luiz Vieira, Ivana Bentes and Carlos Alberto Mattos, 'Da chanchada à orfandade, passando pelo cinema novo', *Cinemais* 33, January–March 2003, pp. 87–113 (p. 92).
29 Carlos Augusto Calil goes as far as to call the *chanchada* an imported genre. Calil, 'Panorama histórico da produção de filmes no Brasil', p. 20.
30 Vieira, Bentes and Mattos, 'Da chanchada à orfandade', p. 100.
31 When pretending to be an accomplished European painter in *Pintando o sete* (Painting

the Town Red, 1959), Oscarito is asked what he thinks of concrete art, to which he replies: 'It depends, logically, on the quality of the cement.'

32 Bastos, *Tristezas não pagam dívidas*, pp. 107–8.

33 Although no official records of box-office receipts were kept in Brazil until 1966, the press coverage of the long-awaited premieres of the *chanchadas* and the many magazines devoted to their stars give ample evidence of their popularity.

34 Rick Altman, *The American Film Musical* (Bloomington and Indianapolis: Indiana University Press, 1987), p. 332.

35 Andrew Tudor, 'Genre', in Barry Keith Grant (ed.), *Film Genre Reader II* (Austin: University of Texas Press, 2003), pp. 3–10 (p. 9).

36 Ibid., pp. 8–9.

37 Paulo Emílio Salles Gomes, *Cinema brasileiro: uma trajetória no subdesenvolvimento* (Rio de Janeiro: Paz e Terra, 1986), p. 91. The publication of this book marked the turning point in the critical reception of the *chanchada*.

7 *CINEMA NOVO*

1 For a more detailed analysis of the *cinema novo* than the present volume permits, the following English-language texts are particularly useful: Randal Johnson, *Cinema Novo X Five: Makers of Contemporary Brazilian Film* (Austin: University of Texas Press, 1984), Ismail Xavier, *Allegories of Underdevelopment: Aesthetics and Politics in Modern Brazilian Cinema* (Minneapolis: University of Minnesota Press, 1997) and the short but useful Robert Stam and Ismail Xavier, 'Transformation of National Allegory: Brazilian Cinema from Dictatorship to Redemocratization', in Michael T. Martin (ed.), *New Latin American Cinema: Studies of National Cinemas* (Detroit, MI: Wayne State University Press, 1997), pp. 295–322. There are a large number of texts in Portuguese on the subject, including Glauber Rocha, *Revolução do cinema novo* (Rio de Janeiro: Alambra/Embrafilme, 1981), Ismail Xavier, *Sertão-mar (Glauber Rocha e a estética da fome)* (São Paulo: Brasiliense, 1983) and Fernão Ramos, 'Os novos rumos do cinema brasileiro, 1955–1970', in Fernão Ramos (ed.), *História do cinema brasileiro* (São Paulo: Arte Editora, 1987).

2 Johnson, *Cinema Novo X Five*, p. 217.

3 As well as its own production and distribution company, Difilm, *cinema novo* had its own collective manifesto, *Luz e Ação*, but the movement is most associated with Glauber Rocha's 'An Aesthetics of Hunger'. Both 'manifestos' are included in English translation in Randal Johnson and Robert Stam (eds), *Brazilian Cinema* (New York: Columbia University Press, 1995).

4 It was after the release of Ruy Guerra's *Os cafajestes* (*The Unscrupulous Ones*, 1962) that the term *cinema novo* began to be used by critics: Alexandre Figueirôa, *Cinema novo: a onda do jovem cinema e sua recepçãao na França* (Campinas: Papyrus, 2004), p. 21.

5 See Chapter 5.

6 For more information, see Randal Johnson, *The Film Industry in Brazil: Culture and the State* (Pittsburgh, PA: University of Pittsburgh Press, 1987), pp. 88–91.

7 Figueirôa, *Cinema novo*, p. 23.

8 Ibid., p. 24.

9 Ibid., p. 28.

10 Figueirôa (*Cinema novo*, p. 23) stresses that there were other films being made that were not part of the movement but that did contribute to a renewal in filmmaking at the time, such as the work of Walter Hugo Khouri.

11 Dos Santos was also older than the other members of the *cinema novo* group and had already established a name for himself as a film director when the movement got into full swing.

12 Quoted in Randal Johnson, 'The Rise and Fall of Brazilian Cinema, 1960–1990', in Johnson and Stam (eds), *Brazilian Cinema*, p. 379.
13 Ironically, when dos Santos and his crew first went to the North-East to film *Vidas secas*, it began to rain, turning the *sertão* green and lush, to such an extent that crew members suggested that the film should be renamed *Vidas molhadas* (literally Wet Lives): Darlene J. Sadlier, *Nelson Pereira dos Santos* (Urbana and Chicago: University of Illinois Press, 2003), pp. 32–3.
14 It is interesting to note that the title of the film as it appears on screen is *Vidas Secas de Graciliano Ramos.*
15 Although not as overpowering, this blinding light can be seen in other *cinema novo* films set in the *sertão*, such as Ruy Guerra's *Os fuzis* (*The Guns*, 1964) and Glauber Rocha's *Deus e o diabo na terra do sol* (*Black God, White Devil*, 1964).
16 Phase one (1961–64) – 'aesthetics of hunger' codes as examined in *Deus e o diabo na terra do sol*; Phase two (1965–67) – reflections on the installation of the dictatorship and the importance of the intellectual (*Terra em Transe*); Phase three – readjustments in terms of the relationship with commercial cinema and the use of allegory as a way round censorship (*Antônio das Mortes*).
17 Consider, for example, the creative use of music in his films. For more information, see Graham Bruce, 'Alma Brasileira: Music in the Films of Glauber Rocha', in Johnson and Stam (eds), *Brazilian Cinema*, pp. 290–305.
18 As well as a series of important studies of Brazilian cinema, Rocha published poetry and a novel entitled *Riverão Sussuarana* (1977).
19 The *cinema novo* group were fascinated by *cangaço* or social banditry: see, for example, Paulo Gil Soares's important documentary *Memória do cangaço* (*Cangaço* Memories, 1965).
20 For a useful analysis of the film, see Ismail Xavier, 'Black God, White Devil: The Representation of History', in Johnson and Stam (eds), *Brazilian Cinema*, pp. 134–48, and José Carlos Avellar, *Deus e o diabo na terra do sol* (Rio de Janeiro: Rocco, 1995).
21 *Terra em transe* is regarded by many as the best Brazilian film to be produced to date. Its consecration abroad has doubtless been helped by the lyrical but nonetheless brilliant analysis of the film offered by Robert Stam: 'Land in Anguish', in Johnson and Stam (eds), *Brazilian Cinema*, pp. 149–61.
22 See Randal Johnson, *Antônio das Mortes* (Trowbridge: Flicks Books, 1998).
23 See, for example, *Cabeças cortadas* (*Cutting Heads*, 1970), filmed in Spain, and *Der Leone Have Sept Cabeças* (*The Lion Has Seven Heads*, 1971), filmed partly in Braazaville.
24 The incident came to be known as 'Os Oito da Glória' (The Gloria Eight).
25 The legend of Glauber Rocha is lovingly kept alive by his family via the Rio-based museum/archive Tempo Glauber (see www.tempoglauber.com.br). A number of films based on Rocha's life and work have recently been made, including Eryk Rocha's *Rocha que voa* (2002) and Sílvio Tendler's *Glauber o filme: labirinto do Brasil* (2003).
26 Julianne Burton, 'The Old and the New: Latin American Cinema at the (Last?) Pesaro Festival', *Jump Cut* 9, 1975, pp. 33–5.
27 Figueirôa, *Cinema novo*, p. 45.
28 The success of *cinema novo* in Europe also aided the movement in that it led to co-productions with Italy, Germany and France. See Figueirôa, *Cinema novo*, p. 47, for details of these.
29 Interest in *cinema novo* in France and elsewhere in Europe cooled off after the events of 1968, when attentions turned to pressing issues at home: ibid.
30 Ibid., p. 138.
31 Ibid., p. 41.
32 Ibid., p. 45. Glauber Rocha and other *cinemanovistas* featured largely in the regular festivals of New Cinema that *Cahiers du cinéma* organised in the 1960s.

33 Ibid., p. 102.
34 Ibid., p. 46.
35 Rocha, 'An Aesthetics of Hunger', p. 59.
36 The main Rio-based *cinemanovistas* who set forth to film in the North-East were followed by a São Paulo-based group of directors who were linked to producer Thomaz Farkas, which included the aforementioned Paulo Gil Soares. Their filmic journeys are tellingly referred to as the 'caravana Farkas'.
37 Paulo Emílio Salles Gomes, 'Cinema: A Trajectory within Underdevelopment', in Johnson and Stam (eds), *Brazilian Cinema*, p. 252.
38 Ibid., p. 251.
39 Figueirôa, *Cinema novo*, p. 25.
40 Ruy Guerra saw this as co-optation. The other *cinema novo* directors disagreed and, as a result, Guerra was distanced from the group: Johnson, *The Film Industry in Brazil*, p. 101.
41 Ibid., p. 128.
42 Brian Goldfarb, 'Local Television and Community Politics in Brazil: São Paulo's TV Anhembi', in Chon A. Noriega (ed.), *Visible Nations: Latin American Cinema and Video* (Minneapolis and London: University of Minnesota Press, 2000), p. 278.
43 Ibid., p. 275.
44 The Boca do Lixo (Mouth of Garbage) is a district in downtown São Paulo that gained its name owing to the large number of prostitutes and pickpockets who frequented its streets. Foreign film distributors were attracted to the Boca from the 1920s because of its cheap rent and proximity to major coach and railway stations. By the end of the 1950s a number of Brazilian producers were established in the district. Its most active period, in terms of production, was in the 1980s with the advent of hard-core.
45 Fernão Ramos, 'Uma forma histórica de cinema alternativo e seus dilemas na atualidade', 1986, quoted in Patricia Aufderheide, 'Grassroots Video in Latin America', in Noriega (ed.), *Visible Nations*, p. 226.
46 Fernão Ramos, *Cinema marginal (1968–1973): a representaçãcao em seu limite* (São Paulo: Brasiliense, 1987), p. 64.
47 Salles Gomes, 'Cinema: A Trajectory within Underdevelopment', p. 251.
48 This 'marginal' performative style was typified by Paulo Villaça and Joel Barcellos in, among other films, *O bandido da luz vermelha* (*Red Light Bandit*, 1968) and *Jardim de Guerra* (War Garden, 1970) respectively, two of the most striking films of the *cinema marginal* production.
49 Ramos, *Cinema marginal*, p. 40.
50 Robert Stam, 'On the Margins: Brazilian Avant-Garde Cinema', in Johnson and Stam (eds), *Brazilian Cinema*, p. 311.
51 Salles Gomes, 'Cinema: A Trajectory within Underdevelopment', p. 252.
52 See appendix to Ramos, *Cinema marginal.*
53 See Chapters 8 and 11 of the present volume. Ramos characterises *cinema marginal* as being made up of a large number of directors of just one film: *Cinema marginal*, p. 39.
54 Salles Gomes, 'Cinema: A Trajectory within Underdevelopment', pp. 252–3.

8 THE *PORNOCHANCHADA*

1 For more information, see Nuno César Abreu, 'Boca do Lixo', in Fernão Ramos and Luiz Felipe Miranda (eds), *Enciclopédia do cinema brasileiro* (São Paulo: Editora Senac, 2000), p. 59.
2 Randal Johnson, 'The Rise and Fall of Brazilian Cinema, 1960–1990', in Randal Johnson and Robert Stam (eds), *Brazilian Cinema* (New York: Columbia University Press, 1995), p. 384.

3 Randal Johnson, *The Film Industry in Brazil: Culture and the State* (Pittsburgh, PA: University of Pittsburgh Press, 1987), p. 186.
4 See Chapter 11.
5 'E depois da pornochanchada?', *Veja*, 7 January 1976.
6 Johnson, *The Film Industry in Brazil*, p. 176.
7 Quoted in Maria Rita Kehl, 'Entrevista com Paulo Emílio Salles Gomes', *Movimento*, 19 January 1976.
8 For more information, see Stephanie Dennison and Lisa Shaw, *Popular Cinema in Brazil* (Manchester: Manchester University Press, 2004), pp. 129–31.
9 José Carlos Avellar, 'Teoria da relatividade', *Anos 70: cinema* (Rio de Janeiro: Europa Empresa Gráfica Editora, 1979), p. 70. In contrast, José Mário Ortiz Ramos argues that censorship has been overly blamed for shaping Brazilian cultural production at the time: 'O cinema brasileiro contemporâneo (1970–1987)', in Fernão Ramos (ed.), *História do cinema brasileiro* (São Paulo: Arte Editora, 1987), p. 401.
10 Avellar, 'Teoria da relatividade', p. 67.
11 Randal Johnson and Robert Stam, 'The Shape of Brazilian Film History', in Johnson and Stam (eds), *Brazilian Cinema*, p. 40.
12 The title of this film clearly draws on the success of Gerard Damiano's porn classic *Deep Throat*, 1972, and even Alvaro Moya's screen name imitates the name of the director of *Deep Throat* (Gerard Damiano is the screen name of Shaun Costello).
13 Avellar, 'Teoria da relatividade', pp. 84–5.
14 Ibid., p. 75.
15 Ibid., p. 70.
16 Ibid., p. 77.
17 The title *Secas e molhadas* is a play on words on 'secos e molhados', the name given to general stores, or shops that sold everything ('dry and wet goods'), traditionally found in small towns in the interior of the country. By changing the gender of the adjectives, the title appears to refer to the state of sexual arousal of women.
18 Avellar, 'Teoria da relatividade', p. 81.
19 José Carlos Avellar, 'Animal doméstico', *Jornal do Brasil*, 31 May 1973.
20 Johnson, *The Film Industry in Brazil*, p. 144.
21 Ibid., p. 132, *apud* O Estado de São Paulo, 10 September 1980.
22 Johnson, *The Film Industry in Brazil*, p. 144.
23 Paulo Emílio Salles Gomes, 'Cinema: A Trajectory within Underdevelopment', in Johnson and Stam (eds), *Brazilian Cinema*, p. 253.
24 José Carlos Avellar, 'Produto nacional bruto', unsourced clipping, MAM archive, Rio de Janeiro, 16 August 1975.
25 Take, for example, the 1975 film *Bacalhau* (Codfish). The film is set up from the start as being a low-budget, badly made and debased version of *Jaws*: for more information, see Dennison and Shaw, *Popular Cinema in Brazil*, pp. 167–8.
26 This is one of the main issues dealt with by Freyre's *The Masters and the Slaves: A Study in the Development of Brazilian Civilization*, trans. Samuel Putman (New York and London: Knopf, 1956), which was first published in 1933.
27 The use of the word 'Vaseline' in the film's title comes with its own suggestive significance in this respect.
28 Later films were more upfront in depicting this as a straightforward sexual preference: see, for example, *A noite das taras* (Night of Perversion 1980), a later *pornochanchada*, with its plethora of explicit but still simulated sex scenes. It was described by one observer as containing everything considered to be the preferred sexual 'perversions' of Brazilians: sodomy, dirty talk, men lubricating their penises with spit, and so on.
29 Jean-Claude Bernardet, 'Nós, invasores', *Movimento*, 22 December 1976.
30 *Cu* is slang in Portuguese for asshole: a favourite in the word play frequently used by

the *pornochanchada*. For example, one of the characters from martial arts spoof *As massagistas profissionais* (The Professional Masseuses, 1976) is called Fung Ku.

31 Jeffrey Lesser, *A Discontented Diaspora: Japanese-Brazilians and the Meanings of Ethnic Militancy, 1960–1980* (Durham, NC and London: Duke University Press, forthcoming 2007), Chapter 1. Perhaps as a result of their perceived threatening virility, black men do not feature largely in the *pornochanchada*, but space is afforded black and mixed-race women, who invariably play maids in middle-class households.

32 Quoted in Kehl, 'Entrevista com Paulo Emílio Salles Gomes'.

33 Jean-Claude Bernardet, 'A pornô-moral', *Movimento*, 7 July 1975.

34 Jean-Claude Bernardet, 'Uma pornô grã-fina para a classe média', *Última hora*, São Paulo, 29 April 1978. In this article, Bernardet also alludes to such films as *pornochanchadas de luxo*, or luxury *pornochanchadas.*

35 Quoted in 'Luz, cama, ação!', *Revista domingo do Jornal do Brasil*, 3 May 1998.

36 See Chapter 7.

37 Walter Hugo Khouri made a number of important 'erotic' films during this period, but given that he had been making films of a sexual nature since the early 1960s his work has not been subsumed in film histories into the *pornochanchada.*

38 Robert Stam, João Luiz Vieira and Ismail Xavier, 'The Shape of Brazilian Cinema in the Post-Modern Age', in Johnson and Stam (eds), *Brazilian Cinema*, pp. 405–6.

39 Ibid., p. 406. The issue of *sexo explícito* in the cinema, and in particular the arguably outdated view of it as something demanding automatic censorship, was revisited in 1992 in Murilo Salles and Sandra Werneck's short (six-minute) film *Pornografia* (Pornography). The film is made up entirely of explicit sex scenes filmed with politically charged intertitles designed to criticise the then Collor government, and with the national anthem supplying a provocative soundtrack, with the goal of intentionally producing problems with the censor, in as much as it represented an attempt to bring *sexo explícito* into the mainstream. Perhaps as a result of hard-core's association with the near death of national cinema in the late 1980s, the film garnered surprisingly little sympathy among either critics or liberal-minded audiences.

40 Johnson, *The Film Industry in Brazil*, p. 172.

41 It should be acknowledged, of course, that the reasons for the growth in crime in urban areas in Brazil are both numerous and complex and, despite what many conservative observers liked to believe at the time, they cannot be solely laid at the door of the *pornochanchada.*

42 For more information on Mazzaropi, see Chapter 11.

43 Paulo Sergio Markun, 'Cartazes de filmes eróticos causam polemica', *Folha de São Paulo*, 3 March 1985.

44 Johnson, 'Popular Cinema in Brazil', *Studies in Latin American Popular Culture* 3, 1984, p. 92. Most of the actresses associated with the soft-core *pornochanchada* who continued to work in the early hard-core films did so with body doubles appearing in the explicit sex scenes.

9 THE NATION IN CONTEMPORARY CINEMA

1 See Chapter 4, '*Retomada* legislation', pp. 36–7.

2 See, for example, Randal Johnson, 'TV Globo, the MPA, and Brazilian Cinema', in Lisa Shaw and Stephanie Dennison (eds), *Latin American Cinema: Essays on Modernity, Gender and National Identity* (Jefferson, NC: McFarland, 2005), pp. 11–38 (p. 18).

3 João Luiz Vieira, programme for the Banco do Brasil-sponsored event 'Encontro com o cinema brasileiro: periferias urbanas', 13 April 2003. Vieira cites the silent film *Nhô Anastácio chegou de viagem* (*Mr Anastácio Came Back from a Trip*, 1908, Júlio Ferrez) as perhaps the earliest example of this theme in Brazilian cinema. The *chanchada* tradition is analysed in Chapter 6, Mazzaropi's films in Chapter 11.

4 Ivana Bentes, 'The *Sertão* and the *Favela* in Contemporary Brazilian Film', in Lúcia Nagib (ed.), *The New Brazilian Cinema* (London and New York: I.B. Tauris, 2003), pp. 121–37 (p. 121).
5 Paulo Lins, author of the book *City of God*, and former slum inhabitant, collaborated on the film's script.
6 *Carandiru* attracted more spectators during its first weekend than any other film – foreign or Brazilian – had yet attracted that year. *Filme B* 6, 14 April 2003, p. 283.
7 There were just two exceptions; the role of Cenoura (Carrot) was played by Matheus Nachtergaele, known for his work on Brazilian television, acclaimed theatre actor, and star of films such as *O auto da compadecida* (*The Dog's Will*, Guel Arraes, 2000), *Me, You, Them* and subsequently *Mango Yellow*, and well-known actor and musician Seu Jorge was cast in the role of Mané Galinha (Knockout Ned).
8 Ivana Bentes, '*Cidade de Deus* promove turismo no inferno', *O Estado de São Paulo*, 31 August 2002.
9 Ivana Bentes, 'O *copyright* da miséria e os discursos sobre a exclusão', *Cinemais* 33, January/March 2003, pp. 189–201 (p. 199).
10 Johnson, 'TV Globo, the MPA, and Brazilian Cinema', p. 34.
11 Lúcia Nagib, 'Talking Bullets: The Language of Violence in *City of God*', *Third Text* 18, 3, 2004, pp. 239–50 (p. 245).
12 Walter Salles, cited in Nayse Lopez, '*Cidade de Deus*, inferno dos homens', *Público* Y, 28 March 2003, pp. 22–4 (p. 24).
13 Nagib, 'Talking Bullets', p. 244. Guti Fraga, director of the 'Nós do Morro' theatre group, set up over ten years ago in the Rio de Janeiro shantytown of Vidigal, collaborated in the project, and was in charge of selecting actors for the film from among the inhabitants of several Rio *favelas.*
14 Fernando Meirelles in interview with José Carlos Avellar, 'Fernando Meirelles: do *Cine Olho* à O2 (passando pelo Olhar Eletrônico)', *Cinemais* 35, July–September 2003, pp. 121–49 (pp. 137–8).
15 Filming in Cidade de Deus itself was impossible owing to the instability caused by rival drug gangs, and the fact that the district's physical characteristics had been altered over time. Lopez, '*Cidade de Deus*, inferno dos homens', p. 24.
16 Quoted in ibid., p. 23.
17 Ismail Xavier, 'Angels with Dirty Faces', *Sight and Sound*, January 2003, pp. 28–30 (p. 28).
18 Beatriz Jaguaribe, 'Favelas and the Aesthetics of Realism: Representations in Film and Literature', *Journal of Latin American Cultural Studies* 13, 3, December 2004, pp. 327–42 (p. 334).
19 David Treece, 'Soundtrack of an Alternative Black Consciousness? *City of God* and Contemporary Afro-Brazilian Music', unpublished manuscript.
20 Ibid.
21 João Luiz Vieira, programme for the Banco do Brasil-sponsored event 'Encontro com o cinema brasileiro: debate com Alexandre Borges e exibição do filme *O invasor*', 15 April 2003.
22 Lúcia Nagib, 'Is This Really Brazil? The Dystopian City of *The Trespasser*', *New Cinemas: Journal of Contemporary Film* 2, 1, pp. 17–28 (p. 17).
23 Ibid.
24 Luiz Zanin Oricchio, *Cinema de novo: um balanço crítico da retomada* (São Paulo: Estação Liberdade, 2003), p. 178.
25 Ibid., p. 179.
26 Sabotage also appeared in Hector Babenco's *Carandiru*, before his murder in January 2003.
27 Verônica Ferreira Dias, 'A Cinema of Conversation: Eduardo Coutinho's *Santo forte*

and *Babilônia 2000*', in Lúcia Nagib (ed.), *The New Brazilian Cinema*, pp. 105–17 (p. 106).
28 Ibid., pp. 107–8.
29 Jaguaribe, 'Favelas and the Aesthetics of Realism', p. 336.
30 Ibid., p. 337.
31 Interview with Felipe Lacerda, University of Leeds, 11 February 2005.
32 Ibid.
33 Lorraine Leu, 'Delinquency, Representation and Remembrance in Rio de Janeiro', paper given at LASA (Latin American Studies Association) XXVI International Congress, San Juan, Puerto Rico, 15–18 March 2006.
34 Ibid.
35 Jaguaribe, 'Favelas and the Aesthetics of Realism', p. 329.
36 Bentes, 'The *Sertão* and the *Favela* in Contemporary Brazilian Film', p. 125.
37 Such as *Central Station, Me, You, Them* and *Behind the Sun.*
38 Waldemar Lima, interviewed by Camilo Soares in the magazine *Continente*, cited in Oricchio, *Cinema de novo*, p. 132.
39 Walter Salles, quoted in Lúcia Nagib (ed.), *O cinema da retomada: depoimentos de 90 cineastas dos anos 90* (São Paulo: Editora 34, 2002), p. 421.
40 The first person we see dictating a letter is Socorro Nobre, an elderly woman and former prisoner about whom Walter Salles made an earlier documentary.
41 Walter Salles, quoted in Nagib (ed.), *O cinema da retomada*, pp. 420–1.
42 Paulo Passos de Oliveira, 'Salles e Lima Jr: *A ostra e o vento* e *Central do Brasil*: o não-lugar e o lugar', *Cinemais* 17, May/June 1999, pp. 135–54 (p. 151).
43 Lúcia Nagib, *A utopia no cinema brasileiro: matrizes, nostalgia, distopias* (São Paulo: Cosac + Naify, 2006), p. 71.
44 Casé is the well-known presenter of TV Globo's series *Brasil Legal* (Cool Brazil) and *Movuca* (Mess), which deal with amusing and poignant real-life stories.
45 Andrucha Waddington, in interview with Marcelo Janot, 'Do sertão para o mundo', *Veja Rio*, 18–24 August 2000, pp. 10–11 (p. 11).
46 Information given in interviews with the director and the cast in the Extras section of the DVD.
47 The plot is based on that of a novel by the Albanian writer Ismail Kadaré.
48 Interview with Walter Salles, Brazilian DVD of *Behind the Sun.*
49 Santoro came to the attention of TV audiences all over Brazil when he played the role of a young priest, Father Malthus, whom a female prostitute falls in love with, in *Hilda the Hurricane* (1998), a TV miniseries set in the 1950s.
50 José Carlos Avellar, 'Pai, país, mãe, pátria', *Cinemais* 33, January/March 2003, pp. 55–85 (pp. 67, 70).
51 Ibid., p. 66.
52 Nagib, *A utopia no cinema brasileiro*, p. 57.
53 Oricchio, *Cinema de novo*, p. 147.
54 Bentes, 'The *Sertão* and the *Favela* in Contemporary Brazilian Film', pp. 124–5.
55 Ibid., p. 129. This tradition began with Humberto Mauro's *Favela dos meus amores* (1934), see pp. 51–2.
56 Arnaldo Jabor, *O Estado de São Paulo*, 16 April 2002, cited in Oricchio, *Cinema de novo*, p. 181.
57 Johnson, 'TV Globo, the MPA, and Brazilian Cinema', p. 35.
58 Jaguaribe, 'Favelas and the Aesthetics of Realism', p. 338.

10 THE STARS OF THE *CHANCHADAS*, 1933–60

1 João Luiz Vieira, 'Foto de cena e chanchada: a eficácia do "Star System" no Brasil', Master's dissertation, Universidade Federal do Rio de Janeiro, 1977, pp. 40–1, and Fernão Ramos and Luiz Felipe Miranda (eds), *Enciclopédia do cinema brasileiro* (São Paulo: SENAC, 2000), p. 36.
2 Franz Fanon, *Black Face, White Mask* (New York: Grove Press, 1967).
3 Darién J. Davis, 'Racial Parity and National Humor: Exploring Brazilian Samba from Noel Rosa to Carmen Miranda, 1930–1939', in William H. Beezley and Linda A. Curcio-Nagy (eds), *Latin American Popular Culture: An Introduction* (Wilmington, DE: Scholarly Resources, 2000), pp. 183–200 (p. 188).
4 Fernanda Bicalho, *Cinearte 1926–1930: a política do estrelismo*, Papéis Avulsos, no. 21 (Rio de Janeiro: Centro Interdisciplinar de Estudos Contemporâneos, UFRJ, 1989), p. 6.
5 Ibid., p. 7.
6 Ibid., pp. 7, 11.
7 *Cinearte*, 21 March 1928, p. 6. Quoted in Bicalho, *Cinearte 1926–1930*, p. 16.
8 Bicalho, *Cinearte 1926–1930*, p. 11.
9 Sheila Schvarzman, *Humberto Mauro e as imagens do Brasil* (São Paulo: UNESP, 2003), p. 35.
10 Ismail Xavier, 'O sonho da indústria: a criação de imagem em *Cinearte*', in *Sétima arte: um culto moderno* (São Paulo: Perspectiva – Secretaria da Cultura, Ciência e Tecnologia do Estado de São Paulo, 1978), pp. 167–97.
11 *Cinearte* 198, 11 December 1929, p. 28.
12 Ana Pessoa, *Carmen Santos: o cinema dos anos 20* (Rio de Janeiro: Aeroplano, 2002), p. 18.
13 *Cinelândia*, October 1956, first fortnight.
14 'Tez *levemente* morena', *Cinelândia*, January 1955, first fortnight. Our emphasis.
15 Bryan McCann, *Hello, Hello, Brazil: Popular Music in the Making of Modern Brazil* (Durham, NC and London: Duke University Press, 2004), pp. 187–8.
16 The scene in which she performs the song 'What has the *baiana* got?' in this film was, however, reused in the follow-up production from the Sonofilmes studio, *Laranja da China* (Orange from China, 1940), in recognition of Miranda's box-office appeal and star status.
17 See Ana M. López, 'Are All Latins from Manhattan? Hollywood, Ethnography and Cultural Colonialism', in John King, Ana M. López and Manuel Alvarado (eds), *Mediating Two Worlds: Cinematic Encounters in the Americas* (London: BFI Publishing, 1993), Ana Rita Mendonça, *Carmen Miranda foi a Washington* (Rio de Janeiro: Record, 1999), and Helena Solberg's biographical film *Carmen Miranda: Bananas Is My Business* (1994).
18 Mendonça, *Carmen Miranda foi a Washington*, p. 23.
19 *Cinearte*, 15 May 1935, p. 10.
20 Mendonça, *Carmen Miranda foi a Washington*, pp. 12–13. As Mendonça points out, in March 1940, during her first year of success in the States, Carmen sang for President Franklin Roosevelt at the White House (p. 13).
21 McCann, *Hello, Hello, Brazil*, p. 145.
22 Mendonça, *Carmen Miranda foi a Washington*, p. 18.
23 Ida Zeitlin, 'Sous American Sizzler', *Motion Picture*, September 1941. For a detailed analysis of Miranda's representation of ethnicity in Hollywood see Shari Roberts, '"The Lady in the Tutti-Frutti Hat": Carmen Miranda, a Spectacle of Ethnicity', *Cinema Journal* 32, 3, Spring 1993, pp. 3–23.
24 José Ligiero Coelho, 'Carmen Miranda: An Afro-Brazilian Paradox', Ph.D. dissertation, New York University, 1998.

25 Ibid., p. 77. Here there is a direct contrast with her ultra-modern, masculinised costume when performing 'Radio Singers' in *Hello, Hello, Carnival!*.
26 Ibid., pp. 136–40.
27 Ibid., p. 141. Lapa was Rio's bohemian night-life and red-light district in the 1920s and 1930s.
28 Mendonça, *Carmen Miranda foi a Washington*, pp. 18–19.
29 Ibid., pp. 19–20.
30 A term coined by Robert Stam, *Tropical Multiculturalism: A Comparative History of Race in Brazilian Cinema and Culture* (Durham, NC and London: Duke University Press, 1997), p. 84.
31 Coelho, 'Carmen Miranda', pp. 49–53.
32 This photograph is reproduced in Ana Rita Mendonça's book *Carmen Miranda foi a Washington*. Grande Otelo refers to this tradition in an interview with Jairo Severiano and Elisete Cardoso recorded at the Museu da Imagem e do Som, Rio de Janeiro, 24 October 1985.
33 Coelho, 'Carmen Miranda', pp. 76–7. Coelho explains that 'Tar Doll' was first performed in a theatrical revue in 1930 by Aracy Cortes and João Martins, who appeared in blackface. Although Brazil had no tradition of minstrelsy, the show's co-writer, Oduvaldo Vianna, had travelled to the USA the previous year and brought back this idea from the Broadway shows that he had seen. Ibid., p. 76.
34 López, 'Are All Latins from Manhattan?', p. 77.
35 *Correio da manhã*, 13 August 1939.
36 Luiz Carlos Merten, 'Eliana', *Estado de São Paulo* (*Caderno 2*), 20 June 1990, p. 3.
37 Richard Dyer, *Stars* (London: BFI, 1979).
38 *Cinelândia*, February 1956, first fortnight.
39 Maite Conde, 'Cinematic Encounters in Premodernist Brazilian Literature', Ph.D. dissertation, UCLA, 2004, p. 217.
40 *Cinelândia* 14, 1953. Similarly, she is described as 'our Jeanne Crain' in *Cinelândia*, March 1953.
41 Vieira, 'Foto de cena e chanchada', p. 36. Stam, *Tropical Multiculturalism*, p. 103.
42 This phenomenon of 'parallel stars' was not unique to Brazil, of course.
43 'Assim é Eliana', *Cinelândia*, December 1955, second fortnight.
44 *Cinelândia*, February 1956, first fortnight.
45 Stam, *Tropical Multiculturalism*, pp. 102–3.
46 *Cinelândia*, June 1952.
47 See, for example, an article entitled 'Oscarito: quando o filme nacional tinha ídolos e público', *Visão*, 8 August 1990, p. 58.
48 Interview (História do Cinema Brasileiro, series) with Oscarito by the Museu da Imagem e do Som, Rio de Janeiro, 11 September 1968.
49 Jerry Palmer, *Taking Humour Seriously* (London and New York: Routledge, 1994), p. 150.
50 Alan Dale, *Slapstick in American Movies* (Minneapolis and London: University of Minnesota Press, 2000), pp. 14–15.
51 *Cinelândia*, February 1956, first fortnight.
52 *Cinelândia*, January 1956, second fortnight.
53 *Cinelândia*, February 1956, first fortnight.
54 Interview (História do Cinema Brasileiro, series) with Oscarito by the Museu da Imagem e do Som, Rio de Janeiro, 11 September 1968.
55 *Cinelândia*, October 1957, first fortnight.
56 *Cinelândia*, December 1958, first fortnight, p. 68.
57 Stam, *Tropical Multiculturalism*, p. 88.
58 Roberto Moura, *Grande Othelo, um artista genial* (Rio de Janeiro: Relume Dumará, 1996), p. 7.

59 This anecdote is recounted in Eduardo Giffoni Flórido, *As grandes personagens da história do cinema brasileiro, 1930–1959* (Rio de Janeiro: Fraiha, 1999), p. 78.
60 He replies: 'Mim star alemon de Santas Catarrinas' (Me Geeerman star from Santas Catarrinas) – Santa Catarina, a southern state in Brazil, where most German immigrants settled in the nineteenth century.
61 Genésio Arruda was synonymous on the popular stage with the figure of the *jeca* or country bumpkin. He went on to star in three of Mazzaropi's films in the 1960s.
62 Moura, *Grande Othelo, um artista genial*, p. 23.
63 According to Flórido, *As grandes personagens da história do cinema brasileiro*, p. 78, it was Jardel Jércolis who in 1933 put the 18-year-old on stage, singing in English, under the English stage name of The Great Othelo.
64 Moura, *Grande Othelo, um artista genial*, pp. 38–9.
65 Ibid., pp. 94–6.
66 McCann, *Hello, Hello, Brazil*, p. 149.
67 Vieira, 'Foto de cena e chanchada', p. 42.
68 Kathryn Castle, London Metropolitan University, 'Blacking Up in Britain: Minstrelsy and Blackface Performance on the British Stage', seminar given in the School of History, University of Leeds, 14 March 2005.
69 Stam, *Tropical Multiculturalism*, p. 103.
70 Moura, *Grande Othelo, um artista genial*, p. 43.
71 Stam, *Tropical Multiculturalism*, p. 92.
72 He subsequently appeared on screen alongside other white co-stars, such as Zé Trindade, Ankito and Costinha, in films produced by other studios.
73 Stam, *Tropical Multiculturalism*, p. 95.
74 Isabel Cristina Mauad, 'Olho de Macunaíma', *O Globo*, 10 June 1990, p. 5.
75 Stam, *Tropical Multiculturalism*, p. 92.
76 Stephanie Dennison and Lisa Shaw, *Popular Cinema in Brazil* (Manchester: Manchester University Press, 2004), p. 233.
77 Stam, *Tropical Multiculturalism*, p. 103.
78 Carl N. Degler, *Neither Black nor White: Slavery and Race Relations in Brazil and the United States* (Madison: University of Wisconsin Press, 1986).
79 Robert Brent Toplin, *Freedom and Prejudice: The Legacy of Slavery in the United States and Brazil* (Westport, CT: Greenwood Press, 1981), p. 93.
80 See Chapter 6.

11 ICONS OF POPULAR CULTURE POST-1960

1 For example, the formats of the two most popular TV genres in Brazil, the soap opera (*telenovela*) and the variety show (*programa de auditório*), have changed relatively little since the 1960s, and many TV presenters (Xuxa, Faustão, Ana Maria Braga and Sílvio Santos, for example) have been prime-time staples for at least twenty years.
2 'O palhaço do Brasil', *Veja*, 13 July 1983.
3 Felipe Bragança, 'Didi, o cupido Trapalhão', *Contracampo*. Available at www.contracampo.com.br/criticas/didi-cupido.htm (accessed 8 August 2006).
4 See Chapter 12.
5 It is impossible not to reflect on the irony of the 'social theme' dealt with in Aragão's 2004 solo film *Didi quer ser criança* (Didi Wants to Be a Child), given Aragão's link with the mighty Globo network and his use of product placement and merchandising aimed at children. In the film Didi plays the owner of a small toy factory, struggling to survive against competition from big businesses that ultimately force him out of the market because 'children just want what they see on adverts'.
6 'O palhaço do Brasil'.

7 Carla Ferreira, 'Renato Aragão reclama da falta de salas para filmes populares'. Available at http://ofuxico.uol.com.br/Materias/Noticias/noticia_9432.htm (accessed 8 August 2006).
8 Eduardo Valente, 'Didi quer ser criança', *Contracampo*. Available at www.contracampo.com.br/64/didicrianca.htm (accessed 8 August 2006).
9 Aragão proved his commitment to continuing to make movies by setting up his own studios in 1999, where a number of his films were produced, before the studios were sold in 2005 to TV Record.
10 A ratings winner throughout the 1990s in TV Globo's daytime slot.
11 For more information on the *circo-teatro*, see Stephanie Dennison and Lisa Shaw, *Popular Cinema in Brazil* (Manchester: Manchester University Press, 2004), pp. 13–16.
12 Nuno César Abreu, 'Anotações sobre Mazzaropi, o Jeca que não era Tatu', *Filme Cultura* 40, August/October 1982, p. 38.
13 Http://lobato.globo.com (accessed 12 August 2006).
14 Although this is not acknowledged in the film credits, Antonio Querino Neto claims that Mazzaropi bought the right to use the Jeca Tatu character from Medicamentos Fontoura: 'Mazzaropi', *Revista Set Cinema e Video*, 5.5, p. 56, quoted in Eva Bueno, 'The Adventures of Jeca Tatu: Class, Culture and Nation in Mazzaropi's Films', *Studies in Latin American Popular Culture* 18, 199, p. 52.
15 These include *E a vaca foi para o brejo* (My Cow Is Stuck in the Mud, 1981), starring Polêncio, and the largely ignored *A volta do Jeca* (Jeca's Return, 1984), starring *caipira* comedian Chico Fumaça and directed by Mazzaropi's director of choice, Pio Zamuner. More recently, Luis Alberto Pereira released *Tapete vermelho* (Red Carpet) in 2005, a homage to Mazzaropi and *caipira* culture. But Jeca's most successful reincarnation can be found in the guise of the naive but honest and healthy Chico Bento, the country bumpkin of Maurício de Souza's ever-popular *Mônica* comic books and animated films.
16 See, for example, *O menino da porteira* (The Porter's Child, 1976), a film based loosely on the plot of a very popular country music song of the same name; Nelson Pereira dos Santos's 1980 *Na estrada da vida: José Rico e milionário* (*The Highway of Life*), a semi-autobiographical film starring two popular *sertanejo* singers, and the box-office smash *Dois filhos de Francisco* (Two Sons of Francisco) of 2005, a film produced by and based on the rise to fame of Zezé di Camargo e Luciano, Brazil's most popular *dupla sertaneja* or country music duo.
17 One PAM Filmes insider commented that the quality of the films Mazzaropi starred in dropped significantly after he took over production, because, as he saw it, his films became little more than Mazzaropi star vehicles: Glauco Barsalini, *Mazzaropi: o Jeca do Brasil* (Campinas, Brazil: Atamo, 2002), p. 55.
18 The drawers of Mazzaropi's office were said to be full of the scripts from popular plays. Mazzaropi produced film scripts based on this material, but most of his own lines were ad-libbed on set: Barsalini, *Mazzaropi*, p. 38.
19 Barsalini, *Mazzaropi*, p. 66.
20 Towards the end of Mazzaropi's career he was obliged to alter this release date owing to competition from the Trapalhões films.
21 Barsalini, *Mazzaropi*, p. 75.
22 Bueno, 'The Adventures of Jeca Tatu', p. 49. Mazzaropi did, however, surround himself with practitioners of popular culture: circus performers and directors, popular theatre producers and so on.
23 Quoted in Armando Salem, 'O Brasil é meu público', *Veja*, 28 January 1970. Available at www.museumazzaropi.com.br/hist.htm (accessed 1 September 2006).
24 Given his films' commercial success, Mazzaropi would have received cash prizes from the INC for one. See Chapter 3.

25 Quoted in Salem, 'O Brasil é meu público'. As Bueno ('The Adventures of Jeca Tatu', p. 49) puts it, 'the Brazil where Mazzaropi's work fits is not the Brazil that goes to Cannes'.
26 Quoted in Barsalini, *Mazzaropi*, pp. 78–9. Mazzaropi similarly had little respect for the filmmaking approach of the *cinema novo* group: 'You can't make films without money. It's stupid to talk the way they all do – work of art, a camera in the hand – that's for fools. It's amateur, it's a joke.' Quoted in 'Nunca fui chupim do governo', *Valeparaibano*, 16 September 1979.
27 Bueno, 'The Adventures of Jeca Tatu', p. 39.
28 Ibid., p. 47.
29 Ibid., p. 49.
30 Ibid., p. 43.
31 Jeffrey Lesser, *A Discontented Diaspora: Japanese-Brazilians and the Meanings of Ethnic Militancy, 1960–1980* (Durham, NC and London: Duke University Press, forthcoming 2007).
32 Quoted in Barsalini, *Mazzaropi*, p. 77.
33 Ibid., p. 95.
34 Quoted in ibid., p. 77.
35 Quoted in Salem, 'O Brasil é meu público'.
36 Barsalini, *Mazzaropi*, p. 78.
37 *Jornal do Comércio*, 9 January 1984, quoted in Bueno, The Adventures of Jeca Tatu', p. 40.
38 It is worth mentioning here the work of Ivan Cardoso, who has produced a (small) number of comedy-horror films, the most important of which is *O segredo da múmia* (*The Secret of the Mummy*, 1982), in which Coffin Joe appeared. Cardoso's style is often described as *terrir*, a play on the words *terror* (horror) and *rir* (to laugh).
39 Marins is frequently included in anthologies of Brazilian *cinema marginal* (see Chapter 7), but he should be seen more as a precursor or inspiration to the movement, given the ideological divergence between his own work and that of his fellow *paulistas*.
40 Interview with José Mojica Marins: www.jt.estadao.com.br/noticias/98/04/25/va4.htm (consulted 1 May 2003).
41 www.oxum.com.br/quimbanda.asp (consulted 11 August 2006).
42 Even the use of an item of clothing borrowed from *Quimbanda* would have been considered very daring: Alexandre Agabiti Fernandes, 'Entre a demência e a transcedência: José Mojica Marins e o cinema fantástico', *Cinémas d'Amérique Latine* 10, 2002, pp. 117–28 (p. 124).
43 By the mid-1980s Mojica Marins was earning a living by performing in character as an MC for an amusement park. He had become a parody of himself, 'a kind of clown': *World's Weirdest Movies: Coffin Joe* (documentary).
44 See, for example, Ivan Finotti and André Barcinski, who have ultimately produced a kind of hagiographic 'weird star' biography that has been very much in vogue in Brazil since the early 1990s: *Maldito: a vida e o cinema de José Mojica Marins, o Zé do Caixão* (São Paulo: Editora 34, 1998).
45 Despite these features, Mojica Marins's horror films did still follow the European and US tradition of practically all-white casts, and on occasion the naked bodies of females were shot in such a way that they looked whiter than they really were.
46 Coffin Joe's voice was dubbed in all his films, because Mojica Marins himself had a speech impediment, like a number of other popular entertainers in Brazil. The director played on this impediment in *Delírios de um anormal*, in which he plays himself, but with perfect, confident speech.
47 He may be evil but even Coffin Joe defends children and old people in his films, with a sentimentality that is perfectly acceptable to Brazilian audiences.
48 Mojica Marins did not escape imprisonment altogether during the dictatorship: he was

jailed for twenty-four hours and beaten in 1970 for allegedly having sex with an underage girl. Interview with José Mojica Marins: www.jt.estadao.com.br/noticias/98/04/25/va4.htm (consulted 1 May 2003).

49 Fernandes, 'Entre a demência e a transcedência', p. 118.

50 Dolores Tierney, 'José Mojica Marins and the Cultural Politics of Marginality in Third-World Criticism', *Journal of Latin American Cultural Studies* 13, 1, 2004, pp. 63–78 (p. 74).

51 Barcinski and Finotti, *Maldito*, p. 155.

12 BOMBSHELLS: PIN-UP ACTRESSES POST-1960

1 Colour, rather than race or ethnicity, given that racial and ethnic origins do not, as a rule, affect the way stars are 'consumed' in Brazil. The racial origins of Sônia Braga and Norma Benguel, for example, are similar, but their look and representation of colour on screen are very different.

2 By the mid-1970s nudity had also found its way into primetime soap operas: Sônia Braga was one of the first to get naked in the very successful *Gabriela, cravo e canela* (Globo, 1975). Although nudity has not disappeared from screens completely, the sense no longer exists that, without full frontal female nudity and X-rated sex scenes, a national film will not sell.

3 Even wholesome children's entertainer Xuxa posed naked in *Playboy* at the beginning of her career in the early 1980s. The notable exception to this rule, ironically, was Norma Benguel, the first full frontal nude of Brazilian cinema in *Os cafajestes* (*The Unscrupulous Ones*, 1962).

4 First published in 1958.

5 In 1976 Bruno Barreto released *Dona Flor e seus dois maridos* (*Dona Flor and Her Two Husbands*), the hugely popular film based on Jorge Amado's 1966 novel of the same name that was set in Salvador in the North-East of Brazil in the 1940s. It still holds the record for the (recorded) largest number of spectators for a national film.

6 In *Dona Flor* press notes (undated, microfiche on Sônia Braga, BFI, London).

7 Edward Telles, 'Ethnic Boundaries and Political Mobilization among African Brazilians', in Michael Hanchard (ed.), *Racial Politics in Contemporary Brazil* (Durham, NC and London: Duke University Press, 1999), p. 83.

8 Michael Hanchard, 'Black Cinderella: Race and the Public Sphere in Brazil', in Hanchard (ed.), *Racial Politics in Contemporary Brazil*, p. 68.

9 According to the 2000 census, out of a population of just under 170 million, just over 66 million citizens declared themselves to be *pardos* or of mixed race, with 90.5 million self-identifying as white and 10.5 million as black. Brazilian Institute of Geography and Statistics website, http://www.ibge.gov.br (accessed 1 March 2002).

10 Telles, 'Ethnic Boundaries and Political Mobilization among African Brazilians', p. 84.

11 Angela Gilliam, 'From Roxbury to Rio – and Back in a Hurry', in David J. Hellwig (ed.), *African-American Reflections on Brazil's Racial Paradise* (Philadelphia, PA: Temple University Press, 1992), pp. 177–8.

12 Braga was criticised in some circles in Brazil for being too white to play Gabriela in the 1970s soap opera, while by contrast a review of *Dona Flor* in New York's *Variety* (14 September 1977) described the title character as a 'lovely mulatto woman'.

13 Donald Pierson, *Negroes in Brazil: A Study of Race Contact at Bahia* (Chicago, IL: University of Chicago Press, 1942), pp. 136–7. Pierson goes on to quote statistics that suggest that the *morena* is more often than not racially a *mulata*. That said, it is worth bearing in mind that Brazilians do not necessarily see *morenas* as being non-white.

14 Quoted in *Dona Flor* press notes.

15 Quoted in *Dona Flor* press notes.

16 See, for example, the notorious scene in *A dama do lotação* when she carefully removes her underwear in the street before heading off to pick up strangers on buses.
17 João Luis Vieira alludes to Penelope Cruz's mimicking of Braga's screen 'look' in *Woman on Top* (2000): 'All-Purpose *Latina*: Penelope Cruz's Travelling Body', paper delivered at New Latin American Cinemas: Contemporary Cinema and Filmmaking, University of Leeds, 30 June 2005.
18 It is interesting to note that, in her frequent discussions of this issue in the press, Braga does not make reference to skin colour. In fact her comments, while useful for the promotion of her own type of beauty, are not wholly accurate: while blondes are undoubtedly over-represented and *mulatas* and black women are under-represented, it is the white-skinned brunette that has always dominated numerically TV and film screens in Brazil.
19 Roberto DaMatta, 'Cores: homenagem a Oracy Nogueira', http://www.jt.estadao.com.br/noticias/99/09/05/cdamatta.htm (accessed 3 March 2002).
20 Hamilton Almeida Filho, '*Playboy* entrevista: Sônia Braga', *Playboy* (Brazil), Unmarked magazine clipping, MAM Film Archive, Rio de Janeiro.
21 Ruben George Oliven, 'Brazil: The Modern in the Tropics', in V. Schelling (ed.), *Through the Kaleidoscope: The Experience of Modernity in Latin America* (London and New York: Verso, 2000), p. 63.
22 Darlene Glória has recently made a return to TV acting.
23 Blumenau is regarded as one of Brazil's most Germanic towns, having attracted a large number of German immigrants in the late nineteenth and early twentieth century. It hosts the nation's annual Oktoberfest.
24 Fischer recently appeared on stage in Rio de Janeiro as Mrs Robinson in a stage version of *The Graduate*.
25 Richard Dyer, *White* (London and New York: Routledge, 1997).
26 Such strong reaction to Benguel's visit to Itamar Franco may have been provoked by the fact that the then president was a notorious womaniser, and that rumours were rife at the time that Benguel had in her youth slept with a president. Norma's honesty and morality continue to be questioned as a result of recent run-ins with the law regarding her overspending and alleged misappropriation of funds during the making of her notorious flop *O Guarani* (The Guarani Indian, 1996).
27 Vera Fischer appears more frequently in facial close-up than Sônia Braga, which conforms to the age-old cliché of the *morena/mulata*'s beauty being located in her body.
28 *Manchete*, 12 May 1982, pp. 13–16.
29 *Manchete*, 14 July 1980, pp. 20–2.
30 The tradition of topless bathing has never really taken off in Brazil and the white or merely lighter-skinned markings left by the tiny triangles that cover the breasts and bottom in the famous 'dental floss' bikinis are considered sexually attractive.
31 Xuxa is therefore perceived as being whiter than the average white Brazilian of Portuguese descent. The fact that all of Xuxa's grandparents were foreign is also significant for Brazilians, as having a European grandparent usually means having the right to a foreign passport (and thus an alternative, 'first-world' identity).
32 Amélia Simpson, *Xuxa: The Mega-Marketing of Gender, Race and Identity* (Philadelphia, PA: Temple University Press, 1993), p. 15. See also Amélia Simpson, 'Representing Racial Difference: Brazil's Xuxa at the Televisual Border', *Studies in Latin American Popular Culture* 17, 1998, pp. 197–221.
33 Randal Johnson and Robert Stam, 'The Shape of Brazilian Film Industry', in Johnson and Stam (eds), *Brazilian Cinema* (New York: Columbia University Press, 1995), p. 16.
34 Carla Perez, who starred in *Xuxa requebra*, was the first so-called *Loira do Tchan* (blonde dancer in the popular 1990s Bahian group É o tchan!, whose departure

prompted a national competition to find a replacement). She starred in a minor hit film based loosely on her rise to superstardom called *Cinderela baiana* (Bahian Cinderella, 1998). Many other iconic blondes have starred in Xuxa's films, including her main competition on TV, Angélica (in *Xuxa e os duendes*), and Vera Fischer (in *Xuxa e os duendes II*).

35 Full frontal nude shots of Xuxa posing in *Revista Status* currently sell on the internet for around £50, and the 1982 edition of *Playboy* in which she appeared is a collector's item.

36 Simpson, *Xuxa*, p. 30.

37 Xuxa tried to have the film withdrawn from circulation. In June 1991 she won a judgement prohibiting (temporarily, at any rate) the distribution of the film on video. While it may be rare, it is possible to find a subtitled DVD version of the film.

38 Simpson, *Xuxa*, p. 14.

39 See, for example, her interview for Brazilian *Playboy* magazine in 1982.

40 Simpson, *Xuxa*, p. 30.

FILMOGRAPHY

This filmography provides a list of all the films referred to in this book, together with a translation of each title. For Brazilian films that have been exhibited abroad under an English title, the latter is given in italics. Each title is followed by the year of production and the name of the director. Indefinite and definite articles (*um*, *uma*, *o*, *a*, *os* or *as* in Portuguese) have been ignored in the alphabetical ordering of films.

7 de Setembro de 1936 – Dia da Pátria (7 September 1936 – Independence Day/ Fatherland Day), 1936, Humberto Mauro.
À meia-noite levarei sua alma (*At Midnight I'll Take Your Soul*), 1964, José Mojica Marins.
Abril despedaçado (*Behind the Sun*), 2002, Walter Salles.
Acabaram-se os otários (No More Suckers), 1929, Luiz de Barros.
Aguirre, Der Zorn Gottes (*Aguirre, Wrath of God*), 1972, Werner Herzog.
Ai no corrida (*In the Realm of the Senses*), 1976, Nagisa Oshima.
Alô, alô, Brasil! (Hello, Hello, Brazil!), 1935, Wallace Downey, João de Barro and Alberto Ribeiro.
Alô, alô, Carnaval! (Hello, Hello, Carnival!), 1936, Adhemar Gonzaga.
Amarelo manga (*Mango Yellow*), 2002, Cláudio Assis.
Amelie (*Le fabuleux destin d'Amélie Poulain*), 2001, Jean-Pierre Jeunet.
Amor, estranho amor (*Love, Strange Love*), 1982, Walter Hugo Khouri.
O amuleto de Ogum (*The Amulet of Ogum*), 1974, Nelson Pereira dos Santos.
Um anjo Trapalhão (An Angel Trapalhão), 2000, Alexandre Boury and Marcelo Travesso.
Um apólogo – Machado de Assis, 1839–1939 (A Tribute – Machado de Assis, 1839–1939), 1939, Humberto Mauro.
Argila (Clay), 1940, Humberto Mauro.
Arraial do Cabo, 1960, Paulo Cesar Saraceni.
Arrivée d'un train à La Ciotat (*Arrival of a Train at La Ciotat Station*), 1895, August and Louis Lumière.
Aruanã, 1938, Líbero Luxardo.
At Play in the Fields of the Lord, 1991, Hector Babenco.
O auto da compadecida (*The Dog's Will*), 2000, Guel Arraes.
Aviso aos navegantes (Calling All Sailors), 1950, Watson Macedo.
A b . . . profunda (Deep A[ss]), 1984, Geraldo Dominó.

Babilônia 2000, 2000, Eduardo Coutinho.
Bacalhau (Codfish), 1975, Adriano Stuart.
Baile perfumado (*Perfumed Ball*), 1997, Paulo Caldas and Lírio Ferreira.
Banana da terra (Banana of the Land), 1939, Rui Costa.
Banana mecânica (Clockwork Banana), 1974, Braz Chediak.
O bandido da luz vermelha (*Red Light Bandit*), 1968, Rogério Sganzerla.
Barro humano (Human Mud), 1928, Adhemar Gonzaga.
Bem-dotado: o homem de Itu (Well-Endowed: The Man from Itu), 1977, José Miziara.
Berlim na batucada (Berlin to the Samba Beat), 1944, Luiz de Barros.
Berlin, Die Symphonie einer Grossstadt (*Berlin, Symphony of a Great City*), 1927, Walter Ruttmann.
Bicho de sete cabeças (*Brainstorm*), 2000, Laís Bodanzky.
Bonequinha de seda (Little Silk Doll), 1936, Oduvaldo Vianna.
Bonitinha mas ordinária (Pretty but Wicked), 1981, Braz Chediak.
Bossa nova, 2000, Bruno Barreto.
Brasa dormida (Dormant Embers), 1928, Humberto Mauro.
Brasiliana (series of seven short films, made between 1945 and 1956), Humberto Mauro.
Cabeças cortadas (*Cutting Heads*), 1970, Glauber Rocha.
O caçula do barulho (The Topsy-Turvy Kid), Riccardo Freda, 1949.
Cada um dá o que tem (Each One Gives Whatever He Can), 1975, Sílvio de Abreu, John Herbert and Adriano Stuart.
Os cafajestes (*The Unscrupulous Ones*), 1962, Ruy Guerra.
Caligula, 1979, Tinto Brass and Bob Guccione.
Canção de amor (Love Song), 1977, Gilda de Abreu.
Câncer (Cancer), 1972, Glauber Rocha.
Candinho (Little Candide), 1953, Abílio Pereira de Almeida.
O cangaceiro (*The Bandit*), 1953, Lima Barreto.
O cangaceiro (*The Cangaceiro*), 1997, Aníbal Massaini Neto.
O cangaceiro Trapalhão (The Bandit Trapalhão), 1983, Daniel Filho.
Carandiru, 2003, Hector Babenco.
Carlota Joaquina: Princesa do Brasil (*Carlota Joaquina: Brazilian Princess*), 1995, Carla Camurati.
Carmen Miranda: Bananas Is My Business, 1994, Helena Solberg.
Carnaval Atlântida (Atlântida Carnival), 1952, José Carlos Burle.
O carnaval cantado de 1933 no Rio de Janeiro (The 1933 Rio de Janeiro Carnival in Song), 1933, Léo Marten and Fausto Muniz.
Carnaval em lá maior (Carnival in A Major), 1955, Adhemar Gonzaga.
A carne (Flesh), 1924, Felipe Ricci.
O casamento dos Trapalhões (The Marriage of the Trapalhões), 1988, José Alvarenga Jr.
Casseta e Planeta: a taça do mundo é nossa (Casseta and Planeta: The World Cup Is Ours), 2003, Lula Buarque de Hollanda.
O cavalheiro Didi e a princesa Lili (Gentleman Didi and Princess Lili), 2006, Marcus Figueiredo.
Central do Brasil (*Central Station*), 1998, Walter Salles.
Um céu de estrelas (*A Starry Sky*), 1996, Tata Amaral.
Chegada de um trem a Petrópolis (Arrival of a Train in Petrópolis), 1897, Vittorio de Maio.
Chico Fumaça, 1958, Victor Lima.
Cidade baixa (*Lower City*), 2004, Sérgio Machado.

Cidade de Deus (*City of God*), 2002, Fernando Meirelles.
Cidade mulher (Woman City), 1936, Humberto Mauro.
Cinco Vezes Favela (*Favela X Five*), 1961, various.
Cinderela baiana (Bahian Cinderella), 1998, Conrado Sanchez.
Coisas eróticas (Erotic Things), 1982, Rafaele Rossi.
Coisas nossas (Our Things), 1931, Wallace Downey.
Com as calças na mão (With His Pants in His Hands), 1975, Carlo Mossi.
Como é boa nossa empregada (How Good Our Maid Is), 1973, Victor di Mello and Ismar Porto.
Como era gostoso o meu francês (*How Tasty Was My Little Frenchman*), 1972, Nelson Pereira dos Santos.
Como ser solteiro (*How to Be Single in Rio*), 1998, Rosane Svartman.
Convém martelar (Keep Trying), 1920, Manuel F. Araújo and António Silva.
Copacabana, 2001, Carla Camurati.
Coração materno (Maternal Heart), 1951, Gilda de Abreu.
O crime da mala (The Suitcase Murder), 1912, director unknown.
O crime de Paula Matos (The Paula Matos Murder), 1913, Paulino Botelho or Luiz Rocha.
Crime delicado (*Delicate Crime*), 2005, Beto Brant.
Crouching Tiger, Hidden Dragon, 2000, Ang Lee.
A dama do lotação (*Lady on the Bus*), 1978, Neville de Almeida.
Dark Water, 2005, Walter Salles.
De pernas pro ar (Topsy-Turvy), 1957, Victor Lima.
De vento em popa (Wind in the Sails), 1957, Carlos Manga.
O dedo da justiça (The Finger of Justice), 1919, director unknown.
Deep Throat, 1972, Gerard Damiano.
Delírios de um anormal (*Hallucinations of a Deranged Mind*), 1978, José Mojica Marins.
Der Leone Have Sept Cabeças (*The Lion Has Seven Heads*), 1971, Glauber Rocha.
O descobrimento do Brasil (The Discovery of Brazil), 1937, Humberto Mauro.
O despertar da besta, aka *Ritual dos sádicos* (*Awakening of the Beast*), 1969 (released 1983), José Mojica Marins.
Deus e o diabo na terra do sol (*Black God, White Devil*), 1964, Glauber Rocha.
Dia da Pátria (Fatherland Day), 1951, Manoel Ribeiro.
Diarios de Motocicleta (*The Motorcycle Diaries*), 2004, Walter Salles Jr.
Didi, o caçador de tesouros (Didi, the Treasure Hunter), 2006, Paulo Aragão and Marcus Figueiredo.
Didi, o cupido Trapalhão (Didi, the Trapalhão Cupid), 2003, Paulo Aragão and Alexandre Boury.
Didi quer ser criança (Didi Wants to Be a Child), 2004, Alexandre Boury and Reynaldo Boury.
Doida demais (Just Too Crazy), 1989, Sérgio Rezende.
Dois filhos de Francisco (*Two Sons of Francisco*), 2005, Breno Silveira.
Os dois ladrões (The Two Thieves), 1960, Carlos Manga.
Dona Flor e seus dois maridos (*Dona Flor and Her Two Husbands*), 1976, Bruno Barreto.
Down Argentine Way, 1940, Irving Cummings.
O dragão da maldade contra o santo guerreiro (*Antônio das Mortes*), 1968, Glauber Rocha.
A dupla do barulho (The Terrible Twosome), 1953, Carlos Manga.
E a vaca foi para o brejo (My Cow Is Stuck in the Mud), 1981, José Adalto Cardoso.
E o mundo se diverte (And the World Has Fun), 1948, Watson Macedo.

É proibido beijar (Kissing Is Forbidden), 1954, Ugo Lombardi.
O ébrio (The Drunkard), 1946, Gilda de Abreu.
Eles não usam black-tie (*They Don't Wear Black Tie*), 1981, Leon Hirzsman.
Eréndira, 1983, Ruy Guerra.
Essa gostosa brincadeira a dois (This Tasty Game for Two), 1974, Victor di Mello.
Esse milhão é meu (That Million Is Mine), 1958, Carlos Manga.
Esta noite encarnarei no teu cadáver (*This Night I Will Possess Your Corpse*), 1967, José Mojica Marins.
Este mundo é um pandeiro (This World Is a Tambourine), 1946, Watson Macedo.
Os estranguladores (The Stranglers), 1908, Francisco Marzullo.
O estranho mundo de Zé do Caixão (*The Strange World of Coffin Joe*), 1968, José Mojica Marins.
Estudantes (Students), 1935, Wallace Downey.
Eu dou o que ela gosta (I Give Her What She Likes), 1975, Braz Chediak.
Eu te amo (*I Love You*), 1981, Arnaldo Jabor.
Eu, tu, eles (*Me, You, Them*), 2000, Andrucha Waddington.
Euclydes da Cunha, 1866–1909, 1944, Humberto Mauro.
O exorcismo negro (*Black Exorcism of Coffin Joe*), 1974, José Mojica Marins.
Fala tu (*Living Rap in Rio*), 2003, Guilherme Coelho.
A família Lero-Lero (The Lero-Lero Family), 1953, Alberto Pieralisi.
Os fantasmas Trapalhões (The Ghostly Trapalhões), 1987, J.B. Tanko.
Favela dos meus amores (Shantytown of My Loves), 1934, Humberto Mauro.
From Dusk till Dawn III, 2000, P.J. Pesce.
Futebol em família (Family Football), 1939, Rui Costa.
Os fuzis (*The Guns*), 1964, Ruy Guerra.
Gabriela, 1983, Bruno Barreto.
Ganga bruta (Brutal Gang), 1933, Humberto Mauro.
The Gang's All Here, 1943, Busby Berkeley.
Garota de Ipanema (*Girl from Ipanema*), 1967, Leon Hirszman.
Gemidos e sussurros (Moans and Whispers), 1987, Rafaele Rossi.
Gilda, 1946, Charles Vidor.
Glauber o filme: labirinto do Brasil (Glauber the Film: Brazilian Labyrinth), 2003, Sílvio Tendler.
A grande arte (*Exposure*), 1991, Walter Salles.
A grande cidade (The Big City), 1966, Carlos Diegues.
A grande família – o filme (Big Family – the Film), 2007, Maurício Farias.
Grito do Ipiranga, 1917, Giorgio Lambertini.
O Guarani (The Guarani Indian), 1916, Vittorio Capellaro.
O Guarani (The Guarani Indian), 1996, Norma Benguel.
Guerra de Canudos (*Battle of Canudos*), 1997, Sérgio Rezende.
Os herdeiros (*The Heirs*), 1970, Carlos Diegues.
High Noon, 1952, Fred Zinnemann.
O homem do ano (*The Man of the Year*), 2003, José Henrique Fonseca.
O homem do sputnik (Sputnik Man), 1959, Carlos Manga.
A idade da terra (*The Age of the Earth*), 1980, Glauber Rocha.
O império do desejo (In the Realm of Desire), 1980, Carlos Reichenbach.
Inconfidência mineira (Conspiracy in Minas Gerais), 1948, Carmen Santos.
Os inconfidentes (The Conspirators), 1936, Humberto Mauro.

Os inconfidentes (*The Conspirators*), 1972, Joaquim Pedro de Andrade.
Independência ou morte (Independence or Death), 1972, Carlos Coimbra.
Inocência (Innocence), 1915, Vittorio Capellaro and Santiago Giannatasio.
O invasor (*The Trespasser*), 2002, Beto Brant.
Iracema, 1920, Vittorio Capellaro.
It's All True, 1942 (unfinished version), Orson Welles.
Jardim de Guerra (War Garden), 1970, Neville D'Almeida.
Jaws, 1975, Steven Spielberg.
Jeca e a égua milagrosa (Jeca and the Miraculous Mare), 1980, Amácio Mazaroppi and Pio Zamuner.
Jeca e seu filho preto (Jeca and His Black Son), 1978, Berillo Facio and Pio Zamuner.
O Jeca macumbeiro (Jeca Does Voodoo), 1974, Amácio Mazaroppi and Pio Zamuner.
João Ninguém (Johnny Nobody), 1937, Mesquitinha.
Justiça (*Justice*), 2004, Maria Ramos.
King Kong, 1933, Merian C. Cooper and Ernest B. Schoedsack.
Kiss of the Spiderwoman, 1985, Hector Babenco.
Lábios sem beijos (Lips without Kisses), 1931, Humberto Mauro.
O lamparina (The Little Oil Lamp), 1964, Glauco Mirko Laurelli.
Lara, 2002, Ana Maria Magalhães.
Laranja da China (Orange from China), 1940, Rui Costa.
Limite (Limit), 1931, Mário Peixoto.
Lua de cristal (Crystal Moon), 1990, Tizuka Yamasaki.
Lúcio Flávio, passageiro da agonia (*Lucio Flavio*), 1977, Hector Babenco.
Macunaíma, 1969, Joaquim Pedro de Andrade.
Madame Satã (*Madame Satan*), 2002, Karim Ainouz.
Mademoiselle Cinema, 1925, Léo Marten.
Malandros em quarta dimensão (*Malandros* in the Fourth Dimension), 1954, Luiz de Barros.
Maridinho de luxo (Upmarket Hubbie), 1938, Luiz de Barros.
As massagistas profissionais (The Professional Masseuses), 1976, Carlo Mossy.
Os matadores (*Belly Up*), 1997, Beto Brant.
Matar ou correr (Kill or Run Away), 1954, Carlos Manga.
Memória do cangaço (*Cangaço* Memories), 1965, Paulo Gil Soares.
O menino da porteira (The Porter's Child), 1976, Jeremias Moreira Filho.
Mestiça, a escrava indomável (Mestiça, the Untameable Slave), 1973, Lenita Perroy.
Meu Japão brasileiro (My Brazilian Japan), 1964, Glauco Mirko Laurelli.
O mistério do dominó negro (The Mystery of the Black Cape), 1931, Cléo de Verberena.
Moleque Tião (Little Kid Tião), 1943, José Carlos Burle.
A moreninha (Little Dark Girl), 1970, Glauco Mirko Laurelli.
Na estrada da vida: José Rico e Milionário (*The Highway of Life*), 1980, Nelson Pereira dos Santos.
Na onda do iê-iê-iê (On the Wave of Rock 'n' Roll), 1965, Aurélio Teixeira.
Na primavera da vida (In the Springtime of Life), 1926, Humberto Mauro.
Nadando em dinheiro (Rolling in Money), 1952, Abílio Pereira de Almeida and Carlos Thiré.
Não adianta chorar (It's No Good Crying), 1945, Watson Macedo.
Nem Sansão, nem Dalila (Neither Samson nor Delilah), 1954, Carlos Manga.

Nhô Anastácio chegou de viagem (*Mr Anastácio Came Back from a Trip*), 1908, Júlio Ferrez.

A noite das taras (Night of Perversion), 1980, David Cardoso, John Woo and Ody Fraga.

Noites cariocas (Rio Nights), 1935, Enrique Cadícamo.

Os normais (*So Normal*), 2003, José Alvarenga Jr.

Nos tempos da vaselina (In the Days of Vaseline), 1979, José Miziara.

Nossa Senhora da Aparecida e seus milagres (Our Lady of Aparecida and Her Miracles), 1919, Mário Leite.

Notícias de uma guerra particular (*News of a Private War*), 1998, João Moreira Salles.

O noviço rebelde (The Rebel Novice), 1997, Tizuka Yamasaki.

Olga, 2004, Jayme Monjardim.

Onde a terra acaba (The Ends of the Earth), 1933, Octávio Gabus Mendes.

Ônibus 174 (*Bus 174*), 2002, José Padilha.

Orfeu (*Orpheus*), 1999, Carlos Diegues.

Orfeu negro (*Black Orpheus*), 1958, Marcel Camus.

Os paqueras (The Flirts), 1969, Reginaldo Farias.

Partida para a Itália dos reservistas no 1 de julho (Reservists' Departure for Italy on 1 July), 1915, Antônio Campos.

Pátria brasileira (Brazilian Fatherland), 1917, Guelfo Andaló.

Pátria e bandeira (Fatherland and Flag), 1918, Antônio Leal.

Paz e amor (Peace and Love), 1910, Alberto Botelho and Alberto Moreira.

Pega ladrão (Catch the Thief), 1940, Rui Costa.

Pequeno dicionário amoroso (*Little Book of Love*), 1997, Sandra Werneck.

Pinguinho de gente (Tiny Tot), 1949, Gilda de Abreu.

Pixote: a lei do mais fraco (*Pixote*), 1981, Hector Babenco.

Pintando o sete (Painting the Town Red), 1959, Carlos Manga.

Pornografia (Pornography), 1992, Murilo Salles and Sandra Werneck.

O pornógrafo (The Pornographer), 1970, João Callegaro.

Portugal, minha saudade (Longing for Portugal), 1973, Amácio Mazzaropi and Pio Zamuner.

O primeiro dia (*Midnight*), 1999, Walter Salles and Daniela Thomas.

A Princesa Xuxa e os Trapalhões (Princess Xuxa and the Trapalhões), 1989, José Alvarenga Jr.

Uma pulga na balança (Eany, meany, miny, mo), 1953, Luciano Salce.

Pureza (Purity), 1940, Chianca de Garcia.

O puritano da rua Augusta (The Puritan of Rua Augusta), 1965, Amácio Mazaroppi.

O rap do pequeno príncipe contras as almas sebosas (*The Little Prince's Rap against the Wicked Souls*), 2000, Paulo Caldas and Marcelo Luna.

Rien que les heures (*Nothing but Time*), 1926, Alberto Cavalcanti.

Rio, 40 graus (*Rio, 40 Degrees*), 1955, Nelson Pereira dos Santos.

Rio, Zona Norte (*Rio, Northern Zone*), 1957, Nelson Pereira dos Santos.

Rituais e festas Bororo (Rituals and Festivals of the Bororo People), 1916, Luís Tomás Reis.

Rocha que voa (Rocha Takes Flight), 2002, Eryk Rocha.

The Rookie, 1990, Clint Eastwood.

O roubo das calcinhas (The Theft of the Panties), 1975, Sindoval Aguiar and Braz Chediak.

Sai da frente (Get Out of My Way), 1952, Abílio Pereira de Almeida.

Samba em Berlim (Samba in Berlin), 1943, Luiz de Barros.

Samba em Brasília (Samba in Brasília), 1960, Watson Macedo.

Samson and Delilah, 1949, Cecil B. de Mille.

Sangue mineiro (Blood of Minas Gerais), 1930, Humberto Mauro.
Santa Marta – duas semanas no morro (*Santa Marta – Two Weeks on the Hill*), 1987, Eduardo Coutinho.
Santo forte (*Strong Saint*), 1999, Eduardo Coutinho.
São Bernardo, 1971, Leon Hirszman.
São Paulo: sinfonia da metrópole (São Paulo: Symphony of the Metropolis), 1929, Adalberto Kemeny and Rudolf Rex Lustig.
Secas e molhadas (Dried Up and Moist), 1975, Mozael Silveira.
As secretárias . . . que fazem de tudo (Secretaries . . . Who Do It All), 1975, Alberto Pieralisi.
O segredo da múmia (*The Secret of the Mummy*), 1982, Ivan Cardoso.
Sem vaselina (Without Vaseline), 1985, Jose Miziara.
Senta no meu que eu entro na sua (Sit on Mine and I'll Put It in Yours), 1985, Ody Fraga.
Sertão das memórias (*Landscapes of Memory*), 1997, José Araujo.
Sessomatto (*How Funny Can Sex Be?*), 1973, Dino Risi.
Seus problemas acabaram!!! (Your Troubles Are Over!!!), 2006, José Lavigne.
Seven Brides for Seven Brothers, 1954, Stanley Donen.
Sexo às avessas (Sex the Other Way Round), 1981, Fauzi Mansur.
Sinfonia de Cataguases (Symphony of Cataguases), 1929, Humberto Mauro.
Sinhá moça (The Plantation Owner's Daughter), 1953, Tom Payne and Oswaldo Sampaio.
Um soutien para papai (A Bra for Daddy), 1975, Carlos Alberto de Souza Barros.
Super Xuxa contra o baixo astral (*Super Xuxa against Satan*), 1988, Ana Penido and David Sonnenschein.
A superfêmea (Superwoman), 1973, Aníbal Massaini Neto.
Tapete vermelho (Red Carpet), 2005, Luis Alberto Pereira.
Terapia do sexo (Sexual Therapy), 1978, Ody Fraga.
Terra em transe (*Land in Anguish*), 1967, Glauber Rocha.
Tesouro perdido (Lost Treasure), 1927, Humberto Mauro.
That Night in Rio, 1941, Irving Cummings.
The Three Caballeros, 1945, Walt Disney.
Tico-Tico no fubá (Tico-Tico Bird in the Corn Meal), 1952, Adolfo Celi.
Toda nudez será castigada (*All Nudity Shall Be Punished*), 1972, Arnaldo Jabor.
O Trapalhão na arca de Noé (The Trapalhão on Noah's Ark), 1983, Del Rangel.
Os Trapalhões e o mágico de Oroz (The Trapalhões and the Wizard of Oroz), 1984, Victor Lustosa and Dedé Santana.
Os Trapalhões nas minas do rei Salomão (The Trapalhões in King Solomon's Mines), 1977, J.B. Tanko.
Os Trapalhões no reino da fantasia (The Trapalhões in the Land of Make-Believe), 1985, Dedé Santana.
Treze cadeiras (Thirteen Chairs), 1957, Francisco Eichhorn.
Tristezas não pagam dívidas (Sadness Won't Pay Your Debts), 1944, José Carlos Burle.
Turistas/Paradise Lost, 2006, John Stockwell.
Urutau, 1919, William H. Jansen.
Valadião, o cratera (Valadião, the Rogue), 1925, Humberto Mauro.
Vamos com calma (Let's Go Quietly), 1956, Carlos Manga.
Vent L'est (*East Wind*), 1970, Jean-Luc Godard.
Vereda tropical (Tropical Paths), 1980, Joaquim Pedro de Andrade.
Viciado em C . . . (Addicted to A . . .), 1985, David Cardoso, aka Roberto Fedegoso.

A vida do cabo João Candido (The Life of Corporal João Candido), 1912, Carlos Lambertini.

Vidas secas (*Barren Lives*), 1963, Nelson Pereira dos Santos.

A *virgem e o machão* (The Virgin and the Macho Man), 1974, J. Avelar (José Mojica Marins).

A volta do Jeca (Jeca's Return), 1984, Pio Zamuner.

A voz do carnaval (The Voice of Carnival), 1933, Adhemar Gonzaga and Humberto Mauro.

Woman on Top (2000), Fina Torres.

Xica da Silva (*Xica*), 1976, Carlos Diegues.

Xuxa abracadabra, 2003, Moacyr Góes.

Xuxa e o tesouro da cidade perdida (Xuxa and the Treasure of the Lost City), 2004, Moacyr Góes.

Xuxa e os duendes (Xuxa and the Elves), 2001, Paulo Sérgio de Almeida and Rogério Gomes.

Xuxa e os duendes II: no caminho das fadas (Xuxa and the Elves II: The Fairies' Path), 2002, Paulo Sérgio de Almeida and Rogério Gomes.

Xuxa e os Trapalhões em o mistério de Robin Hood (Xuxa and the Trapalhões in the Mystery of Robin Hood), 1990, José Alvarenga Jr.

Xuxa popstar, 2000, Paulo Sérgio de Almeida and Tizuka Yamasaki.

Xuxa requebra (Xuxa Gets Down), 1999, Tizuka Yamasaki.

INDEX

A library at your fingertips!

eBooks are electronic versions of printed books. You can store them on your PC/laptop or browse them online.

They have advantages for anyone needing rapid access to a wide variety of published, copyright information.

eBooks can help your research by enabling you to bookmark chapters, annotate text and use instant searches to find specific words or phrases. Several eBook files would fit on even a small laptop or PDA.

NEW: Save money by eSubscribing: cheap, online access to any eBook for as long as you need it.

Annual subscription packages

We now offer special low-cost bulk subscriptions to packages of eBooks in certain subject areas. These are available to libraries or to individuals.

For more information please contact webmaster.ebooks@tandf.co.uk

We're continually developing the eBook concept, so keep up to date by visiting the website.

www.eBookstore.tandf.co.uk